Afrikan Mothers

Nah Dove

Afrikan Mothers

Bearers of Culture

Makers of Social Change

State University of New York Press

Production by Ruth Fisher
Marketing by Fran Keneston

Published by
State University of New York Press, Albany

For information, address the State University of New York Press,
State University Plaza, Albany, NY 12246

Library of Congress Cataloging-in-Publication Data

Dove, Nah.
    Afrikan mothers : bearers of culture, makers of social change /
Nah Dove.
        p.   cm.
    Includes bibliographical references and index.
    ISBN 0-7914-3881-3 (HC acid-free). — ISBN 0-7914-3882-1 (PB acid-
free)
    1. Women, Black—Great Britain—Interviews.   2. Women, Black—
United States—Interviews.   3. Afrocentrism—Philosophy.
4. Education—Africa—Philosophy.   5. Africa—Civilization—Western
influences.   I. Title.
HQ1593.D68   1998
305.48'896—dc21   97-41264
                                                            CIP

10 9 8 7 6 5 4 3 2 1

To the hundreds of millions of Afrikan lives lost in the struggle against European domination, and to those Afrikan women, children, and men who struggle today, and to those yet unborn.

To the lives of millions of First Nations' women, children, and men who died in the struggle against European domination and to those who struggle today and to those yet unborn.

To those who fight against injustices such as these.

Contents

Acknowledgments

My work is the result of a collective effort. My mother, Dorothy, has been instrumental in helping to support me in every way. My father, Raymond, was there when I needed him. I could not have written this book without the love and spiritual support of my dear children: Siona-Ankrah, Nadu, Ali, Olatunji, Akua, and Hope-Olani. I cannot forget my darling grandchildren, Nadu's daughters, Adjowa and Abena, who love me as nana. My soul-mate Mwalimu Shujaa has guided me in my work.

I give thanks to the women in the American Studies Department, SUNY at Buffalo, for offering me a place in the Women's Studies component. Endesha Holland was instrumental in this move. Hester Eisenstein and Liz Kennedy must be remembered, as well as my sisters from the Black women's graduate group. I thank the department for awarding me the Rockefeller Humanities Fellowship that enabled me to gather data and work with my ideas from the summer of 1993 to the summer of 1994.

Thank you to Lawrence Chisolm, for believing in my ideas, and especially, for your guidance, you will always be remembered, and Barbara Shircliffe, and Peggy Bertram, who read my work.

Thank you, Yvonne Dion Buffalo and John Mohawk, for the friendship and education that I have received from you. I want to express my gratitude to James Turner, Molefi Asante, Kariamu Welsh Asante, and Ama Mazama, who have been critical to my academic survival. Thank you Asa Hilliard for your inspiration.

xi

I offer a special thank you to the wonderful Afrikan mothers whose stories are the central focus of this book. I was honored to hear your words, and I am honored to present them so that other women will be inspired to become institution builders.

Finally, I thank Herbert Ekwe-Ekwe, a mentor and editor, and Femi Nzegwu for your support. There are many whose names I have not included but I love you and thank you for your love.

Introduction

Once a young girl danced beneath the Afrikan sky and the
sun kissed her bones. She saw her reflection in the lake and
understood her spiritual connection. She never betrayed her
mother Afrika.

—Nah Dove

The objective of this book is to address the need to recognize the
critical role of Afrikan[1] women, especially as mothers, in attempting to humanize a world that has debased Afrika,[2] her peoples, her
descendants and everything associated with her. With this in mind,
the intention is to argue that Afrikan mothers as bearers of culture
have been the backbone of the struggle to resist the European
conquest of Afrika, her resources, and her peoples' energies.

To carry out this task, I use ideas and experiences that can serve
as a model to analyze both the devastating effect that western or
European-oriented culture and societies have on Afrikan people as
well as some of the ways that Afrikan-oriented culture has sustained Afrikan survival.

This world is one in which millions of people suffer in their
struggles to survive the aftermath of conquest. Their voices are ignored, silenced by a belief in a western concept of progress, an ideology that advances the notion that some members of humanity
deserve to live without access to, or control over, their resources.

Many have come to believe that some members of humanity have earned the right to control the resources and energies of others as if ordained by a higher order. These ideas are founded on a European-centered interpretation of reality. They provide the basis of and support for the present world order. This book is written in opposition to such ideas. Unfortunately, many of us, particularly those who benefit from western-designed privileges, have become, through a process of deculturalization[3] and misinformation, complacent and accepting of injustice.

In respect for the memory of those women, men, and children who have perished, this book looks at the world from an Afrikan-centered perspective. In this way, it is hoped that this work will add a necessary dimension to the ongoing restoration and reconstruction of an Afrikan worldview that will ultimately benefit all humanity.

This work is grounded in my research; personal experiences; the knowledge that has been given to me by all the people I have met in this lifetime; the experiences of Afrikan women, men, and children that I have witnessed and learned about; the academic and scholarly research of Afrikan people that I have read and investigated; and my spiritual link with Afrika through my ancestors. My task is to understand the global Afrikan condition. It is not possible to make sense of what is happening to Afrikan people in London and Los Angeles without looking at what is happening in Kingston (Jamaica), Sao Paulo (Brazil), and Durban (South Africa). At the same time, it is not possible to speak of the Afrikan experience without speaking of Europe's role in constructing the racialization of the world, and our role in either perpetuating it or deconstructing European[4] domination. I therefore ask the reader to use this book as a basis for locating one's self and responsibility to cultural allegiance in this evolving global construction.

I attempt to show that there is a need to reinterpret the Afrikan story as it has been told. The European-centered construction of "history," whether masculine or feminine, has overlooked the cultural significance of sources of information that need to be investigated for linkages toward a more complete understanding of our Afrikan story. The European argument, mostly male-centered, is not historically credible because it is based on information that has excluded other experiences, including those of European women. Hazel Carby elucidates that for Afrikan women:

History has constructed our sexuality and our femininity as deviating from those qualities with which white women, as the prize objects of the Western world, have been endowed. . . . [O]ur continuing struggle with history began with its discovery of us. . . . We cannot hope to reconstitute ourselves in all our absences, or to rectify the ill-conceived presences that invade herstory from history, but we do wish to bear witness to our own herstories. (1982a, 212)

Thus, Carby's intention is to recognize a female-centered perspective for Afrikan women that can be extricated from that of European women. She argues that the Afrikan story of resistance to European oppression includes the struggles waged by Afrikan women. It follows that one must be cognizant of the reciprocity of Afrikan female and male power relations prior to invasion. In this way, the construction of herstory, moves toward an authentic representation of the Afrikan story.

For Afrikan women and men, it is critical to understand the nature of our relationship to European women and men. Inconsistencies in the European version of our story raises questions and doubts about the validity of European history concerning global relations. There is much information that suggests that Afrikan contacts with Europeans were culturally beneficial to Europeans. I attempt to show this reality in order to develop a challenge to misinformation. In this way the antithetical cultural argument that I develop can be seen as having some material and ideological bases outside the European paradigm.

Prior to the capturing and enslavement of Afrikan women, men, and children, we could feed, clothe, and shelter ourselves; develop philosophies and spiritual, mental, and medicinal health care; construct institutions of every type from the state to the village; create technologies and civilizations; be creative in all the art forms; travel and trade across continents; and be self-determining as a people. It is evident that we are no longer in control of our resources, our energies, and therefore our destiny. As Chancellor Williams (1984)[5] has argued, it is clear that a great tragedy of catastrophic proportions has befallen Afrikan people.

In order to change the conditions that we find ourselves in as a people, it is urgent that we work toward unraveling the nature of circumstances that have led to this state of existence. The contemporary situation of Afrikans as conquered and oppressed peoples can be traced to the power relations that evolved between Afrikan and European people from antiquity. The differences between the belief and value systems of these two cultural groups have had a critical effect on the development of their societies. I write with the belief that a clash of cultures has occurred, the ramifications of which we are only beginning to clarify.

Resistance to oppression is the central theme of this book. The Maafa[6] and its fallout are still firmly ensconced in the cultural memory of Afrikan people. Afrikan women, men, and children have continuously resisted European inhumanity at the cost of countless lives. Social change has taken place as a result of Afrikan warriorship. Even Europeans, caught up in struggles against their own ethnic conflicts, class divisions, sexist oppression, and discrimination of any kind, have been inspired to challenge their conditions, because of the unrelenting struggles of Afrikan women, men, and children.

How then do these struggles manifest in the everyday lives of ordinary Afrikan people? This book looks at the life-herstories of twenty-one Afrikan mothers from the Caribbean, Afrika, the United Kingdom, and the United States. Of the twenty-one women, seventeen have chosen to send their children to African culturally affirming[7] schools in the United Kingdom and the United States and four from the United States have chosen to use European schools. In order to understand the significance of their stories, I have contextualized their narratives in a his/herstory of Afrikan struggle and resistance against white supremacy/European domination.

The analysis of their narratives is guided by the questions that shape the book:

1. How were Europeans able to take institutional control of the world's peoples and resources?

2. What has happened to Afrikan people as a result of conquest?

3. What are the cultural ramifications for Afrikan peoples and others?

4. How can we move forward?

In chapter 1, I lay out the methodology of this research by explaining the concepts used to understand the tension between European peoples and Afrikan peoples. At the same time I explain the process that guided this study.

Chapter 2 develops a background to the herstories of the Afrikan mothers who live in the United Kingdom. While not all the mothers who live in the United Kingdom are from the Caribbean, the effects of the Caribbean influence on the lives of Afrikan people residing there have been substantial. The intention is to make connections between the U.K. mothers' stories and the complex dynamics which account for the treatment of Afrikan people in the United Kingdom.

Chapter 3 speaks for itself, it tells the herstories of the Afrikan mothers who live in the United Kingdom.

In chapter 4, I define the U.S. context of the Afrikan experience by including the construction of the Americas[8] and the holocaust of the indigenous, First Nations[9] people. In this way it is possible to understand the role of schooling in support of this societal entity.

Chapter 5 looks at the herstories of the Afrikan mothers who live in the United States and use the Sankofa Afrikan-centered school.

Chapter 6 looks at the stories of Afrikan mothers from the United States who decided not to send their children to the Afrikan-centered school.

In chapter 7, I analyze these stories from an Afrikan-centered perspective. My intention is to link the mothers' decisions to send their children to culturally affirming schools to the process of personal transformation that has evolved from their struggles to survive and maintain their dignity and integrity in the face of tremendous odds.

The purpose of Chapter 8 is to validate the intellectualism and knowledge of these mothers as a critical part of the continuing attempt to free ourselves globally from the manacles of European control over our spirituality, minds, bodies, energies, and resources.

It is my hope that this book brings together some concepts that are in keeping with the integrity of Afrikan women, men, and children. With this in mind, these ideas are woven throughout the book so that the reader gains clarity, through the voices of Afrikan mothers, about the nature of white supremacy and its sometimes subtle and often blatant, barbaric impact upon Afrikan women, men, and children and other cultural groups throughout the world.

Importantly, I recognize myself as a learning, growing person who is in a process of development. Thus, mistakes may be attributed to my level of comprehension concerning the social reality of Afrikan humanity and my role in it.

①

Methods of Research

A conceptual framework is important for understanding the thinking and motivation behind the study. Every person has a perception of reality grounded in experiences and knowledge of his/herstorical cultural orientation.

Marimba Ani (1994) has provided perhaps the most concise definition of culture in her book *Yurugu*. Culture affects the way we perceive the world, and the way we think and behave in the world. For Afrikan people, as Ani and others show, it is vital to understand the nature of European domination because culture is a critical element that is used as a weapon in domination. For Afrikan and other subject people, particularly in the United States and the United Kingdom, imposed alien European values and beliefs shape and manipulate behavior to serve the interests of the governing group.

My entry into higher education was triggered by a desire to study the nature of European domination/white supremacy in order to make sense of why and how Afrikan women, men, and children have been persecuted and debased for so long. My involvement as a child and parent in the British public school system led to my

1

commitment to Black parent and teacher organizations and the development of supplementary schools as a self-determining salvation for our children.

The European answers to questions concerning the treatment of Afrikan people were and still are quite inadequate and illogical for any Afrikan person to accept. However, over centuries of violence and the appropriation of Afrikan resources and energies, Afrikan people have been forced to accept alien interpretations of Afrikan realities. In order to bring clarity to the situation it became critical for me to read and immerse myself in the research and ideas of Afrikan people. Receiving funding and attending university provided me with the time and opportunity to access documentation of the Afrikan experience from our own vantage point. In this light, I have used ideas from this body of knowledge along with my own experiences and that of others to fashion a conceptual framework. These ideas guided my choice to look at the relevance of Afrikan-run, culturally affirming schools to the liberation of Afrikan people, although I already had a sense of their significance because I was involved in the movement. However, I did not know the background of their existence from a historical viewpoint and as I grew more knowledgeable it seemed logical to begin to look at the types of mothers who chose to use these schools.

It is not unique for Afrikan people or any people to wish to reproduce their culture. This is how any people survives. However, it is extremely difficult for Afrikan people to see the need to reproduce Afrikan values and beliefs while living under the supremacy of a European cultural collective that debases and devalues Afrikan people in every area of social reality. Eurocentric beliefs of this nature imply that a return to values of the Afrikan past has little or no relevance to the present. How then could these mothers see outside the European construction of Afrika and her people and understand the importance of culturally affirming schools to the emotional, spiritual, and academic development of their children?

In reality, the retention of Afrikan cultural forms has been an important feature of Afrikan survival and resistance against the continuing Maafa. These forms range from the spiritual to the material. In this way, Afrikan people have held onto notions of justice and humanity from an Afrikan-based morality. These ideas have been the bedrock of the struggle against injustice perpetrated by the aggressor. In other words, the struggle for liberation is based upon Afrikan ideas of social reality, not on European ideas of progress.

Important research on cultural retention has been carried out by Ani (1995), Asante and Welsh-Asante (1985), Diop, (1959/1990), Herskovitz (1958/1990), Holloway (1991), Richards (1980), Tedla (1995), and others. In this light, the task of Afrikan-centered thinkers is to reclaim, reconstruct, elevate, and dignify Afrikan cultural values and beliefs as a mode of resistance to life under white supremacy. Afrikan-centered or Afrocentric[1] ideas and knowledge are significantly different from those that elevate Afrikan people as a racial/genetic group while at the same time derogate Afrika and her culture or fail to see the importance of Afrika.

For the purpose of building a liberationist agenda, there can be no separation between Afrikan people wherever they live and their cultural link to Afrika. In reality, Afrikan people are still wrestling with alien concepts of humanity, spirituality, male/female relations, and family values. This has had a pervasive and insidious effect upon the Afrikan psyche. W. E. B. Du Bois (1903/1969) brought this to mind when he spoke of "double consciousness" as reflecting a state of being when, the Negro looks at herself through the eyes of others. This imposed condition has, to a degree, successfully undermined the ability of Afrikan people to reproduce our values and beliefs on a consistent basis.

Using Diop's cradle theory (1959, 1990) and his concept of cultural unity, one is better able to define the nature of European domination (white supremacy) and its effects upon Afrikan people. Diop theorizes the development of two distinct cradles of civilization that created modes of societal structures almost antithetical to each other. The Southern cradle, Afrika, where humanity began, produced matriarchal societies. Over time, the migration of peoples to the colder climates of the northern cradle produced patriarchal, male-centered societies. Quite simply he attributes matriarchy to an agrarian lifestyle in a climate of abundance and patriarchy to nomadic traditions arising from a harsh environment. In time the patriarchal culture would develop, as Diop states,

instincts necessary for survival in such an environment . . . man must obtain his bread by the sweat of his brow. Above all, he must learn to rely on himself alone. . . . He could not indulge in the luxury of believing in a beneficent God who would shower down abundant means of gaining a livelihood; instead he would conjure up deities maleficent and cruel, jealous and spiteful: Zeus, Yaweh among others. (1974, 112)

Conversely, the concept of matriarchy highlights the complementary aspect of the female-male relationship or the nature of the feminine and the masculine in all aspects of social organization. The woman is revered in her role as the mother who is the bringer of life, the conduit to the spiritual regeneration of the ancestors, the bearer of culture and the center of social organization. Thus, according to Diop, to speak or behave inappropriately in front of a mother is tantamount to committing sacrilege. It is believed that such behavior will be known in the ancestors' realm and the repercussions will fall upon the families of the perpetrators. As a result of her powerful role, the mother wishes to use her power wisely and will often be a tolerant person toward her children and her partner (Diop 1990, 70–71). In the context of western patriarchy this tolerance may be exploited and viewed as a weakness rather than a strength.

The role of motherhood or mothering is not limited to mothers or women even in contemporary Afrika (Tedla 1995). Motherhood depicts the nature of the communal responsibilities involved in the raising of children and the caring of others. However, while the role of women and mothering in the process of reproduction is critical to the continuation of any society and culture, in a patriarchal society this role is not ascribed with the value that it bears in a matriarchal society.

In antiquity, as Diop (1990) explains, the European or Indo-Aryan woman is considered little more than a burden that the man drags behind him. Beyond her function of child-bearing, her role is nothing. As a person of less value, she must leave her clan to join her husband, unlike the matriarchal custom, which requires the man to join her family (p. 29). The differences that arise from these two cultural orientations may be viewed as significant. The debasement of women in one culture and the respect for women in the other, mark important distinctions that should not be ignored when analyzing the contemporary difficulties for Afrikan people, especially Afrikan women living in western-oriented societies.

There is plenty of evidence to show that Afrikan women in antiquity and even after the last major European conquest of Afrika,[2] held key positions in the political, legal, spiritual, agrarian, economic, and health arenas. Researchers like Diop, Ivan Van Sertima, Barbara Lesko, Merlin Stone, Charles Finch, David Sweetman, Hazel Carby, Rosalyn Terborg-Penn, Filomina Chioma Steady, Ifi Amadiume, and others bring clarity to this reality. This is a critical part of the Afrikan woman's cultural heritage. What does today's subjugated Afrikan woman have to contend with under European cultural imposition? She not only suffers as a woman, but she suffers first as an Afrikan person, degraded primarily by her color, features, and hair texture.

The racialized dynamics of her experience may also be attributed to European culture. From Diop's cradle theory (1959/1990) and Ani's understanding of Yurugu (1994), the xenophobic (fear of foreigners) behavior Europeans exhibited during the conquest of the world's peoples may be related to the imbalance of the feminine and masculine principles. The unequal power relationship between the male and female coupled with the fear of the "other" may be considered significant in the development of hierarchical and unequal power relations among European ethnicities. These inequalities later provided the basis for defining the social positions of other cultural groups. It is possible to view the inequalities exhibited in today's western-oriented societies as reflective of this condition.

The concept of race has been constructed to differentiate and measure the value of humanity in accordance with the moral structure of Europeans. From an Afrikan-centered perspective, it has played a critical role in falsely dividing humanity, according to European notions of inferiority and superiority, using genetic characteristics based on color distinctions. This concept has enabled Europeans to unite as "white" people in the fabrication of "white" supremacy over the "Red," "Yellow," "Brown," and "Black" peoples of the world.

Within the western world, the ideology of "white" supremacy has developed in concert with the conquest of Afrika and her people. The Afrikan woman has been constructed as a woman of the "Black" race and all the negative connotations that Europeans have attached to that definition. Conceptually, she has been separated from her cultural base, Afrika. To facilitate the authenticity of this belief, Afrika and her people have been debased. The process of deculturalization has played a vital role in constructing this ideology. Now the Black woman can be manipulated into thinking that she is a "Black" Briton, U.K. "Black," "Black" American, "Black" Brazilian, "Black" German, and so on. As a citizen of these places, not only does she not have the same human rights afforded her as her white counterparts, she is also viewed as not deserving them. As a Black citizen, she fights for the right to exist as a debased European national. Ironically, she will always be perceived by Europeans as an Afrikan in the most negative way whether she understands this or not. Culturally affirming schools serve to nurture the belief in Afrikaness as a critical component in humanness and personhood from an Afrikan-centered or Afrocentric perspective. This knowledge has the possibility of helping the Afrikan woman to connect with her proud cultural heritage.

Diop's research (1959/1990) suggests that when the European and Afrikan cultural groups met, the xenophilic (love of people) attitude of Afrikan people versus the xenophobic (fear of foreigners) of Europeans may well have been Afrika's downfall. In effect, it is possible to view the values and beliefs of Afrikan people and European people as standing in direct opposition. What was considered a strength in one civilization was viewed as a weakness to be exploited by the other. Subsequently, European ethnicities under the auspices of "white" supremacy were able, as a cultural entity, to undermine, annihilate, and subjugate those who exhibited the values of matriarchy.

Diop's concept of cultural unity (1959/1990) addresses the ability of any cultural group to reproduce itself through the intergenerational transmission of its values and beliefs. In this way, the contemporary societies of these two major cultural groups, the European and the Afrikan, can be seen to demonstrate many of the same values as their ancestors did thousands of years ago. A focus on the distinctions between European patriarchal and Afrikan matriarchal cultures provides the basis for understanding the contradictions between these value systems. Their in-built moral systems are, to their creators, perfectly justified, neither appearing morally deficient. However, the severe ramifications for Afrikan women and men as a result of patriarchal morality is a continuing matter of life and death. In reality, we are dealing with a clash of cultures and therefore a clash of moral systems. By using the clash of culture as a paradigm, we can more easily make sense of some contemporary conditions. In this war of cultural domination, the mothers who send their children to culturally affirming schools may be perceived as warriors conditioned to understand the nature of the war.

Background

Contextualized by the Southern cradle origins of the herstory of Afrikan women, my project presents a new model of analysis that looks in-depth at reasons for the choice that Afrikan mothers have made to send their children to culturally affirming schools in the United States and the United Kingdom. The major questions relating to their decisions are:

1. Why do these mothers, in the face of the debasement of Afrikan people, perceive Afrikan culture to be of any relevance to their children's lives?

2. What types of women have made the choice to send their children to culturally affirmative schools?

I interviewed twenty-one mothers, thirteen in the United States and eight in the United Kingdom. Of the thirteen mothers in the United States, eight mothers sent their children to a full-time independent Afrikan-centered school called Sankofa. It was the first full-time Afrikan-centered school to operate in a northeastern city where over one-third of the population is Afrikan. One mother was the head teacher[3] of Sankofa and her children, who attended the local university, assisted her when she needed their help. Three of the remaining four mothers sent their children to public schools and the fourth sent her child to a private European (i.e., western-oriented) day care center. The eight mothers interviewed in the United Kingdom sent their children to culturally affirming supplementary schools. Supplementary schools are part-time schools, run by Afrikan people, usually operating on Saturdays and after state school hours. Just as not all independent Black schools in the United States are culturally affirmative Afrikan schools, so not all supplementary schools in the United Kingdom are culturally affirmative Afrikan schools. Of the eight mothers in the United Kingdom four mothers sent their children to Queen Nzinga School and four to Marcus Garvey School. Both schools are situated in London.

The model that I have designed as an analytical tool suggests reasons why these mothers send their children to culturally affirmative schools as well as why the four U.S. mothers chose not to send their children. In both cases my goal was to find out whether there is a more personal experiential reason for making these decisions in view of the significance of what a culturally affirmative school represents. I was also interested in the nature of their respective choices. In this context my objectives were to determine:

1. Whether their choice to send their children to an Afrikan-centered school can be construed as part of a resistance movement against racism in the public/state system.

2. Whether their choice not to send their children is indicative of a level of consciousness concerning what they perceive to be the effects of racism on their children or themselves.

These questions overlap and interrelate in the analyses of the lives of the twenty-one women involved in the study. On one hand, some parents who send their children to culturally affirmative schools may not be fully cognizant of the devastating effects of racism on their children. On the other hand, parents who do not send their children to these schools may be fully cognizant of the effects but may have reasons for not sending their children that pertain to some perceived shortcomings in the schools themselves. Since the majority of parents in the United States, and the United Kingdom, do not send their children to these schools, what makes these parents different? The exploratory look at the backgrounds of the four parents who do not send their children to culturally affirmative schools provide some insights that may be useful in helping to define some of the differences. This information may also provide some ideas about how or whether Afrikan-centered schools can be made more appealing. However, the major focus of this work is on the life herstories of seventeen mothers who committed themselves to supporting the schools for reasons that relate to the levels of their consciousness concerning the broader struggle of Afrikan people. It is clear that while these women come from diverse backgrounds ranging from the Caribbean, the United Kingdom, the United States, and Afrika with a variety of survival experiences, in general, they are not only consciously aware of the state's attempt to falsify information about the his/herstory of Afrikan people but are also aware of the impact of this miseducation on their children's lives.

This work is influenced by two earlier studies, one carried out in the United Kingdom and the other in the United States. The first study focused on the use of supplementary schools by Afrikan people in the United Kingdom (Dove 1990). These part-time schools, administered by Afrikan people, mainly Afrikan Caribbeans, emerged from the 1960s as a result of the large numbers of Afrikan-Caribbean children placed in "special" schools better known as Educational Sub-Normal (ESN) schools. The study was intended to give credence to parents as intellectual resources whose voices are given little validity in the planning and policy development aspects of state/public schooling.[4] Furthermore, the study viewed the development of these schools as an act of Afrikan resistance against the racism inherent in the state/public school system.

The second study carried out by Joan Ratteray and Mwalimu Shujaa (1987) was an investigation of parental perceptions about their involvement in independent neighborhood schools. The report from this study, *Dare to Choose,* focuses on the development and use of full-time independent schools, which like supplementary schools have arisen as a result of parental dissatisfaction with public schooling. Not all the schools in these two studies can be considered to be Afrikan-centered schools. However, all the schools constitute Afrikan-run alternatives to state/public schooling and thus involve serious considerations made by parents to use these schools. This applies whether they are part-time schools as in the United Kingdom or full-time schools as in the U.S. study. I reanalyzed the data from these two studies to contextualize the ideas for the present study.

Rationale and Method

This study builds on methods of interviewing developed during my previous supplementary school study done in the United Kingdom (see Dove 1990). In the current study I also focus on parental perceptions regarding the effects that racism in state schooling has upon their children. However, I believe that in-depth interviews undertaken for the present study look more deeply into reasons why parents have chosen culturally affirming schools. Rather than looking solely at the impact of schooling on their children, I look at the herstories of these mothers and try to make links between their experiences, and their understanding of racism, to their decisions about their own children's schooling and education.

I have been greatly influenced by the models used in three important studies carried out by Afrikan women about Afrikan women living in the United States and the United Kingdom. Influenced by their experiences as scholars, their approaches moved away from European-centered concepts and perspectives regarding the relationship between the researcher and the people who share information with them. One approach was developed by Joyce Ladner, whose sociological study *Tomorrow's Tomorrow,* carried out in 1964 in St. Louis, Missouri, and published in 1971, looks at the lives of young Black women growing up in an impoverished Afrikan community. Describing the significance of her study, Ladner wrote:

Few authorities on the Black community have written about the vast amount of strength and adaptability of the people. They have ignored the fact that this community is a force which not only acts upon its residents but which is also acted upon. (Ladner 1971, xv)

She shows the strengths of these young women who were living and raising children in family structures infected by white supremacy with low levels of life expectancy.

The second study, *The Heart of the Race,* published in 1986 and authored by three Afrikan women living in the United Kingdom, Beverly Bryan, Stella Dadzie, and Suzanne Scafe, is based on herstories of contemporary Afrikan women whose ideas and actions illuminate the critical role that women exercise in making social change in the United Kingdom. As researchers, they have set the context for Afrikan women to speak for themselves because these voices have been ignored or not clearly represented. Without this perspective, the story of Afrikan people is incomplete. With this in mind, they speak of the cultural significance of the Afrikan woman's experience:

> Our African origin is the cornerstone of our lifestyle and our perception of the world, the internal dynamic which has enabled us continuously to resist new assaults on our way of life. In responding to these assaults, we have had to create and recreate new definitions of ourselves as a people. As such our culture has become subversive, for through it we have always had to challenge, combat and find new ways of winning. (p. 183)

The third study, *The Habit of Surviving*, published in 1991 and written by Kesho Yvonne Scott, contrasts the lives of five "successful" Black women born in the United States in the 1930s. This model emphasizes the personal herstories of these women. These life stories were acquired through in-depth interviews that focused on the techniques invented by these women throughout their lives as victims and survivors.

> I could begin to see that we as black people (and especially black women) had some good habits and some bad habits, and that both played a role in our survival. I could finally make a theoretical leap from survival by means of group practices in every day life (and in my own life) to the design of an oppressive society to exert control over not only the material world but the hearts, minds and spirits of oppressed people, especially black women. (Scott 1991, 10)

I have transposed these designs into the model that is molded by my own theoretical framework, which highlights, in particular, the cultural context of the Afrikan woman's experience from antiquity into the future. At the same time it is apparent that the ideal Afrikan family cannot exist under European control and that its deficiency is a characteristic of the cultural war being waged against

Afrikan people's potential to strive toward spiritual, mental, social, political, and economic self-determination. This study highlights women who not only act against their oppressors but hold a vision of a future within which being Afrikan provides the basis of a new world order.

The focus on Afrikan women as parents is related very much to the fact that women are the vanguard in both the development and use of Afrikan culturally affirming institutions. Their involvement in this process defines them as warriors and leaders, who, as I have previously explicated, have for centuries been the backbone of resistance movements against European control and domination. As Afrikan mothers, women have always played the central role in building the family and in nurturing and helping in their children's growth, physically, mentally, and spiritually.

Historically and of necessity, the family has been under siege under white supremacy. For this reason, Hazel Carby importantly views the Afrikan family as the site of struggle and argues that

> [w]e would not wish to deny that the family can be a source of oppression for us but we also wish to examine how the black family has functioned as a prime source of resistance to oppression. We need to recognize that during slavery, periods of colonialism and under the present authoritarian state, the black family has been a site of political and cultural resistance to racism. (Carby 1982a, 214)

It is Carby's contention that the survival of Afrikan people has been predicated on the strength of the family and its ability to challenge the injustices of white supremacy.

The role of women and men in the establishment of the family has been severely debilitated by the continuous attempt to subjugate Afrikan people through political, economic, psychological, and spiritual means. This systematic effort has had an impact on the development of the family and, therefore, the Afrikan child's growth. It is compounded by the ability of the father to provide the economic resources for his family and especially in relation to the access of the prospective mother to proper health care, schooling, employment, housing, marriage and human rights even before she conceives. Moreover, the obstacles that Afrikan women and men face in being raised in, and raising children in, white supremacist patriarchy is devastating, as the works of W. E. B. Du Bois, Robert Staples, Robert Hill, Andrew Billingsley, Antonio McDaniel, Harriette Pipes McAdoo, James Stewart, Niara Sudarkasa, K. Sue Jewell, Wade Nobles, Asa Hilliard, and others show.

Under European domination the process of deculturalization has had serious ramifications for the thinking and behaviors of oppressed peoples, especially those whose cultural values are grounded in matriarchal belief systems. Difficulties in the face of patriarchy, especially for Afrikan people, center around the ability to maintain the family, venerate the woman, revere the role of motherhood and fatherhood, and respect the integrity of girls and boys as the wealth and future of the society. As a mother, the Afrikan woman must contend with the racism that devalues the humanity of her people as well as the sexism that devalues her womanhood and therefore her status. As bearers of culture the Afrikan mother's responsibility for retaining cultural unity has been beset with myriad dangers. I have therefore tried to show the resilience of some Afrikan mothers who, in the face of such tremendous obstacles, are able to see the value of their Afrikaness and knowingly transfer that understanding to their children.

For this study, I view those supplementary schools that focus on cultural affirmation in their pedagogies as similar to Afrikan-centered schools in the United States. Moreover, I believe that in both cases, Afrikan-based institution building is rooted in the attempt to challenge the immorality of European supremacy. The women who have chosen to build these schools have made a decision about the types of influences they wish their children to be exposed to. This sets them apart from other women who send their children to state/public schools or to other private schools. To believe that an Afrikan-based cultural emphasis is important to their children in the face of the derogation of Afrikan people and culture is a reflection of the ability of Afrikan people to maintain their values even under the most extreme attempts at deculturalization.

The U.S. school in this study is tuition based. This means that these women and their families must raise the finances to send their children. If they are unable to do so, they can participate in the school and exchange skills for the finances that they are unable to provide. They may teach part-time, watch the children during lunchtime or playtime, or help to carry out administrative tasks. In this regard, the critical questions are: Do the fees dictate and determine the type of women who build these schools? Does the financial situation prevent more women from making this decision?

My earlier U.K. study (Dove 1990), coupled with data from the U.K. parents involved in the present study, goes some way toward answering these questions. In the United Kingdom most supplementary schools are free or charge minimal fees (Dhondy 1982; Jones 1984; Best 1990; Dove 1990). However, the majority of Afrikan parents, whether rich or poor, do not subscribe to these schools. So, I speculate that the fee-paying aspect of the Afrikan-centered school may not entirely account for why some parents do not use this school or other schools like the one in this study. In the U.S. city where the Sankofa School is located, there is a substantial Afrikan middle-class. However, overall and in the main, middle-class parents are not the main users. Generally, if they use private schools, they send their children to western-centered schools.

In the supplementary school study (1990) with the use of questionnaires, I asked parents if they would send their children to these schools if they became full-time. An overwhelming majority of the sixty questionnaires returned showed that they would. Furthermore, half of the parents said they would be prepared to pay for this service. This is interesting because the majority of parents who use supplementary schools in both the 1990 study and the present one are poor. It may be true to say that more parents would send their children to fee-paying Afrikan-centered schools if they could afford to do so. Given the London findings, it is also reasonable to argue that the parents who send their children to culturally affirming schools constitute a minority of parents who, I believe, have made a radical, political decision.

The history of supplementary schools in the United Kingdom developed out of the movement among Afrikan Caribbean parents, in particular, who were dissatisfied with the racism of state/public schooling. The commitment of parents to send their children to these schools relates to their awareness of the racist dynamics of the state system. As Faroukh Dhondy (1982) states when describing the conditions surrounding the establishment of the early supplementary schools:

The State, itself aware that a powerful political base could be built through the Supplementary schools, used police and education officials to harass them. Pressure was put on owners and caretakers of the buildings used. Parents were visited by the police and questioned as to whether they knew their children were in the hands of Black Power fanatics. The children themselves were harassed by the police who would frequently visit the schools and question what was taking place. (1982, 33)

Discrimination of this kind did not end with police harassment. Parents have confided that their children suffer discrimination from mainstream teachers if it is known that they attend these schools. This is one reason why some parents do not use supplementary schools. In the United States Afrikan-centered or culturally affirmative institutions pose a similar threat to the establishment in the sense that such schools also offer a powerful political base for Afrikan activism. Parents, who therefore make a commitment to send their children to schools administrated by Afrikan people appear to take a militant stand. I would argue that although parents pay tuition for their children to go to Sankofa and schools like it, their commitment goes beyond the financial aspects of obtaining a private school education. I believe that the eight Afrikan women interviewees who chose to send their children to an Afrikan-centered school and the eight women whose children attend the two culturally affirming schools in the United Kingdom have taken a radical stance and made a radical choice. Based on their interviews, their choice has less to do with money and more to do with helping their children navigate this world with Afrikan principles and philosophies to guide them.

Evaluating My Respect for My Sisters

The question of trust in Afrikan people as educators is an important factor in the decision to send a child to a culturally affirming school, particularly in the climate of the debate about whether these schools are segregationist and developing anti-white sentiments. When I went to the United Kingdom to begin this study, this work was in reality a continuation of my earlier study of 1990, carried out when I was a student. I visited some of the same schools and met some of the same mothers that I had been involved with. Thus, I did not have to undergo much of my earlier experiences. However, it is important that you understand some of my earlier experiences from 1990 so that you may see how I was able to build upon them.

In 1990, the trust factor was extremely important given the his/ herstory of harassment towards the development of supplementary schools as a challenge to the racist state school treatment of Afrikan children. Parents were aware of the hostility felt against them both by the public/state school system and the community at large. In my case, when I went to interview the school directors, parents and children, I was aware of the climate of mistrust. As a school co-director and educator, I was leery of persons investigating these schools. As Afrikan people we have a tradition of encountering agent provocateurs whose mission is to destroy Afrikan unity that appears to challenge the ideologies of the dominant group.

In fact, the first school I visited was one of the first supplementary schools founded in London. I was refused access to parents by the board of directors because of a prior investigation carried out by another student whose study challenged the credibility of supplementary schools. Although I was hurt at the insinuation, I fully understood the feelings of suspicion held against "outsiders" carrying out "investigations" about the school.

Thus, for this study, it was important for me to present myself as a credible person in looks, dress, and carriage. Even before providing a personal explanation of my research after the phone and letter contact, I felt that I had to present myself as mature and competent enough for the work. For seven years prior to this investigation I had grown my hair in "dreadlocks." Although I had cut my hair a year earlier, I had allowed it to grow back without locks and I kept a color rinse in it to look younger. For this investigation, I allowed the gray to show through. I felt that being natural, as an older woman, I would be far more acceptable as a serious and conscientious person. Not only that, I also felt that looking older would remove the idea that I was a novice or entirely new to the arena.

Interestingly, five of the parents from this 1990 study became interviewees for the herstories of the present study. These interviews with the U.K. mothers took place in London in November 1993. I was invited by the administrator of Queen Nzinga School to speak to interested parents and teachers from all over the country about the development of full-time Afrikan-centered schools. My intention was to carry out the interviews during my one-month stay. Before my arrival, I informed the administrator of Queen Nzinga School of my intention to interview mothers. She had spoken to parents and they gave me permission to approach them. At the same time, I made contact with Adoaha, a mother from Marcus Garvey School who had introduced me to three mothers from my 1990 study. These four mothers had helped me to pilot my study of that time and advised me on my questionnaire categories (see Dove 1990). Adoaha spoke to them about my research and they agreed to be interviewed again.

In the United States, as a founding member on the board of directors of Sankofa School, I became acquainted with the parents and their children on my visits to the school. Some of the parents that I interviewed were also founding members like myself. Therefore, I was very familiar with them as colleagues before the interviews. I believe that these relationships had a bearing on the interviews because trust had been established earlier. My role as a founding member gave me some credibility as a researcher with those parents who did not really know me. Thus, my role as an active member of Sankofa School enabled the parents to feel that I had no interest in undermining them or the school. To my mind, as an Afrikan woman whose allegiance lies with my people, it was not possible to attempt to interview women who I viewed as sisters and activists, with objectives outside those that I felt obliged to reveal.

Arrangements were made to interview parents at Sankofa School after the board had granted permission for me to carry out my investigation. I called parents and notified them of my intention to carry out this study. In both the United States and the United Kingdom my approach was one of genuine humility and respect because I felt honored that these women would be prepared to trust me with private information about their personal lives. As an Afrikan woman growing up in the West, and a single parent with a history of little or no financial stability, I felt that I could identify with the participants on any level as a sister. In fact, there were moments when I felt emotionally overcome with either the joy or sadness produced by some of the experiences that were narrated. Indeed, some situations reminded me of my own experiences. In some strange way, when one is relating one's story to another it provides a time of reflection and analysis as one sees where one has come from and where one is. It is generally rare that an opportunity arises when one can look at one's self. Reflecting on the Afrikan struggle generally, and the injustices meted to our children, often, there are many moments of sadness.

There were different depths of information given and I can relate this to the closeness of my relationship to the interviewees. For instance, I was privy to some very sensitive personal information. I related this sharing of life experiences not only to the trust built up during the interview but also to the context of the relationship prior to the interview. I did not press any person to tell me anything that she felt was too personal. I allowed each mother the freedom to choose what she wished to speak about after laying out the types of things that I wished to find out. Thus my questions were open-ended but structured in that I was looking for specific kinds of experiences.

The U.S. interviews at Sankofa School took place in February and March of 1992. The U.K. interviews at Queen Nzinga and Marcus Garvey Schools took place in November 1993. Prior to the interviews, each mother was briefed on the objectives of the interviews and the methods that I would use. The interviews were taped and ran from one and a half to two and a half hours. I followed up interviews with phone calls if anything needed clarification. Before the recording, I introduced myself and established the questions and the types of information that I wanted for the study. In this way, I wanted to create a reasonably relaxed situation in the context of the seriousness of the interview.

I believe that my questions dealing with the experiences of growing up as Afrikan women and experiencing the racism and sexism that this entails were profound. All of the women who sent their children to the culturally affirming schools, took their decision seriously and the interviews themselves were thoughtful. During the course of the interviews, I tried to elicit ideas from the women that reflected their own political feelings about some of the critical issues going on in the Afrikan community. The interviews were therefore not generally of a happy-go-lucky superficial nature, nor did I want them to be. My study was to focus on the gravity of growing up and raising children in this society.

My Credibility as a Researcher and a Sister

Although the interviewees and I acknowledged that we as Black/ Afrikan women could come together in understanding the experiential similarity of living in western society, we were different in the sense that our origins and language were rooted in other places. Moreover, learning to become an academic in the Eurocentric system of higher education has required that I develop a level of proficiency in the English language in order to understand the subtleties of its uses especially concerning Afrikan people. My continental Afrikan roots and European experience must have played a part in my communication with the sisters.

When I arrived in England from West Afrika, in the early 1950s, I was six years old and could speak two Nigerian languages, Igbo and Yoruba. Within a short period of time, these languages lost their validity in an English context. As an isolated Afrikan child growing up in England it became critical that I understand the oppressor language and speak it as well as I could, as soon as I could. I learned the language as a necessary part of a survival technique. Understanding the meanings of the oppressor's language enables one to present an argument or case to defend or fight for the rights of self or others. My work in the state school system has required that I also understand the language of "education," which excludes those who are not of the teaching profession. Thus, understanding has helped in the challenge to, and struggle against, racism in the schools, as implicated in the processes that undermine Afrikan teachers, students, and parents.

Having lived in Brixton among predominantly Afrikan people from Jamaica, I learned to understand that language especially well since I was once a member of the Twelve Tribes Rastafarian organization. Each of the Caribbean islands has its own distinct language that has developed out of the colonizers' languages. The language of the Afrikan American is similar in that it has arisen as a way of communication that is used in the interests of Afrikan people who have designed it. These languages maintain characteristics of speech that came from Afrika. Moreover and importantly as Herskovitz (1958) showed, many of the words used by Afrikan nations, which replaced European words in the construction of Afrikan-based languages under European domination, were in fact very similar to the English words. As a result, early Eurocentric scholars believed that Afrikan people were mispronouncing European words when they were in fact using Afrikan words. For example, the Mende word *suwango,* "to be proud," was seen as a mispronounciation of the word *swagger.* The Wolof word *lir,* meaning *"small,"* was viewed as a corruption of *little.* The Twi word *fa,* *"to take,"* was seen as a mispronunciation of *for* (p. 277). Ignorance of this type has served to invalidate Afrikan speech within the public school system (see the Oakland School District's debate on Ebonics).

Although I speak the "downpressor" language in the style of the oppressor, I have subverted its use so that it can serve the interests of the oppressed. New languages or dialects that arose out of oppressive power relations are used to undermine the oppressor. At the same time, I believe that the language of the oppressor can itself be subverted. After all it would be ridiculous to believe that to speak the language of the conquered necessarily means that the user is actively trying to change oppressive social conditions. Similarly, it would be nonsense to believe that people who speak the language of the oppressor work to support oppression or are themselves oppressors. However, to preserve a language, in the face of the continued attempt to impose standards as a way of inferiorizing that language, must be considered an act of subversion. While language is an integral part of culture, we who have learned to exploit it have the potential to reconstruct meanings to suit the values that pertain to our Afrikan cultural orientation.

In the context of these interviews, the women with whom I communicated did not appear to have a problem with the fact that I am an Afrikan who speaks like a European. They spoke English in a similar manner, although for some English was a second language. Though I must have missed some of the subtleties of communicating in one's own language, what was of the utmost importance was that the mothers trusted me because they knew the nature of my work. Their trust was not based on my familiarity with their language. This is not to deny the importance of the familiarity and trust that can be gained from speaking the same dialect or language. However, part of the work, as I see it, is to form bridges, to create unity among Afrikan people in spite of the imperialist languages that have been learned. In this vein I try to show the similarities in the experiences of these women living in western patriarchal racist societies. This unity is critical for providing a basis for a liberationist agenda.

For the purpose of reporting my findings I have changed the original names of the schools and of these beautiful women to hide their identities and to suit the impressions that I formed as a result of getting to know them. Three of the women already use Afrikan names. The chosen names among the U.S. mothers are: Ayoluwa (joy of our people); Aisha (life); Aidoo (arrived); Binta, (beautiful daughter); Camara (one who teaches from experience); Dalmar (versatile); Adaeze (princess); Ezigbo (beloved); Ife (lover of art and culture); Jaha (dignity); Kumiwa (brave); Mawasi (in God's hands); and Nalo (much loved). The chosen names among the U.K. mothers are: Abebe (we asked and got her); Adoaha (daughter of the people); Amal (hopes); Diallo (bold); Enomwoyi (one who has grace); Fugo (she brings wholeness); Kesi (born when father had difficulties); Nzinga (she is beauty and courage).

I took these names from *The Book of Afrikan Names* (1991) by Molefi Kete Asante, whose work on Afrocentricity has been paramount among activists and scholars, particularly in the academic arena, for the purpose of reclaiming and developing Afrikan-based knowledge. He purposely did not identify the languages because he felt that in a Pan-Afrikanist way it is critical to our survival that we begin to see ourselves as Afrikan people in a more global way than in the narrower context of a particular ethnic or national group.

Finally, the interviews were long and very detailed. I used content analysis to code them in ways that relate to the specific areas that are germane to this study. Obviously there is a wealth of information, but not all of it could be used here. The key areas that I focus on are:

1. Upbringing
2. Schooling
3. Experiences with racism
4. Children's schooling
5. Feelings about culturally affirmative schooling

In discussing my analysis of the interviews, I use these areas as guidelines. I also employ information gleaned from the other studies mentioned earlier to contextualize these findings.

Ultimately, I present a culturally based model for analyzing the impact of racism and sexism on the cultural continuity of Afrikan people. Based on this model, I correlate the interviewees interpretations of racism, in particular, to their decisions to use or not use these schools. It is the case that while sexism has a pervasive impact upon the lives of Afrikan women, men, and children, the values of European patriarchy have, as I have previously argued, been the basis for a devaluation of humanity that is reflected in the historical process and achievement of the racialization of the world. Therefore, racism and the devaluation of Afrikan humanity takes priority in the minds of these Afrikan women concerning their children's survival and for that matter the survival of Afrikan people.

I have divided the interviews into the two groups: Women, from the United Kingdom and women from the United States. In order to understand the similarities in their struggles as Afrikan women living in these countries as subjugated people, I provide an his/herstorical context to their stories.

②

A Context for the
United Kingdom Herstories

This chapter provides a herstorical background for the experiences of some of the U.K. mothers, the majority of whom come from the Caribbean and whose stories are the central theme of this book. My intention is to make a link between the liberation struggles of Afrikan women and men, from antiquity to the present day. I hope that it is feasible to view this ongoing struggle from European control as a critical feature within the Afrikan cultural collective memory that cannot be erased until just power relations exist between Afrikan and European peoples. For this undertaking, I shall present

1. A background of the political conditions that undergird socioeconomic reasons for entry into the United Kingdom of large numbers of Afrikan people from the continent and from the Caribbean

2. A view of the impact of nineteenth-century ideological influences of scientific racism on the immigration and educational political policies that influenced the post war period in the United Kingdom

3. A brief historical view of the British schooling system as the context for the experience of Afrikan children in the United Kingdom

The capture and enslavement of Afrikan women, men, and children was fundamental to the accumulation of wealth for the development of capitalism in Western Europe (Williams 1966). It was Karl Marx who provided the world with a comprehensive model of how capitalism functions as a system of production. This form of European economic profit-making was, he believed, the most effective exploitation of human energies. From his analysis, we understand that this type of economy—with its complete disregard for humanity—exacted the most effort from humans in the shortest possible time. In the Caribbean, it provided Europeans with an abundance of wealth for centuries at the cost of millions of Afrikan lives. The average life expectancy of an Afrikan person was seven years (Marx 1976, 915). The constant supply of people from the Afrikan continent made the plantation economy a viable enterprise from which Europeans of all classes could ultimately profit.

While it is important to highlight the role of Afrikan labor power and the genocide associated with it in the development of capitalism, it is critical not to ignore how the Caribbean islands were violently stolen from the First Nations peoples (indigenous people) who populated these islands. Cristobel Colon's (Christopher Columbus) heinous treatment of the Tainos of Guanahani (renamed Indians of Hispaniola) set a precedent for the trail of destruction that was to follow his "discovery" of the "New World" (Carew 1994). The genocidal atrocities committed against these people are an important part of the equation concerning Europe's accumulation of wealth. This issue is discussed in more detail in chapter 4. The repopulation of the islands by enslaved Afrikan people was an attempt to replace the lost energies of the indigenous peoples with forced labor to yield a profit from the plantation system that would eventually be instituted all over the Americas. In the long run, Afrikan and First Nation people's resistance to this form of inhumanity proved the inefficiency of this system.

Resistance to European domination, "white" supremacy, took place in many forms. Afrikan women, particularly in their roles as mothers, have always been and continue to be the vanguard of this movement. The stories of their bravery and defiance have yet to come to light. In the plantation system throughout the Americas, women worked alongside men suffering the same abuses and tortures. Pregnancy made little difference either to punishment or the workload. The horrors of this indifference comes alive in movies such as *Quilombo* (1987) and *Sankofa* (1994), and in the literary encounters of Stella Dadzie (1990), Gloria Joseph (1981), and Angela Davis (1984).

In the Caribbean, the eventual reduction in the labor pool forced an economic value on "breeding" thus incentives were devised to stimulate the growth of labor energies (Dadzie 1990). These incentives—more food, better working and birthing conditions, payment for surviving children and so on—failed to raise the reproduction rate substantially. Although, as Dadzie points out, theories to account for this drop in reproduction have linked this state of affairs to the poor diet, bad treatment, marital instability, and such; in reality, the reasons were related to the women's determination not to reproduce as an act of defiance. The women's cultural knowledge from Afrika of healing through plants was used to prevent conception and to induce abortion. Breast-feeding for lengthy periods and the killing of their children were also ways in which mothers resisted and defied the economic exploitation of their reproductive powers (Dadzie 1990, 28–31). I would add that while matriarchal values, retained from Afrika, were still powerful, it was the decision of both women and men not to have children because of their inability to provide the correct parenting under these inhumane conditions. At the same time, the decision to have children was very likely based on a belief that such children would be the makers of social change.

Women's roles in resistance were varied. They ranged from working as spies, committing suicide, active participation in uprisings, to the poisoning of owners. From Dadzie's research in Jamaica, we have various examples of women warriors. She writes of Minelta, a girl of fifteen years, who was sentenced to death for attempting to poison her master. On hearing her sentence, she showed no emotion then laughed as she left the "courthouse" (Dadzie, 32). In the early 1700s women like Nanny the Maroon, grounded in the tradition of the "Ashanti warrior-priestess," provided the leadership that led to the founding of Nanny Town or "women's town" in the Blue Mountains (Dadzie, 34). The action and roles of such women clearly indicate their matriarchal Afrikan origins, particularly in light of the great fighting tradition of female Afrikan warriors like the Candaces, Queens of Kush, who were never conquered by invading Europeans like the Greeks and the Romans who conquered Kemet (Ancient Egypt) from 332–323 B.C.E. (Finch 1990). Queen Nzinga of Angola (1581–1663) was a great military leader who fought against the Portuguese colonial oppression. Donna Beatrice (1682–1706) was a political and spiritual leader who opposed Portuguese domination by her challenge to their belief in white Christian supremacy. She promoted Afrikan consciousness through her re-Afrikanization of biblical characters. In Ghana, Yaa Asantewa (1840/60–1920) fought against the British invasion in 1900 (Sweetman 1984). Warriorship, as these examples show, is shaped by the conditions of the time.

The role of women, especially as mothers, has always been integral to the struggle for freedom and as Dadzie states: "The most powerful and enduring of these was their role as primary conveyers of culture" (Dadzie, 33). Thus, the transference of cultural values and beliefs in both the past and the present may be viewed as an aspect of female warriorship. It is those values and beliefs that have sustained Afrikan life, while at the same time, challenged the injustices placed upon Afrikan people by a cruel, immoral conqueror.

Afrikan resistance in the Caribbean, on the Afrikan continent and in North and South America was a reflection of the intolerable conditions and status that Europeans had violently imposed. Given the African development of deep and profound spirituality, the Afrikan person could only view her oppressor as the human embodiment of everything that was antithetical to all that she held sacred. Hart (1980) argues that it was the resistance of enslaved Afrikan people against their oppressors that led to the abolition of "slavery."

Europeans as a cultural collective worked diligently to support each other in maintaining control over the energies and resources of Afrikan peoples on a global scale. After the abolition of "slavery" in the Caribbean, the consolidation of a colonial relationship between Afrikan people and their metropolitan rulers took place. In fact, slavery as an economic structure did not end, rather it took on a new form. The capitalist markets that had evolved from enslaved labor like coffee, sugar, cotton, tobacco, food crops, and labor continued to be developed under the auspices of what became known as "freed labor." In reality, women and men remained tied to the production of these crops under the same rulership. This transitory phase was often painful. Craton says of Britain's colonies:

> [T]he newly freed were continually harassed by the extension of British police, vagrancy, and masters and servants laws, applied by justices of the peace who were usually planters or by stipendiary magistrates strongly under plantocratic influence. The freedmen's ambitions to be peasant freeholders were hampered by relatively high prices for lands, taxes that grossly favored the large landowners, and the enforcement of laws against squatting. Political expression was stifled, and where there were elections the franchise was denied to the black masses by loaded property qualifications. Though they could no longer control the larger economy, the colonial whites also made sure that they remained a large oligarchy, controlling all wholesale and most retail trade and obtaining legislation against the former slaves' network. (Fryer 1988, 98)

As a result of these inequities, uprisings continued all over the British-run Caribbean islands right up until the beginning of World War II (Fryer 1988), the most violently repressed of which took place in Jamaica. Paul Bogle, a Baptist preacher and small holding farmer, led the rebellion against unfair land distribution and judicial injustices. The British militia were involved and seven Afrikan persons were killed. The courthouse was burned and one Black magistrate and eighteen white people were killed. Governor Eyre, a highly respected member of the Anthropological Society of London, ordered the execution of 439 Afrikan people. Bogle was hanged, 600 Afrikan women and men were flogged barbarically, and 1,000 homes were burned. "Ah my man!" said a captain of the Kingston Volunteers to one of his prisoners, "we shall take a thousand of your black men's hearts for one white man's ear" (Fryer 1988, 99–100).

As previously implied, after so-called emancipation, Europe maintained its economic relations of dependency. Profits continued to depend on markets created through the violent exploitation of enslaved and colonized Afrikan energies. This state of affairs, in turn, forced the islands to depend upon this type of economy to survive. These Caribbean economics continued to be controlled by Europeans although they were managed by Afrikan men who took on a neocolonial role.[1]

At the same time, untold atrocities were committed against Afrikan women and men on the continent of Afrika during European colonization, which for the most part entailed the forcible, violent use of captured energies and resources. In some ways, to speak of colonization as though it was a rather mundane and progressive experience has the effect of diluting the impact of white supremacy on Afrikan peoples (and others) and their social structures. From at least the 1500s, during the Portuguese colonization of Afrika, but especially at the Berlin conference in 1884–85 during the division of Afrika among other European countries like, Britain, Germany, Belgium, France, and Italy, the subjugation of Afrikan people was taking place. According to Peter Fryer's (1988) research on Britain's colonies, Britain alone had taken parts of Afrika beginning in 1662 with the Gambia. In 1807, Sierra Leone became a colony. Lagos was occupied in 1861,

and the southern Gold Coast (Ghana), annexed in 1874. In southern Africa, the Cape of Good Hope had been occupied since 1806 and Natal since 1843; and Basutoland had been annexed in 1868. . . . Bechuanaland (Botswana) was made a "protectorate" in 1885. The occupation of Nigeria was formally complete by 1886. . . . Somaliland was occupied in 1886; Zululand was annexed in 1887; then Kenya the following year.
    Rhodesia came under British rule in 1888–93, Zanzibar in 1890, Uganda in 1890–96 and Nyasaland (Malawi) in 1891. Ashanti was conquered in 1901. . . . Egypt occupied in 1882. . . . British capital, and the international banking groups associated with it, also dominated the Portuguese African colonies of Angola, Mozambique and Portuguese Guinea; and British interests had a substantial share in the exploitation of the Belgian Congo. (Fryer 1988, 34–35)

This is not to speak of Britain's colonies in the Caribbean or any other part of the world. Certainly by the time of the Berlin conference, the machine gun had been invented and this force added to greed was devastating for Afrikan people as Fryer cogently points out (p. 34). The Congo was controlled by both the French and the Belgians. A French Congolese official commented:

> The dead, we no longer count them. The villages, horrible charnel-houses, disappear in the yawning gulf. A thousand diseases follow in our footsteps. . . . And this martyrdom continues. . . . We white men must shut our eyes not to see the hideous dead, the dying who curse us, and the wounded who implore, the weeping women and the starving children. We must stop our ears not to hear the lamentations, the cries, the maledictions which rise from every foot of land, from every tuft of grass. (Morel 1920/1969, 138)

According to Chinweizu (1975) in the Congo Free State, mostly owned and controlled by the king of Belgium, Leopold II, barbaric torturous treatment of Afrikan people managed to cut the population within a twenty-year period from over 20 million to half that.

> In the process, slavery and disorder were visited upon the African inhabitants of the Free State. Leopold simply declared the land and the people his own; he made the produce of the land his own, wrecked the trade of the land, and made slaves of those natives he did not kill. And of them he demanded rubber, more and ever more rubber. (62)

"Independence" from European atrocities was, for colonized countries, an ideological concept rather than a material and spiritual reality. For instance, during the European war, World War II, according to Chinweizu, Britain acquired funds through "borrowing" 3,000 million pounds from her colonies (Chinweizu 1975). These were called "reserves." Ironically for Afrikan people, Britain saw this money as a contribution to the defense of the empire—an empire built on extraction of wealth from its colonized peoples. Moreover, the Caribbean, like Afrika and the United States, provided servicemen who fought for Europeans during that war. Their contribution was not recognized. Afterwards, argues Chinweizu, Britain did not repay its debt. Instead, colonies were asked to provide more money. Between 1947 and 1948, marketing boards were established to protect the colonies' farmers from global market fluctuations by guaranteeing stable prices. Monies accrued from the "good" years were invested and impounded (Chinweizu 1975, 272).

The arrival of Afrikan women and men from the Caribbean to the United Kingdom during the late 1940s and early 1950s is/was his/herstorically linked to the state of economic affairs existing in both the United Kingdom and the Caribbean. In the Caribbean, as Eric Williams argues, there had been a rise in the standard of some people's living resulting from this economic relationship (Williams 1975, 500–501). More importantly, however, chronic unemployment and underemployment intensified as a result of population growth, rising wages, and capital-intensive technologies. The rebuilding of Western Europe was dependent on monies from its colonies and aid from the United States to save the British economy. The labor shortage in Britain demanded workers from the Caribbean to enter industries.

Afrikan workers from the Caribbean were actively recruited by London Transport from Barbados, Trinidad, and Jamaica. The British Hotels and Restaurants Association also recruited from Barbados. Although many Afrikan people coming to the United Kingdom were skilled workers, they were offered the lowest, most menial jobs. Over 46 percent of men and 27 percent of women were skilled manual workers (Fryer 1984, 373–74). Glass's research revealed that the illiteracy rate among 16,089 "immigrants" from the Caribbean in 1954–55 was less than 2 percent (Ogbu 1978, 242). Due to this migratory pattern, restriction on the movements of Afrikan labor became the focus of government discussions in Britain. A cabinet task force was set up to obtain information from the police and Labor Exchange[2] staff (Fryer 1988, 118–19).

The exploitation of Afrikan women and men in the Caribbean has played a critical role in accumulating wealth for Britain's economy. The control of Afrikan energies and resources from enslaved labor to paid labor has been carefully orchestrated by the British government to facilitate Britain's economic development.

More recently, since the end of World War II, the status of Afrikan people as immigrant labor has been critical for determining a position in Britain's socioeconomic hierarchy and, thus, the quality of life affordable. Immigration control is linked to the eugenics movement (Cohen 1985), and is a critical component of the legal conditions of Afrikan women and men living in the United Kingdom. The following paragraphs will elucidate this state of affairs.

Race and Immigration Policy

The eugenics movement has perhaps been most well known for its promotion and advocacy of "scientific" racism. The basic assumption is that hereditary racial differences in humans assume a psychological dimension. The idea that "intelligence" is an innate characteristic whose level can be measured in individuals and "races" was developed by Francis Galton (1822–1911). During the 1900s this idea led to a European obsession with measuring an entity defined as "intelligence" and the development of IQ testing to determine its various levels. Greatly influenced by his cousin Charles Darwin and the concept of evolution, Galton founded the study of eugenics in 1883. The concept of evolution was critical to scientific racism and the subsequent development of IQ testing since it was based on the idea of change as movement relating to progress and progression. The concept of progress allowed Europeans to construct criteria that sought to differentiate humanity on the grounds of its closeness or distance from early humans. The monkey was seen as the progenitor of humankind. The perceived closeness to the monkey of early humanity was defined by Europeans. They supposed that they were distant enough from those origins to classify themselves as superior. Their criteria for this distinction was largely based upon genetic differences like skin color, physiology, hair texture, and so on.

Charles Darwin popularized the concept of evolution. His ideas were influenced by and served to influence the racism of the time. Stephen Jay Gould points out that in Darwin's *Descent of Man*, he wrote of a future time when "the gap between human and ape will increase by the anticipated extinction of such intermediaries as chimpanzees and Hottentots" (Gould 1988, 36). The derogatory Dutch name "Hottentot" that Darwin employs refers to an Afrikan people, almost annihilated by the Dutch invasion in South Afrika, who know themselves as Khoi Khoi. Far from being "intermediaries" between monkeys and men, they are oppressed laborers and many are revolutionary fighters against the system of apartheid in South Afrika.

Eugenics, through IQ testing underpinned by the belief in innate inferiority/superiority, had an important influence on the history of immigration and educational policy in the United Kingdom and the United States. According to Cohen (1985), the 1905 Aliens Act is associated with the eugenics movement's ideological concepts in relation to the notion of improvement in the efficiency of nation and empire (pp. 73–74). This act encouraged the separation of so-called races on the grounds that inferiority innately transferred and that the transference of inferiority was bad for the British nation, the race, and the empire. The right to exclude "immigrants" from Britain on economic or health grounds was later enacted during the 1920s against Jewish immigrants (Cohen 1985, 89–90). At the same time in the United States, according to Gould, the results of the intelligence testing of 1.75 million service men during the 1914–18 European war led to the Immigration Restriction Act of 1924. This act curtailed the entrance of immigrants on the grounds of their national genetic inferiority.

Alongside the fear of a declining intelligence due to the entry of "inferior" races such as Jewish people, Turks, Greeks, and Italians, was the ever present fear of the "Negro." The racialized breakdown of the army tests showed that 89 percent of Afrikan service men were "morons." In reality, these figures reflected the levels of cultural bias in the tests, the unfamiliarity with test taking, and the rate of illiteracy among Afrikan persons. These "findings" provided the "scientific" data to support the continuation of selection and segregation. These data were used to justify the testing of all children and the restricted entry of Black children into higher education in the United States (Gould 1988, 228–32). In the British context, IQ testing became a major determining factor in assigning children to their racialized and for that matter, racially gendered, socioeconomic roles through the schooling system.

Coming Home to Roost

The racialized power relations consolidated by the accumulated wealth on which the United Kingdom grew as an industrialized nation did not become visibly apparent until the entry of large numbers of Afrikan women and men from the Caribbean and Afrika around the time of my arrival in 1952. At this time, the movement of Afrikan people was of prime importance to Britain's global economic power. On the other hand, Britain's open invitation for Afrikan people from the Caribbean to enter Britain was directly related to a need to rebuild Britain. Britain needed to replenish the labor power necessary to carry out the most menial tasks, regardless of the laborers' skills and academic qualifications. On the other hand, the entry of continental Afrikan people (mostly men) into the universities and colleges was a reflection of the preparation for the neocolonial roles and occupations that would be needed in Afrika to build and maintain European institutions. As Ekwe-Ekwe (1993) argues, the independence struggles of Afrikan peoples from European domination did not prevent the consolidation of European institutions. The newly constructed Afrikan nation-states designed by colonial powers served to continue the holocaust started by European invasions even after their physical departure. As recently as the last thirty-three years, six million Afrikan people have died in the postcolonial conflicts (Ekwe-Ekwe, 72). This was and continues to be the context for the entry of Afrikan women, children, and men from the Afrikan continent into the United Kingdom.

Cohen (1985) argued that the eugenicist ideology of the 1880s underpins modern political arguments for the control of "immigrants" into Britain based on the fear that Black people were diseased, would take white employment, and would live off welfare. This control was consummated in the 1953 Aliens Order (pp. 89–90). Britain's indigenous population had little historical understanding, as a result of miseducation, of the real nature of Europe's and in particular Britain's exploitative relationship to Afrikan people. They perceived Afrikan people as swarming into the country from the jungles with objectives like stealing their jobs, homes, wealth, welfare, women, and men.

Knowing Our Rightful Place in Britain's Schools

The 1944 Education Act heralded a new era of full-time educational provision by the state for the majority of children who had previously been excluded because they were too poor to afford to go to school. Compulsory education signified the new extensive role of the state. All children, it was felt, should receive the education best suited to their individual requirements. Three types of secondary education were proposed, grammar school for the most academically able, secondary modern school for developing vocational skills, and technical school for the more industrially motivated pupils.

The 1943 White Paper on Educational Reconstruction (para 28 [4]) was concerned about the suitability of grammar school with its academic foundation for some children because

[t]oo many of the nation's abler children are attracted into a type of education which prepares primarily for the University and for the administrative and clerical professions; too few find their way into school from which the design and craftsmanship sides of the industry are recruited. If education is to serve interests both of the child and the nation, some means must be found of correcting this bias and directing ability into the field where it will find its best realization.

Thus, while secondary education implied an equal education, it was clear that this tripartite system was to differentiate children into middle and lower socioeconomic strata, while the public (private elite) schooling would remain the bastion of white male and white female elitism. In reality, the tripartite system was a four-part system, where the elite schooling would continue to educate the children of the ruling elite, who would one day continue to control and direct the schooling, and the so-called education, of the masses.

In this way, the fundamental feudal class power relations could remain intact. However, new classes had evolved from the massive accumulation of wealth that had accrued from the dominated peoples of the world. The wealth that had fed into the industrialization era, now consolidated these classes through the new schooling system. It is clear that the government's political objective was to tie "education" to Britain's socioeconomic needs, so that children would be schooled into their social positions. Importantly, the question of how to achieve the smooth transition of children into their correct social positions in the hierarchy was answered by the mental testing of nonelite children.

As already noted, the eugenicists had developed IQ testing during the early 1900s. A leading eugenicist, Cyril Burt, educational psychologist for the London County Council and later the chairperson of the Department of Psychology at the University of London, played a role in the formulation of ideas concerning the tripartite schooling system (Gould 1988, 234–35). The 1944 Education Act required that children take the IQ test at the age of eleven years. This examination was called the eleven plus. It would channel children into their respective secondary schools. Through this process, it was believed that the child would receive the most suitable education according to his or her intellectual ability.

When IQ testing was implemented, it primarily dealt with white children and differentiated them on the grounds of class and sex. However, the fundamental tenets of eugenics rested upon the notion of the innate inferiority of the so-called races and the Afrikan/Black race in particular. This would not become obvious until the later entry of Afrikan people from the Caribbean and Afrika. Our level of "intelligence" now had to fit into our politically determined socioeconomic roles. An example of how the notion of Afrikan inferiority was implied even among white children is revealed in Burt's study of working-class children in London. He notes that

exceptionally prevalent in those whose faces are marked by developmental defects—by the round receding forehead, the protruding muzzle, the short and upturned nose, the thickened lips which combine to give the slum child's profile a negroid or almost simian outline. (Burt 1937, 186)

Although his work was later discredited because of contrived evidence, it influenced the work of other leading eugenicists. Arthur Jensen from the United States used Burt's figures as crucial data for substantiating the supposed inherited differences in intelligence between Afrikan people and Europeans in the United States, during the 1960s (Gould 1988, 235). Burt's position as educational psychologist for London schools had a powerful impact on the role of psychologists within the British school system, especially in controlling African children's energies through the Educational Psychological Services during the 1960s until the present date.

"Special" Immigrant Education

By the 1960s, the schooling of Afrikan children had become an important political issue. The status of the immigrant had become integrally bound up with being Black or of Afrikan descent and not British. The entry of millions of white South Afrikans and Australians was not an issue. The official sanctioning of the treatment of immigrants can be related to the fear engendered by the ideology of white superiority directed into the state politics of British and white nationalism and perpetuated to cement the indigenous population to its rulers. Thus people of Afrikan descent were/are perceived as alien, foreign, and inferior.

Other characteristics of the immigrant group were/are its economic role as cheap labor, its implied temporary nature as a alien body, and the availability of its use or misuse in comparison with indigenous labor. For Afrikan people the historical "legal" relations with Europeans have been confined to the status of "enslaved," "colonized," and "immigrant." These legal political statuses denied the significance of Afrikan energies and resources in the development of capital accumulation in the metropolitan center and therefore the right of equal access to any of the so-called benefits of a welfare state system including health care, housing, employment, and education. As a result, Afrikan people were viewed as foreign for no matter how much our energies and resources had been exploited to provide wealth for Europeans or how long we had resided in or whether we were born in Britain.

The early reports on immigrant children not surprisingly referred to Afrikan Caribbean children as coming from inferior cultures and homes (Carby 1982; Dove 1988). Afrikan children were found to be consistently "failing" in the schooling system. Figures on examination results and reading tests showed that this was the case. The underattainment, underperformance, and underachievement of Black children became a concern raised by Afrikan parents not happy with these conditions. After all, Afrikan parents who had been raised in the Caribbean had seen their people in positions of leadership similar to continental Afrikan people. It did not make sense that these children were doing so poorly in schools. In reality, most children did not do well in the school system because of the fundamental need to maintain racialized socioeconomic and gendered inequalities. Afrikan children, particularly the boys overall, were doing less well than white children overall. In line with the socioeconomic needs and racist expectations of British society, Afrikan children were being failed by the schools. Due to the racism of the system of schooling supported by the majority of "teachers," Afrikan children were/are prevented from fulfilling their potential regarding the acquisition of the basic academic skills.

The eugenicist ideas, so fundamental to IQ testing, played an important role in the schooling of Afrikan children. It was not surprising that during the 1960s an inordinate number of Afrikan children were being referred to Educationally Sub-Normal (ESN) schools. In 1971, according to the report of the Parliamentary Select Committee (1973, 38), 5,500 immigrant children were put into "special" schools throughout England and Wales designed for those considered mentally retarded. Afrikan Caribbean children represented 70 percent of these children. In Greater London, 25 percent of all Afrikan Caribbean children were in these schools. For instance, in the borough of Brent 60 percent of primary school children and 70 percent of secondary school children in ESN schools were Afrikan Caribbean. In the borough of Haringey, although Afrikan Caribbean children made up 10 percent of the school population, they accounted for 25 percent of those in ESN schools (Ogbu 1978, 249–50). It was discovered that some children were entering these schools in Haringey directly upon arrival from the Caribbean (Dhondy 1982, 27) That same year, Bernard Coard articulated, and substantiated, the serious concerns of the Black communities.

His book *How the West Indian Child Is Made Educationally Sub-Normal* focused on the deficiency of the education system by highlighting the dynamics of racism through culturally biased testing. Coard explained that

the one way to insure no changes in the social hierarchy and abundant unskilled labor is to adopt and adapt the educational system to meet the needs of the situation: to prepare our children for the society's future unskilled and ill-paid jobs.

It is in this perspective that we can come to appreciate why so many of our black children are being dumped in ESN schools, secondary moderns, the lowest streams of the comprehensive schools and "Bussed" and "Banded" about the school system. (Coard 1971, 35–36)

It was this situation that led concerned parents and teachers to develop supplementary schools as a mode of resistance to this racism. These parents were no longer interested in leaving their children's education totally in the hands of a white racist schooling system.

Some fourteen years later, like Coard's, the work of Cecile Wright (1985a & b) supported what Afrikan children and parents knew experientially. Her major study defined the nature of the racist dynamic involved in the relationship between white teachers and Black pupils. She examined methods of streaming and banding (tracking), and the ways in which referral procedures and suspensions were conducted. She also looked at the school setting and the use of remedial units. Her findings showed that the Afrikan children in the study, particularly those from the Caribbean, entered the secondary schools with a higher reading age than all other groups. However, behavior, based on teacher recommendations, was used to allocate children to bands. In this way, Afrikan students were downgraded so that a ranking hierarchy occurred whereby those of the Afrikan diaspora were placed at the bottom. No Afrikan children were placed in higher bands than their examination performances, yet there were instances where Asian (Indian) or European children were allocated higher positions than their examination results warranted. Wright linked misallocation to teacher perceptions that determined and affected the eligibility of Afrikan students for public examination groupings. Consequently, their academic ability and educational opportunity were restricted by inappropriate groupings directed by the teachers.

In her interviews with the pupils, Wright found that they believed that the system was "rigged" and that "bad" behavior was related to "bad" treatment rather than, as teachers claimed, a result of underachievement (Wright 1985a, 17). In summarizing the student's experiences, Wright concludes: "To the West Indian, the school seemed to be seen as a "battleground," a hostile environment insofar as it rejects their colour and their identity" (Wright 1985b, 12). Wright's work offers an Afrocentric perspective that challenges many of the studies on underachievement previously carried out by white researchers who, steeped in their own racism, have ignored the significance of the racist determinants and dynamics of British society as viable variables (Dove 1990). However, there was an aspect of this work and most works on underachievement that went unstudied.

These studies did not include a breakdown by male and female of differential treatment and academic results. Importantly, the gendered aspects of Britain's socioeconomic conditions influence the way that boys and girls are stratified and treated. As Finch (1984) argued, more white boys were channeled into grammar schools because of their expected social roles. In the case of girls of Afrikan descent, the study by Jeffrey Driver (1980) first raised the issue of some Black girls performing academically better than Black boys and white girls and boys. The work of Mac an Ghaill (1988) also revealed that Afrikan girls managed to get better grades than Afrikan boys. He linked this to their strategies against racism, which were different from the boy's strategies in that they incorporated a "pro-education," "antischool" stance. This enabled them to appraise their own abilities regardless of teacher evaluation. The form of resistance was attitudinal and covert rather than attitudinal and overt like that of the boys. In this way they took a challenging approach to curriculum content rather than direct teacher confrontation (Mac an Ghaill, 26–36).

Many of the differences between the results of the boys and the girls are, to my mind, related primarily to patriarchal values. It is important to understand that we are engaged in a cultural war whereby the oppression of Afrikan people is paramount so that energies and resources can continue to be controlled. For instance, Afrikan males in a patriarchal society are considered to be a powerful threat to white supremacy because of their potential as warriors. The expectations of males within patriarchy include being aggressive, protecting the family, the society, and the culture, and earning enough money to take care of the material needs of the family. In the western classroom setting, Afrikan boys are perceived to be a physical danger, especially if they carry out the European, Northern cradle roles of masculine aggression expected within a patriarchy. They appear to be more of a threat to the social order than the girls, who under patriarchy are expected to be dominated, inferior, and subservient.

Both white male and female teachers have patriarchal expectations of Afrikan pupils. This is apparent when looking at the higher ratio of Afrikan boys to girls sent to do time in special education units for behavioral disorders, the numbers referred to educational psychologists, and the numbers expelled and suspended. However, the figures from an Inner London Education Authority (ILEA) report, *Characteristics of Pupils in Special Schools and Units* (1988), show an overrepresentation of both Afrikan boys and girls in these units. One Afrikan male educational psychologist working in a London borough confided to me that white women were the most responsible for the number of referrals relating to Afrikan male students. The action taken by white women "teachers" to control Afrikan male students may be viewed as reflective of the cultural solidarity of white women and males to control the energies and actions of Afrikan people.

Secondly and importantly, the results I believe also reflect the racism and sexism that define the value of their gendered labor power. Ironically, as devalued labor, Afrikan female labor is the optimum labor power. Maria Mies (1987) argues succinctly that on a global scale, "Third World" women are the optimal labor power because the cheaper the labor energies, the more profit they can produce. Ironically, in the West, at this time the energies of the Afrikan male are those which are most unnecessary, undesired, unemployed, and underemployed. As a male, in a patriarchal society, technically, he should be paid more than the Afrikan woman. However, his Afrikanity devalues his maleness. Since, Third World labor power brings capitalists maximum profits, Afrikan males within the capitalist centers of the West are undesirable. On the one hand, in order to maintain patriarchal cultural cohesiveness and stability, European males are privileged above others. On the other hand, consistent with racist ideology, the Afrikan female's labor energies may be the most exploited and devalued. The racialized and gendered socioeconomic determinants of U.K. society are played out in the school system. It is Afrikan young men, who, of necessity, challenge most openly the abusive conditions that relegate them to the bottom of the social hierarchy in terms of status, dignity, and integrity.

In any case, and in spite of the repressive controlling mechanisms of the state, Afrikan young men in particular have achieved a reputation for taking to the streets to challenge policing practices and the right to be employed. As a result, other disenfranchised peoples receive some benefit.

Conclusion

Overall, I have focused primarily on the European-Afrikan relationship, with regard to the enslavement and colonization. This has provided a necessary context for understanding how Afrikan movement has been/is structured and controlled globally. The "immigrant" status accorded to the Afrikan person, particularly in the United Kingdom, has been shaped by the eugenicist ideology of race. In this way, skin color and status have become synonymous with inferior and superior mental, psychological, and cultural attributes, which in turn validate the master-slave power relations regardless of the historical moment. The racialized socioeconomic political structure between the Caribbean and the United Kingdom was largely built upon the genocide of First Nations populations, stolen lands, and the captured and colonized energies of Afrikan people. The United Kingdom exploited the energies and resources of Afrikan people to fulfill the state's needs from the 1940s onward.

This status facilitated the transference of Afrikan skills from the Caribbean and Afrika to Britain while maintaining and perpetuating the same power relationship between Europeans and Afrikan women, men, and children. This relationship has been reflected in the schooling of Afrikan children, who are required to fit at the bottom of the racialized European social hierarchy.

I focus on Afrikan people from the Caribbean because the majority of Afrikan people living in the United Kingdom come from that his/herstorical experience. Moreover, the majority of the United Kingdom life-herstories are grounded in the Caribbean experience. However, I do not ignore the experiences of Afrikan people who hail from the continent. This chapter offers a context for analyzing the influences that impact on their lives as Afrikan women growing up under "white" supremacy. Their experiences have shaped their roles as mothers who have decided to send their children to culturally affirmative schools. Chapter 3 provides insight into the types of women who have made the decision to promote their cultural links to Afrika.

③

The Herstories of Afrikan
Mothers in the United Kingdom

Mothers Who Send Their Children
to the Marcus Garvey School

Nzinga ("She is beauty and courage")

Nzinga is thirty-nine years old. She is married and has two daughters and two sons. She lives with her husband and three of her children. Her first daughter was adopted from birth. At the present time, Nzinga is a cook in the school that her youngest son attends. She is tall and statuesque with natural hair, beautiful eyes, and a soft lilting voice. Nzinga was raised with her sister by her grandmother in the Caribbean on the island of St. Kitts until she went to the United Kingdom at the age of eleven years where she was raised by her father. Her husband is from the island of Nevis (in the Caribbean).

Nzinga loved her grandmother dearly. She was the most important person in Nzinga's life and it was she who had the most positive influence in her upbringing. Just outside the house where she was raised stood a crucifix, set up in memory of working men

who had gone on strike and been shot and killed by "the whites."
She was brought up to understand that these men had stood up for
what they believed in, and that they were an example of how she
must live. Nzinga was made deeply aware of the color-coded discrimination that was instituted in the Caribbean as a result of
European colonization. Indeed, it not only manifests as part of the
social hierarchy but has an effect even within families.

> My sister was very fair. I was the dark one. She had sort of
> straightish hair. We used to go to a sort of private school when
> I was much younger and these people were Libyans, from
> abroad [who ran the school]. . . . [M]y sister was invited to
> tea . . . but I wasn't invited. She got all dressed up to go and
> my grandmother said, "Well, where are you going?" She said
> she was going to visit and she said, "Well, wait for your sis-
> ter." She said that I wasn't invited. My grandmother said, "I
> beg your pardon, not invited, why not?" "She is not like
> me." . . . [W]e was only little then. My grandmother said, "What
> makes you thinks she's not, you got same mother, same fa-
> ther, come from the same family, why is that?" "My hair is
> different." She said, "That is what's stopping you from going
> with your sister?" She said "Yes." My grandmother cut off her
> hair every bit of it, cut clean off".

The grandmother made the girls look out of the window at the
crucifix, with tears streaming down their eyes, she reminded them
of those who were shot dead by the whites because they went on
strike.

> My grandmother . . . she said, "Look, you are no different. If I
> was to cut off all your skin and cut off mine, you'd be the
> same." . . . And that was one thing that stuck in my mind of
> how it is important to see yourself as yourself. You cannot
> judge another Black person because your hair or skin is dif-
> ferent. It undervalues you, it hurts the other person inside, it
> destroys them.

This act brought the sisters closer together. Nzinga's sister never
grew her hair again.

Nzinga's grandfather's family owned most of the estates in St. Kitts. Because her grandfather was very light-skinned and had married her grandmother who was very dark, he was disinherited. They had four children, two girls and two boys, the youngest of whom was Nzinga's father. The father's relationship with Nzinga's mother did not work out in part because her family was wealthy and disagreed with the union. Eventually, the father left for England and remained there. In the meantime, Nzinga's mother stayed in the home of her grandmother.

My mother decided she didn't want to have no more to do with my father's family. She didn't want us by then and she leave us in what you call a pasture and she just walked away and she never looked back since. And my grandmother had the task of bringing us up.

Nzinga, who was five years old at the time, has a vivid recollection of that moment when she saw her mother walk out of her life.

Early experiences of schooling in St. Kitts before the age of four were with Mrs. Claxton. Mrs. Claxton was a large Afrikan lady. Parents paid a shilling to have their children taught by her. They were taught to love and appreciate themselves and Mrs. Claxton cornrowed the children's hair and cooked while she taught them how to read and told them stories of Afrika. Mrs. Claxton, like Nzinga's grandmother, still spoke in an Afrikan language. Most children did not go to public or private school until around seven or eight years of age and from then they learned nothing more about Afrika. Nzinga became separated from her sister when she was sent to England to go to school because she was considered to be a "bright" child.

She came to London and lived with her father. She remembers that going to school in London was agony. There was a particular white female teacher who gave Nzinga a phobia about her hair.

You know, we had to grease our hair, we call it grease in the Caribbean, oil it. And every time she would pass she would put her hands in my hair and she would take it and wipe, you know [gestures an exaggerated wiping off the oil from the hand] and it annoyed me and I could never learn. I just couldn't face that sort of act every morning that I was totally different.

Not speaking English with a posh (upper-class) accent was another drawback; she was often criticized for this. Furthermore, her father believed that the teachers were always right when they complained about her behavior, although it is true to say that he marched to the school and told off the teacher who wiped her hands through Nzinga's hair.

While Nzinga was feeling the alienation of leaving her grandmother and her cultural roots in the Caribbean, she was also trying to deal with the hostile schooling system in London. At the same time, she was living with a father who began to abuse her. All of this made her existence in London a "living" nightmare. Her father beat and sexually molested Nzinga from the time of her arrival at the age of eleven years. She was kept as his housekeeper and "slave." No relatives were allowed to visit their home. At the age of fourteen years Nzinga gave birth to her first daughter. Her own father was the father of her child, whom she delivered herself. Up until the point of delivery, she had no idea that she was pregnant and barely understood what was happening to her.

I was not prepared for the fear and the emotional pain. I felt no [physical] pain when I delivered the baby.

She began to hemorrhage and neighbors made aware of her dilemma called an ambulance. Nzinga said that the social services assigned to the hospital knew who the father of the child was and the school was aware that she was receiving beatings. However, there was no more than a warning given to the father from the social services. Her daughter was adopted and she never saw her again.

I was scared, he had taken everything from me, the ultimate right that I had to be myself. I felt like nothing. I contemplated dying.

One day, when she was able to choose her moment, Nzinga walked out of her home and, as she said, "I never looked back." From there she stayed with friends and later an uncle who helped her to organize her life and get into college.

Nzinga married when she was twenty-five years old to a man from the island of Nevis whom she describes as a "real West Indian."

He is very supportive and has been very active in helping her raise their daughter and two sons. "When I look at my husband, I do not see my father. If I don't want to cook he will get up and cook for me, even after work. If I am sick or in pain, he is there for me."

The raising of Nzinga's children has not been restricted to the home. She has been extremely involved in their public/state school life. Because of her own experiences of racism at school and at college, Nzinga has never trusted the schools to take care of her children:

> You see when you give your child to other people, other cultures, and other places to look after, whatever they feel about your child or yourself, is going into that child. And they tell them, "Oh, stop speaking like that, because that's not the way to speak," and so I say, "Well I speak like that in the house with my children." So I stop work to look after my children. I wanted my children to believe in what I am and what they are gonna be, you know.

From the time Nzinga's eldest child was in school, she gave up good jobs in offices and at the post office to spend time with her children at home and in school. She began as a classroom helper for no money when her daughter was in junior school[1] and become a school cook so that she could keep an eye on her children and others. She has seen how the children react to racist treatment and believes that her presence makes a significant difference in the behavior of the teachers.

> They know I know. So when I'm there they behave themselves cos, if they don't, I'm not going to let them do any nonsense and think I'm just gonna shut my eyes . . . if they can do that to that child what are they doing to mine?

While her daughter Magano ("she is a gift") was still in junior school, her white female math teacher refused to give her any homework even after Nzinga's insistence. She believed that Magano was incapable of understanding this level of math. At this time Magano was attending a culturally affirming supplementary school and was doing math at a higher level than in her mainstream school. Both Nzinga and her husband visited the head teacher and insisted that their daughter could do the math. The head teacher challenged the parents and asked that they allow their daughter to sit for a test. The math teacher in question asked the school governors and the chairperson of the board of governors to be present at that time. Under these conditions and to the shock of those present, Magano completed the test successfully. They had to apologize. Their plan to humiliate the family had failed. It served to show their own racism and stupidity as far as Nzinga was concerned.

Her second child, the eldest son, is nine years old. He is very bright and confident and has his own ideas. He is interested in learning and is therefore always asking questions. As a result, his teacher confided in Nzinga that Mahluli ("this a victor") has a lot of problems. She advised that he be sent to a special school.

Right now, I just drop me battle eyes there because I knew where she was coming from. Why should I put him in another school, can't he read, can't he write? But there's a lotta other kids in your class who hasn't got the standard of education of my son, so why should my son move out?

Nzinga decided to get another opinion and met with a child psychologist. The psychologist assured her that her son had no problem, just a lot of opinions, moral opinions, race opinions, and political opinions. After this conclusion, Nzinga reported the teacher to the authorities. The teacher was most offended, Nzinga remembers, but in one week had a change of heart and decided to introduce some Black books to her predominantly Afrikan class.

The youngest child, a son, is in infant school, where he gets bored.

And when I said to them, that is not good enough, they get very defensive . . . you are out there to educate, my job is to mother him and look out for him. And at the present moment I'm taking him away from this school because I just feel to myself that they're walking all over us. They're forcing them [children] into a position where they have to underachieve. I say, "Hold up a minute, you're getting paid!" I mean, I raise funds for the school, then they don't buy any Black books. They put me in a position I have to defend us. I don't think I should have to tell teacher in this society that nine out of every ten chile in that school is Black. So why aren't you buying any Black books?

There was a point when Nzinga felt that her children needed more cultural information about Afrikan people than they were getting. Bothered by the emotional abuse of the system, she sent them all to Marcus Garvey School. The changes were immediate. She saw it in their confidence. More than that, her children learned about Afrikan people who have achieved things in all areas of life. These children even teach their teachers in mainstream school. Importantly, Nzinga took the children to St. Kitts where she was born. They loved it and wish to return to go to school there. The visit enabled them to relax and be themselves. Nzinga had not felt so free in a long time.

In terms of her own strengths, Nzinga has been inspired by her grandmother and Mrs. Claxton. She says that Winnie Mandela is one woman whom she would gladly follow.

Black women must have a place in this world, we're not just this or that, even so you have to look at some of the Black men. Them too that they would like to keep us having children and keepin us in our place [laughing]. You can't expect me to have kids and stay at home cos it's not gonna do us any good. Because, we are the real people, we women, we delivers the goods we have the kids you know, not the men, they are there like a falling back stone, if we feel like we had enough and they say let me help you, that is good.

Adoaha ("Daughter of the people")

Adoaha was born in Grenada in 1957. She is slim and delicate in build, around five feet four with natural plaited hair. Her eyes are bright and her mouth looks serious easily and smiles easily. She is a single mother, as of four years ago, with an older son and a daughter. The father of her children was her first boyfriend, whom she met at eighteen years of age. He is an Afrikan born in the United Kingdom of Afrikan Caribbean and European parentage.

Adoaha was born of a single mother and has a brother of a different father. Her mother was one of seven children. Adoaha grew up in the small house of her mother's mother along with her aunts, uncles, cousins, and mother until she was around four or five years old. Her mother's sister had a son eight days apart from Adoaha and they grew up together like twins. She remembers how color was highlighted in Grenada but it failed to separate her from her cousin.

> When I was in the Caribbean growing up, people used to say to me, "What a lovely girl, nice skin and clear skin! My cousin, who I grew up with and love very much, he was totally, very, very dark. . . . We both walking on the road together, "what a nice pretty child, look how clear skinned she is" and that made me love, probably love my cousin even more cos they didn't used to like say nothing to him and you know and it was terrible and I used to say don't touch me. . . . But if you're thing–minded those things could get to you and then you could start thinking that you're better because you're a little lighter.

One day a cousin of Adoaha's mother who was a teacher and lived in a large house in Trinidad was visiting when she saw Adoaha running barefoot in the savannah. She asked for permission to take her to Trinidad and raise her. Adoaha's mother saw an opportunity for what she thought would be a better future than she could offer her child and she agreed to let her go.

> My mum was a very poor woman even when she got married . . . literally the size of my front room was the size of my mum's house. The kids used to come round and it didn't matter what little bit of food my mother had, that food would stretch.

Adoaha went to live with her aunt who then became her mother and raised her from that age. Life in Trinidad, living in a big house with everything she needed, was for Adoaha a "pampered life."

However, being the daughter of a schoolteacher and attending the same school that her mother taught in was difficult. Expectations were high and Adoaha found herself failing to live up to them academically: "[M]y mum being a teacher, God, it was very difficult being in the same school. And my grades were really poor. I used to come last. I used to get licks continuously."

In order to be popular, Adoaha "tiefed" a hundred dollars from her mother and found out how difficult it is for a child to get rid of so much money. Eventually she was found out and got a good beating. During holiday times, Adoaha went home to visit her family and she was very glad to keep in contact. When she was ten years old her mother decided to look for employment in England and left Adoaha with a woman who had a daughter of the same age. Things did not go well for Adoaha, her new guardian used the monies sent from England to support herself and to spoil her own daughter while she neglected Adoaha. Two years later, Adoaha's mother came back from England, officially adopted her and brought her to England at the age of twelve.

After a short stay in London, they moved up to the north of England and lived in a large house with a big garden. It was a time when many jobs were available for people prepared to move out of London. It was very "unnerving" living in this city because there were no Afrikan people. At the school there were only two other Afrikan children. She experienced some racism, mainly from the boys, but really wasn't that aware of it. On one occasion she remembers a boy holding a sink plunger,

> [H]e squeezed it and he goes, this is my lips. . . . I was going, What? It was then that the other Black girl said, "Yeah, he's just a bit stupid and he's just being rude about your lips." In actual fact, this guy, although he was English, his lips were much thicker than mines, you know, it's just that mentality.

Interestingly enough, Adoaha did far better academically in the British school.

> When I came to England I was much brighter than the kids in the British school because I was way ahead. But in Trinidad, academically, the kids there are so advanced, it's unbelievable.

Although I was like a dunce, let's say in Trinidad, when I came to England I was bright, I was one of the brightest in the classroom.

She returned to London at the age of sixteen, went to college, and then became a psychiatric nurse. Adoaha's major difficulties with growing up in London stemmed from being a young woman maturing with a very strict and protective mother. Meeting Birago ("down-to-earth"), the man who became the father of her children, was a point of contention for her and her mother early on in that relationship.

The thing was he wasn't street, he used to make tapes, bring his cassette and we used to go to the park . . . two minutes walk from my mum's house . . . sit in the park and just talk and he'd walk me back home and things. We did it for a year and that was really lovely. [S]he started to relax, because she thought I wouldn't just run off and get pregnant and go and do stupidness. She was very disappointed in me when I was pregnant with Baako, you know, I got the worst, all sorts of names. Although I was with Birago for four years, it was terrible name calling and you should get married and he's got no respect for you. And I suppose it's because I let her down in a way. She wanted me to get married, set up in a proper home, working for lots of money. I was qualified but you have to work for awhile to get to that decent pay. . . . If there was any possibility of me going up the ladder, I dashed it away basically.

With the birth of her son Baako ("first-born"), she began looking for a new home. The parents of the child's father offered them an apartment above the bookshop that they ran. By this time Adoaha was involved in helping to run an independent Black bookshop. Her involvement with this family-owned enterprise was a major turning point in Adoaha's life, it became her life's work.

The bookshop was itself a focal point in Black/Afrikan life in London. It was/is a center for ideas, political movement, and the running of the Marcus Garvey School, a culturally affirming independent part-time school.

[P]eople saw it as a social place. It wasn't just a bookshop . . . they were welcome, we weren't there just to take their money, you know, they would come and say, "Can you recommend me a book?" and for twenty minutes you'd be with this one person who at the end of the day might not even buy a book. But it didn't matter because the mere fact they came out from the street and realized that there are Black people writing books . . . it was amazing . . . people didn't know Black authors existed because there were no Black books in the school. A lot of people used to come into the bookshop and ask, "Where can I get a lawyer?"

Through her work with the bookshop she has become legally astute in knowing how to defend Afrikan people. This plays a role in understanding the rights of parents and children in school. While her son and daughter attend Marcus Garvey, their father, who attended the school some twenty-eight years earlier when his father started it, often teaches in the school. Their children began life with their parents fully aware of the pitfalls of the British school system.

In Adoaha's eyes, Marcus Garvey is not a supplementary school; it teaches the children what they need to know about the Afrikan experience in a global context. Parents who attend the school are carefully screened to make sure that they are prepared to play a major role in their children's education. At the same time, parents are expected to become an active part of the collective. The school also provides a support network for parents who are fighting for their children's rights in the mainstream school system. Some of the teachers are students who have graduated from there. As far as Adoaha is concerned, the effect of the school on her children is obvious. It is critical, she believes, for them to stick to their culture.

There's a warmth with Black people which you don't find with English and European and I try to tell them that and show them that. I said yeah, you know, you'll find there's good and bad in all cultures, in all races wherever you go. But feel the richness. I love my Black friends. It's something which I hope they keep and cherish. I don't want my kids to ever be ashamed of who they are and where they've come from.

As part of their cultural education, she sent both her son and daughter to the Caribbean and they loved it and wish to go back. Adoaha is very proud that her children have managed to form and maintain an allegiance to their people because she believes that for so many children in the United Kingdom it is very difficult to maintain or even to develop such ties.

Adoaha has a good relationship with the father of her children. He has and still plays a positive role in their upbringing. In terms of the future, Adoaha wants her children most of all to be comfortable with themselves and to be happy. She hopes that their education will provide them with choices but not tempt them to aspire to have a lot of money and a big house.

> If they want to sweep the road, they've got a degree . . . it don't matter, they can do that. I have this fear for my boy. Every time my child goes out there I think gosh, you know, will he come home, will he be alright, because of the way the climate is. There's a couple of incidents that have happen to him where somebody like stole his hat and somebody punched him and stuff like that and it really, really worries me and at the end of the day I think, well if he lives to be fifty, I'll be happy, put it that way. I don't know if it's a negative way of looking at things but I've got like a fear in me for my children.

As for herself, Adoaha feels that she has failed to live up to her mother's expectations but she is still close to her and respects her. She is very happy with her close women friends (they are involved in the culturally affirming school) because she feels that she will always be rich in their company. If she has nothing or they have nothing or need help, they just call each other and they are there for each other.

> I'm a very fulfilled person. You know how sometimes people just come around you because you've got money or you've got a fast car. The people who I'm very lucky to be associated with, those things are not even secondary, it's not important.

Diallo ("Bold")

Diallo was born thirty-five years ago, the eldest of six children, in the Caribbean island of Antigua. She is a carpenter by trade and has two sons aged sixteen and eleven. For the last nine years, Diallo has raised her sons on her own. Their father is from the island of St. Vincent. Diallo has lovely eyes that light up her face. She is of medium build, around five feet two or three inches tall. Her father was an engineer in Antigua but when he went to England he was employed as a factory worker. Diallo's mother raised the children and took any employment that she could.

For the first seven years of her life Diallo lived in Antigua. She and her sister were born in a small village where her mother was born. They moved to her father's village. Diallo's father was one of fourteen children. He left Antigua for England in 1959. For a year he hardly ate in order to save enough money to bring over Diallo's mother and younger brother, who was six months old at the time. In the meantime Diallo and her sister stayed with her father's parents and grew up among their many aunts, uncles, and cousins in a tiny house that was located high up overlooking the village. She remembers her grandfather well because he had a great sense of humor and he is still alive and just as much fun. However, it was her grandmother who she clung to when it was time to leave Antigua and go to England to join her parents. Diallo attended school in Antigua from the age of five, and she enjoyed it. The head mistress was very strict and caned anybody who was late. Being a young person in Antigua meant that there were chores to carry out before school. Diallo got up at 5.30 a.m. to fetch water.

> Everybody knew everybody, brilliant, it was a close knit community, you know . . . I can remember walking a far distance to school, I had to take my grandfather's lunch to where he worked. . . . [W]hen it was my turn I was petrified because there was a rock that you had to go past and the stories that were going around that somebody was struck by lightening there.

Her memories of Antigua are happy and it was with great sadness that she left to go to London.

I came to this country in January 1965 which was very cold. In fact I didn't wanna come, I had to be bribed to get on the plane. . . . [W]hen my sister and I got here, it was different from what we were told. We heard the streets were paved with gold . . . there were people there who were nice and you know, you'd get somewhere to live. . . . [S]o we came here believing those things.

When they first came to London the family lived in a large room in an old house. She, her sister, four brothers, and her mother and father did everything in that room, they even bathed in the room because the bathroom in the house was in such a bad state. Eventually Diallo's mother grew tired. She took the children to the Hackney Town Hall where she left them until the family was given proper council accommodation.

So we was dumped there, she went away, we crying and in the end my younger brothers were put into a children's home in order for us to get a flat and that's how we got this flat in Hackney. That was about a four bedroom flat. . . . I tell you it was the pits. We were always in fights, the racism that we had then was just constant, you know, we were on the ground floor and the other little children used to spit on us when we went out and we weren't allowed to go anywhere.

One day her mother had taken as much as she could of the racist abuse from the people upstairs. She marched up four flights of stairs with an axe to "sort them out." The police were called and wanted to search the flat for the "chopper." Diallo's mother invited them in to search while her father "fretted" and Diallo cried. Diallo marveled at the way her mother handled everything, she was "brilliant." The police never found the axe.

The first primary school Diallo attended in London was very disciplined—for example, there was no swearing—but the second school was the opposite. There were fights and name calling and Diallo and her sister found themselves in many fights. She remembers that her sister took far fewer insults than she, so she often fought to support her sister. Their mother was at the schools regularly, defending her children. She found this hostile environment very disturbing.

[B]ecause of all that, right, I had this thing, I was never Black, right, because I was the only Black in the group so that was a way of me thinking that the problem would go away, I wouldn't get no hassle because I looked at myself as white. That went on for awhile. . . . I think it had a lot to do with my parents . . . because they never . . . even though Mum and Dad made us happy, they never taught us anything about Black this and Black culture. . . . I grew up thinking. . . . mind you that stems form the West Indies because I remember my mum sending my sister two dolls, one Black and one white, she didn't want the Black one, I didn't want the Black one, we fought for the white doll and looking back, I think that was really sad.

Throughout her school life in the United Kingdom, Diallo attended predominantly white schools and remained "white minded."

I had one Black friend, she was like me, white minded, and I had a Greek friend. Me and her we always said we was going to marry a white man or a mixed–race man. That's how we went on for years and you know it turned out.

History and religious education were two subjects that Diallo excelled in and in retrospect she still feels angry about this because she believed the information she was told by her teachers. When Diallo first left school she worked in a children's hospital but hated seeing children so ill. Then she worked in a supermarket where her mum was a store detective. Around the age of seventeen years old, Diallo met the young man who would become the father of her two sons. She met him at her first party. Diallo was fascinated—he was a "white West Indian." She could hear him speak but could not see an Afrikan person in the room.

[I]n the end it was bugging me. I said, "Excuse me, where are you from?" He goes, "Why you wanna know?" I said, "I just want to know where you from because you sound Black but you ain't Black." So he goes, "You hear of St. Vincent?" I said, "Of course I heard of St. Vincent." He goes, "That's where I'm from."

He was two years younger than Diallo but mature for his age. They began seeing each other. She did not sleep with him for two years. They carefully planned their first child Muato ("he who searches for truth"). They lived together and the baby's father supported Diallo while she worked part-time exchanging child care responsibilities with her girlfriend. Five and a half years later she gave birth to their second son Solwazi ("he who is knowledge"). When her second son was two years old they agreed to separate and the father settled in Switzerland.

Essentially, Diallo has raised her sons as a single parent for the last nine years. For several years the children visited with their father in Switzerland until they decided not to. Diallo has maintained a close relationship with his family and her sons visit them regularly. They have also traveled to St. Vincent to visit family there.

In terms of her children's schooling, while Solwazi was little, Diallo sent her first son Muata to an all-white church school after she moved away from a neighborhood where the local school was well mixed. The church school had a reputation for "high achievers."

> That school, well, it was all blonde-haired blued-eyed clones, she (head teacher) only took in the few elite token Black children . . . and because it was a good school, um, I had no trouble with Muata being there, but it always used to get to me, I used to sit in assembly and see all this blonde hair and think why have I put him in this school, but because everybody said it was a good school and it was hard to get in, it was sort of a challenge. So I got him in. . . . I must have gone there three or four times, the whole time he was there.

On one occasion Muata had fought back when he was hit and had been the one penalized. Diallo sorted that out to her satisfaction. Although there was little reason to complain about his treatment at school generally, Diallo became involved in the school's parent teacher group and attended all the meetings.

Diallo's later involvement with Marcus Garvey School started as a result of her growing awareness of her "Blackness" around the time Muata was seven years old in 1984. At this time Diallo was looking for a new job and a woman friend of hers suggested that she go to a local women's center run by white women who taught plumbing, electronics, carpentry, and engineering and offered child-care facilities. Diallo decided to train as a carpenter.

> I went there, right, majority of students were Black women and also single parents and I sit down. We used to have tutor groups every week and talk about issues, or they'll bring up a subject and we'll discuss it. Things like lesbianism, which I never knew existed amongst Black people. . . . I asked my tutor, "Is there any Black women lesbian?" All the others are like embarrassed, you know, like looking down . . . and she goes, "Diallo's right . . . she wants to know and we'll tell her." She goes "Yes" and I thought, shock, horror. They taught me, them white women taught me to be proud of my Black skin . . . really weird . . . it was like something just lifted out on me. I was getting all, everything Black to read, there was so much I found out, that Black people from Antigua came from Sierra Leone. . . . It was just weird and I was, what, twenty-seven about, and that was when I found my Blackness.

Some of the white women who ran the center were lesbian and Diallo felt that they were "different people, lovely, lovely women." She joined them in campaigning to prevent the center from closing down and then she moved on to another women's center in Ladbroke Grove that had more Afrikan women teaching. There she became a member of the committee and "it was brilliant." While becoming conscious of her identity as an Afrikan woman, she began to teach her mother. In fact, Diallo felt angry with her mother for never having spoken about being Black.

> It was a battle trying to tell her she was of Afrikan descent and not to use certain words and say certain things. . . . It's taken years though [laughing] but, she's a good woman.

This awareness of her "Black self" led to Diallo's reading more and becoming politically active. It was because of her interest in reading that she went to the Black bookshop and subsequently joined the Black Parents Movement. Her life became filled from that time with marching in demonstrations for women against racism, for the miners, trade unions, boycotting supermarkets selling South Afrikan products, demonstrating against police brutality, and defending her children and others in mainstream schooling. At that time Marcus Garvey had been closed for a while but when it reopened Diallo enrolled her sons. The more Diallo discovered about Afrikan history, the more angry she got. She remembered how she had loved history at school and believed everything that she had been taught.

> When Muata was choosing his subjects at school, I didn't want him to take history. . . . I was angry . . . I remember when we sat down ready to choose, I said, "You're not taking history and if the teachers want to know why, I'll tell em why." Up to this day, he never took history.

She is satisfied that her sons receive the real cultural history that they need from Marcus Garvey School. The school is seen as critical to her son's development. When Diallo first went to the school, she found herself reading the material and learning.

Raising sons in white society has been worrisome for Diallo.

> I see what our men have to go through. Years ago I used to slag Black men off, thinking they're useless and they're thing, but it's not so. . . . A lot of them do try and they get knocked back and I don't want Muata and Solwazi to get knocked back. . . . I'm scared because there are nasty people out there and I don't want my children to get hurt. Sometimes, I'm not glad that I've got boys, I dunno, it's weird, cos I know how Black women are . . . cos the white society are not scared of Black women as such. . . . [T]hat's why they're giving us the jobs. . . . I said to my sons, "You must go out and get, you have to do well. If they do one, two, you do two, three, four, you don't accept any less." That's what I'm trying to drum into them, because I'm scared of how things are going and sometimes I wish I had girl children.

An incident with the police has fed into her fears. About a year ago, while her younger son, who was ten, at the time, and his older friend Baako (Adaoha's son) were on their way to another friend's home, they were stopped by the police. The older boy was carrying his video recorder. Diallo's son was sent away by the police, while the older boy was kept for questioning. When Diallo heard about the incident she was angry because she thought it was irresponsible of the police to send her son away and for her friend's son to be questioned as though he were a thief. She was also upset because her older son had not been with them. When it was all over, the police let Adaoha's son go. When Diallo heard what had happened, she called the police and complained bitterly about their behavior.

> I came out with, "No wonder they're killing your arse down there [in reference to the shooting of a policeman]. . . . I'm telling you if anyone of you touch my boys there's gonna be trouble, you lot are gonna hear of my name and I'm not having it." You don't get anywhere, but I was so angry I thought I was going to cut my hand off.

Generally speaking, Diallo is happy with how her sons are developing. She and other mothers who use the Marcus Garvey School hold sessions with their children to discuss particular issues pertaining to their growth, for instance, how they should treat each other as young women and men. In this way they find out how their children feel about life and how they can work together. As a single mother Diallo does not see herself as particularly strong.

> [W]e deal with all kindsa things, we deal with accounts, we deal with um juggling the children, we deal with all kinda shopping, you know, we've got so many trades in one, it's unbelievable, the things that a lot of us have to put up with— absent men, or even though the men are there they're still not doing nothing and it's still down to us at the end of the day. I wouldn't say I'm strong, I'd just say we do what we have to do.

Kesi ("Born when father had difficulties")

Kesi left her home in Jamaica when she was six years old and went to live in the United Kingdom. She is thirty-nine years old and has two sons and one daughter. Kesi is slim with sparkling dark eyes. She has natural short curly hair. She laughs all the time and is very direct when speaking with you. The father of her first son was from Nigeria and the father of her other two children is from the Caribbean island of Monseratt. Kesi and her sister were raised in Jamaica by their grandmother until she died. Then they moved to their grandfather's home in Hanover between Negrille and Montego Bay before going to live in the United Kingdom.

The death of her grandmother was a traumatic experience for Kesi. She recalled: "Grandmother had gone into the mountains to pick yam and she never came back, just her body." When grandmother was placed in the coffin, Kesi was held over the coffin to see her grandmother for the last time. She believed that she was being placed in the coffin alongside her grandmother. She remembers, to this day, how scared she was. It was her father's idea to send her to live with her grandparents. She really never knew her mother. Her father went to England and sent for her later. Kesi has only vague memories of the first six years of her life in Jamaica. Her grandfather sent her to school but he could not afford the uniform, so after one day of attendance she never returned. Playing with her sister and her cousins is one of her pleasant memories of her life in Jamaica.

Kesi's father sent for her to come to England. He came to meet her at the airport with the woman that she would stay with until she became an adult.

I got off the plane and he says to me, "Call this woman mother," and that was the last thing I knew. Even though I remember having a mother back in the West Indies, I couldn't understand why he was saying these things to me, but that is what he said and I've been calling her mother ever since. . . . She was very vindictive. People say she was doing the best she can in a white society bringing up children and there's no father and going out to work and trying to pay the mortgage and everything else, but to me, that's no excuse. I think that what happened was she resented my father a lot for the way he treated her . . . and I got my father's mannerisms and I got my father personality and she saw my father in me and she used to take it out on me.

Kesi's father paid for her and her sister's upkeep while they grew up with their new mother. He worked in the post office and lived with another woman. Kesi loved her father, although she saw him as a man who was irresponsible toward women. Her sister adored her father. She states: "My father was a rogue [laughing], I tell ya. He was what is known in the trade as a womanizer." Kesi's mother would complain to her father about her behavior, and he was the one who punished Kesi by hitting her. He did this until she was thirteen and then it stopped. Her sister did not get the same treatment from their mother or father and Kesi resented this.

Attending school in London was not a pleasant experience for Kesi. She remembers her first traumatic experience on the day she started school at the age of six.

You didn't know what was going on, your parents didn't prepare you for school, you sort of going to this school, it was cold, you got chilblains. . . . My first day at school in that dinner hall, I could remember I was eating um lettuce, watercress . . . we don't have those things in the Caribbean and the woman sat there and forced those things down my throat and up to this day, I don't eat watercress. She was like a sergeant major . . . she had on black skirt, a pink top, this was like thirty something years ago, she was short, she was fat, she had grey hair . . . she was white and she said "Eat your greens." Black people wasn't around in those days.

School for Kesi was never a good experience. Her speech was always being corrected and she found learning hard.

I wasn't teached in the West Indies so like six years be lost. So when I came over here and did go into a different school I find it took me a long time to read and write. I found education completely different.

At home, Kesi was not encouraged to do her schoolwork:

[W]hen you get home from school you wasn't supposed to do homework, what you are supposed to do, a good girl always cleaned the house, cooked dinner, washed your clothes and you stay there. That was her [Kesi's mother's] attitude, she couldn't understand what education was about, because a good girl don't do those things.

By the time Kesi left school at the age of fifteen years old she was not qualified in anything, that is, she had not passed any examinations. As soon as she left school she worked for an insurance company in the office doing clerical work for three years and then went into computers. At the age of nineteen Kesi, had her first child, a son named Mosi ("first-born"). The father of her son was a Nigerian man with whom she lived for over a year.

He was knocking it off left, right and center with every Tom, Dick and Harry and I left him and I came home to mother . . . After my father I said no man is gonna lay a finger on me, and he was a womanizer, he never beat me, y'know w'a mean, he had women here and women all over the place and I just decided enough was enough and so I left him.

It was during this period that Kesi really thought about the type of man that she wanted to be with.

Her son Mosi was two and a half years old when she met her partner, the man who would become the father of her daughter and second son and would help her take care of her eldest son.

Because of the way my father carried on I decided I didn't want that for my children, their father had to do his bit, he had to look after them, he had to support them, and he had to talk to them. So when we got together, we planned the children and then he had a job where he worked away from home.

When he came home Kesi had everything planned.

So what I used to say to him, "It's your turn now, it's your turn to read to the children, to bathe the children. I'm going out." I think because of his home life . . . because he was shift backwards and forwards as a child I think he understands what I'm saying and his children mean a lot to him. I think that's why it works for us because we probably come from the same background. . . . [H]e works away from home, I am mother, father and everything to those children. When he comes home, he is mother and father to those children [and] I am gone. They have a better relationship with their father. Their father don't hit them, only does he raise his voice. A lot of people think that's very strange, but that's the way it is.

Kesi has had some serious problems with the British school system. She has absolutely no faith in it concerning her two sons. Her first son was expelled from secondary school when he was twelve because he "got into the wrong set of people." After that, he went to another school.

What happens is when your child move from one school to another, automatically he's got a label, O my friend, I don't care what nobody said, he carries a label around with him.

He attended school for one week and then played truant for six months from this school. Kesi had no idea. He was leaving home each day as though he were going to school. When Kesi found out she spoke to him about whether he should go to school or stay away. He virtually stayed at home from the age of thirteen. He is now nineteen years old. His mother saw no point in sending him. From the time he was expelled at the age of twelve, Kesi fought the education authorities. She believes that the system stereotyped and discriminated against her son because he was Black.

There's no support that says to you, "Alright, this is what you do." And I mean when your children are Black, automatically they are stereotyped anyway. Because he's Black, he doesn't want to learn and he's disruptive. It's not good for the other children, so automatically, he had that against him. And I find it doesn't matter if you have a Black teacher . . . a white teacher, pink or whatever color, if you're disrupting the other class you have to go. . . . I think the education system let my son down.

Fighting the education authorities was a full-time occupation for Kesi and as a result she got quite ill. She became a cook in the local junior school while her eldest son attended. Her daughter used to go there and now her youngest son attends. During this time she saw many changes in the school and believes that it is more difficult to challenge school policies especially since the Conservative Party had been in power for so long.

For her daughter Nayo ("we have joy") the system has been quite different. She has had no problems at all. She started nursery school at the age of three and could read at three.

> She was different, she had pencil in her hand from the time she was born. I never had anything bad about her, she says she's going to university and when she finishes she wants to be a drama teacher and when she finish that she going to America. But I think also what's happened in our society, things are more harder for boys than it is for girls. I'm not saying that girls have things easier. It's just that there's always a net for a girl, if she falls there's always somebody to help her because she's a woman. He's supposed to go out in the world and conquer the world and everything is supposed to be easy for him but it's not. I resent that because I don't see any future for my son.

Kesi started her daughter at Marcus Garvey School when she was six. She is now (at the time of the interview) fourteen. She believes that the school has helped her, whereas with her older son it was too late because he did not want to learn by then.

Kesi's youngest son Nwanodu ("may he survive") is six years old and has a speech impediment. Going to school has not helped him because of his frustration with trying to communicate and the teachers' lack of attention to or consideration for his condition. Kesi has very negative feelings concerning her youngest son's education. She has the same feelings about this son's chances of succeeding in life as she does for her eldest son. She does not hold much hope. In fact, she would like him to stop school now because she feels that it does him no good whatsoever.

He does attend the Marcus Garvey School on Saturdays and enjoys it because he has friends there and he receives more individual attention. As a result, he listens and speaks his mind. It would be ideal if such a school could be full-time as far as Kesi is concerned.

I would like a school where there was less children, there was teachers who had time for him, who will sit down and listen to him whingeing because he's a good whiner and give him just time, giving him self-confidence within himself. Those are the only things he needs, once you do that for him, he will excel.

While fighting to get her eldest son back in school, she ran into other parents trying to give her advice as to how to raise her son. As a result of her own experiences with trying to raise sons in this society, Kesi no longer stands in judgment of parents.

Perhaps I used to do it when my child was young and you see other parents go through the same problem and you say well it must be the parents' fault because they didn't spend time. But being through the mill . . . you can only do so much for your child and that is what happens. I dunno, Black people in this country have got very narrow-minded views on things. If you have two children and everything's ok, both of them's got jobs, they seem to think that's ok, they don't seem to think, "Oh well, the system didn't work. [Rather, they will think] "It's ok. I don't see what you're talking about. It worked for mine. You must be going to the wrong school. He must be mixing with the wrong people. You must be living in the wrong area."

Fighting for her first son's rights was very difficult for Kesi: she remembers how much she cried, how painful it was, and how much it made her ill. An added burden for her is the under- and unemployment of Afrikan males in London. At thirty-nine years of age, she has worked all her life and feels that when it is difficult for her to be employed how can she encourage her son when she knows that it is even worse for Black males.

For the last six years Kesi has been involved with the Saturday school, and she has learned a lot about her cultural background and has visited Jamaica and realized her roots. She believes that she has gotten into the "British ways" and that over time she has been gradually losing the Caribbean ways in her eating, speaking, and dressing and that it was dying in her. Kesi believes that the state schools compound this cultural loss by not exposing the children to anything about Afrikan culture and history. As far as Kesi is concerned, "All parents should take their children back home." Her husband and she plan to take her children to the Caribbean to visit Monseratt and Jamaica.

When she returns to Jamaica for a visit this year, she will tell her father just what she thinks of him. Kesi has always been reflective over this relationship and finds time to think about it. It was when Kesi left home that she began to look at the effect her relationship with her father had on her.

I became an adult and I have my own children and our relationship got better because I tried to make our relationship get better. But even now he runs away, if the pressure gets too much, my dad's gone. My father's in Jamaica and I'm going there next year and I'm gonna tell him exactly what I think.

Mothers Who Send Their Children to the Queen Nzinga School

Abebe ("We asked and got her")

Abebe is thirty-two years old. She is a single mother with an eleven-year-old son. She is tall and proud, with natural short hair. Her demeanor is one of confidence. She is serious, though her face lights up easily when she is amused. She is born of a Nigerian father of the Yoruba nation and English mother from London. Her father and mother divorced and married other partners when she was four years old. Her stepfather was also Nigerian and she was raised with three brothers from this marriage, while her father raised her brother and sister and had another daughter. Presently, she works in her son's school as a teacher's aide and is training to become a teacher skilled in the Montessori method. The father of her son was born in the United Kingdom and his parents are Jamaican.

Abebe was born in England and traveled to Nigeria with her mother and brother and sister when she was three years old where she lived for a year with the family of her father. She remembers the early part of her life with her parents as being one of tension. She believes that this tension was set in motion during the time she and her parents lived in Nigeria when her father returned to England alone in order to get employment. Being left with her husband's family while she had no money really angered Abebe's mother. When her mother returned to the United Kingdom her parents began divorce proceedings and a fight for custody of the children ensued that her father eventually won.

I could not accept that I could not be with my mother. I continually ran away from home, from the age of seven until probably nine. My sister and my brother seemed to get on better with my father than I did and um, I got on with my father but I think I had a lot of anger inside me as to why the two of them were playing games on us.

The anger that built up over the constant strife between her parents was only fueled by his response to the birth of her son. His new wife, a Catholic, had reservations about birth outside marriage and he felt that it would create tension in his marriage if he were to condone the situation. At this point, Abebe severed ties with her father because she was deeply hurt. She did not see him for four years, although he always kept in contact with her by sending her birthday cards. One day Abebe received a call from her father's wife, who informed her that her father was terminally ill and had only a short while to live.

I thought, "O my God, he's going to come out with all the reasons now for all this animosity and hate in our lives." We went into the bedroom and it was a real shock to me because I hadn't seen him for four years and he just didn't look the same as I saw him last time. He could just about speak and he only said two lines to me, and that was "Forgive me for what I've done." He actually said [this] to me and I remember looking over and saying, "Yes," but feeling in my heart I would never forgive him. [H]e did not realize that because of his actions he had created a channel of anger and um misunderstanding for generations.

Abebe cried and forgave her father as she relayed the story to me, with great sadness. As a result of his behavior, she had never spoken to her son about his grandfather.

Abebe's schooling experience in London was certainly not easy as she remembers it. She has little recollection of it until secondary school level.

> I remember being in secondary school and being in class where I think it was probably 25 percent Black people as opposed to white students and y'know, the anger was there but they wouldn't talk about it and because they wouldn't talk about it they just keep it, you know, hold it inside, which what Black people have been doing for generations and generations and generations. All I remember about secondary school is that I wanted to get out. I wanted to leave school at fifteen and I was in and out of school for the last year, which is something I am quite angry with my mother about to this day. She went back to work and because she had remarried and had three younger children, I was expected to look after them during the day so I missed almost three-quarters of my last year at school.

Abebe's teachers believed that she was "bunking" from school, hanging in the park and smoking with the local "yobos."

> One reason why I always held a great deal of respect for my father was he wanted us educated. It wasn't so much that he'd like us to do it, it was something necessary for us to do. And I think from his point of view, he wanted us to be educated because he didn't want us to have the life that he had here, working for the Royal Mail and the Hoover company. I don't ever remember him coming home from work saying, "Oh, I had a good day."

After leaving school, Abebe worked as a chartered accountant, a telephonist, and a receptionist, and then worked in offices where she became computer literate. A self-taught person, Abebe eventually ran an accounting agency earning 25,000 pounds a year. This enabled her to purchase her own council flat, which is where she lives now with her son. She met her son's father four months before they went on a trip to Paris with friends. During that vacation she had become pregnant while on the pill. While in the process of getting a termination, she decided to have the child. "I knew it was a decision that was going to create a life, make a life, and make centuries ahead."

The child's father is of Jamaican descent. Although Abebe and he separated after a year, he took full responsibility for his son and has been involved in his life from the beginning. After her son Addae ("morning sun") was born, Abebe was surprised at how welcomed he was by his father's family.

I couldn't believe his father's family's reaction to him. They all came to the hospital [the father's six brothers, one sister, and parents] and they all gave him something even though it was really small. Yet my family was the total opposite and I was like, I've only known these people for a year and look at the warmth they're showing.

Her son spends every other weekend from Friday to Sunday with his father at the grandparents' home. They dote on him. She believes that they provide an important cultural influence in his life, a role that she wished her father had been able to play. She has always worked to maintain a positive relationship between her son and his father and his family.

In looking at the racism involved in her son's schooling, Abebe has a matter-of-fact opinion from her own schooling experiences about teachers' generally being racist. She sees it in particular in the terminology used in his school reports because she is very meticulous in her analysis of what they are saying or implying. For the last three years her son has had problems with his school. At first he just fitted into the system but now, according to Abebe, he analyzes things and he is anti-establishment.

I won't change his thought mode or his politics because of it and I know that's going to cause us problems for the next six years. I don't really care, I see living here is one big problem anyway.

Just two years ago, Abebe discovered that her son has a form of dyslexia. She began to educate herself about dyslexia. As a result of her investigations, she decided to become a teacher. Working with her son at home with his schoolwork has always been a priority. Because of his short-term memory, he must go over his work every evening or else he will forget it. As a teacher's aide in the school that her son attends, she is able to keep an eye on him and the teachers as well as earn teaching hours toward her Montessori training.

There are lots of children in Addae's school that are in exactly the same situation as him and the system has failed them in one way or another and I felt that I would rather work with those children. It's also a good way of analyzing what methods are used to teach children.

When an educational psychologist was suggested for her son, she refused to participate in any psychological counseling.

The child's father has supported Abebe in paying for a qualified dyslexia teacher for two hours a week for over a year. It was he who suggested enrolling their son in the Queen Nzinga School, which he now attends. Abebe feels that Afrikan parents are generally not aware of what is happening to their children in the state school system. It is critical, as far as she is concerned, for children to understand their history, where they come from, who they are, and where they can go.

I don't think there could be anything better for Black people in this country than Afrikan-centered schools. I'd like to go back to Afrika. I want my son to go there.

Abebe has plans to go to the Caribbean with her son this year. It is ironic, she thinks, that her son knows that she is half-Afrikan but because of his father's family's cultural influence, he identifies more with the Caribbean. In fact, she pointed out, he still thinks that Afrikans are Afrikans and Jamaicans are Jamaicans; he does not realize the connection. She remembers that in her own upbringing her father and stepfather were anti–West Indian, while she has West Indian friends who are anti-Afrikan. "I think it's the way British society has made Black people turn on each other here."

Before Abebe decided to teach, she gave up full-time work three years ago and she traveled to Kenya with her partner of the time, who was Italian. After their visit to Afrika, they decided to get married. Having been to Rome to visit his family on three occasions, she felt comfortable enough to leave London with her son and marry her partner, whom she had been living with for a year. She received a rude awakening. While the family had welcomed her, when they met her son, who is very dark, they refused to allow them into their home. She insisted on driving back to London immediately. For three months she was in a state of shock because she was in love with her partner. That incident brought the relationship to an end. There was no way that she could subject her son or herself to that kind of pressure.

She and her son's father are extremely protective over their son. Because he is big for his age, he seems like a man, but he is just an innocent child and she has fears for his safety as an Afrikan boy growing up in a racist society.

I've got five brothers and each one of them has been in and out of prison. They all came out of school totally uneducated and got angry, very, very angry when they first started trying to find work and they couldn't get work cos they weren't educated enough. It's like a metamorphosis of being nice in society, then being pushy, then being angry. It makes me feel really sad because I see their struggle, um until they learn to direct it somewhere they're just going to carry on struggling.

Abebe's plans are to train as a teacher so that she is always there for her son and will eventually take him to Afrika and teach there.

I'd like to go back to Afrika. . . . [M]y father's brother was a chief. The community protected and raised my family. I need to experience it. I want my son to go there.

Amal ("Hopes")

Born thirty-one years ago in the United Kingdom of Nigerian parents from the Yoruba nation, Amal is a woman with great enthusiasm. She has beautiful smooth skin with wide eyes and dreadlocks that she wears under a headscarf when she is in public. Laughter comes quickly to Amal, but it disguises her deep pain. Raising a son and daughter as a single parent has not been easy. The father of her son is from St. Lucia, while the father of her daughter is from Nigeria. She has one sister and one brother who were raised with her in London. Presently, she is studying to become a teacher.

Born in the East End of London, Amal and her sister were fostered when she was two years old until school age. Amal is not clear about why she was fostered, although she has been told many stories. It may have been because her father was an engineering student and her mother was working full-time in any menial work to support him. Perhaps the children would have been a distraction to their father's studies or perhaps children were not allowed to live in the premises where they stayed. At any rate, she deeply regrets this decision by her parents. She spent these unhappy formative years being raised by an elderly white couple in the racist East End of London. At the time, she believes it was the "in-thing" for Afrikan parents to foster their children. However, she remembers seriously questioning her parents' logic when her brother was born and he was not fostered.

From school age, a cultural contradiction developed between school and home for Amal. While at home she was expected to behave like a Nigerian person, but at school she was expected to be English. While her parents spoke Yoruba at home, she was expected to speak English. This only added to the confusion. Her mother later told her that she did not think it was important for the children to speak Yoruba and besides they never seemed to want to.

I remember from five years old I did not want people to call my surname. I was English, I was proud, the color was a thing . . . a problem, but as far as I was concerned I was English. I remember when I was a little older going to shop and I said to my self I wonder if these people see me, I'm the only Black person coming in here. I used to see myself, you know, I must stand out. "God, they're all looking at me." I'm Black because someone said, "You're not white. You can't rub that skin color off." "Oh God, people know I'm Black. People can see me."

Amal and her sister wanted to be English and white. She remembers being ashamed to allow her school friends to enter her home and meet her mother.

When she was ten years old, she and her family went to Nigeria and lived there for a year.

[W]e didn't want to go cos at school we was told that they were swinging in trees and lived in mud huts and there was nothing there but dust and sand and no civilization and we really believed that. . . . It was really at the time, you look back on it and you say how could you, but it's amazing what they can do, what damage can be done at school. I mean the whole way of thinking it ends up with us thinking this is our home . . . this cold England. We're living in this racist society, [but] we prefer that than to go somewhere we didn't know.

They enjoyed Nigeria despite the alienation of not speaking their Yoruba language. Amal particularly liked the fact that the school books reflected Afrikan history and depicted Afrikan people.

For her parents, education was the key to their salvation. While she admired her parents for their focus on education, it was such a tremendous pressure in her life, especially regarding their high expectations, that it had a negative affect on her. Her whole life seemed to be centered around gaining qualifications in school. Since the plan was to return to Nigeria, Amal was training to become a pharmacist. Right from the start, she never wanted to be a scientist, she wanted to be a teacher. Her father's belief in the British school system led him to trust the teachers implicitly and blame his daughters for any supposed misdemeanors, which ultimately led to beatings.

She remembers that the beatings had little effect, because they were often unjust, so she just became clever at avoiding them. Certain teachers took advantage of this home situation as a way of controlling Amal and her sister. Amal witnessed other parents threatening to kill the teachers if they touched their children. She wished her parents were the same way. By the time Amal reached her A-level work, she was pregnant with her son. No beatings, nagging, or restrictions by her parents had worked to prevent her from taking this direction.

> So I met this guy. . . . It seemed alright. My mum was always warning me like, that all those men out there were all devils and I used to think if they were devils they'd have horns. This guy was from St. Lucia. He'd had a terrible life. We could relate to certain things. He had locks, all the things that wasn't right—West Indian, locks, hadn't finished school, didn't have A-levels, not career motivated, all the things I was warned against.[2]

Amal moved out of her home at the age of twenty into a home for poor single mothers and their babies, believing that she would be with this man forever. He left her when she was four months pregnant and only after he had been gone for six months did Amal really believe that he was never returning. Alone and living in a white area in London, she tried to return home. Her mother said she could come home only if the child would be put up for adoption or fostered. By this time her father had returned to Nigeria and left her mother. He had often beaten her mother, who decided that she would be better off staying in London and getting a divorce. The dream of returning to Nigeria seemed no longer feasible. Furthermore, Amal's memory of her foster experience made her determined to keep her son Ako ("the first child") and so she remained alone.

Deeply hurt and disappointed, Amal raised her son. When her son was three years old she met the man who would become the father of her second child. He was a Nigerian man and she felt proud to introduce him to her mother, who promptly warned her to "Watch him."

> He was just like my uncle. When I was pregnant with my daughter . . . there were a lot of things he didn't tell me. I did not know where he lived and I did not think at the time that I needed to know. I'd met the ideal person. He's one of our own. He wouldn't mess me.

Regardless of her mother's concerns, and as with the father of her son, Amal totally trusted this man. He lied to her and left her before she gave birth to her daughter. Amal again slipped into depression: she had failed at school, she couldn't hold onto a man, her self-esteem was low. However, joining Ujima, an Afrikan women's group for single mothers in Finsbury Park, became a turning point in her life. With the support of these women, she was able to develop her self-esteem. By this time, she had moved to Richmond, a white, upper- and middle-class neighborhood where her son still attends school.

For a while Amal was happy with the school because of its record of high academic achievement. However, she was mindful of her son's safety as the only Afrikan child in an all-white school. After a while, she noticed that Ako gravitated toward white people and did not appear to like the company of Afrikan people. When he first attended the culturally affirming school on Saturdays, he was very upset to sit with other Afrikan children and cried. For Amal it was a process of self-realization in terms of her choice to send him to the Saturday school.

I started to realize that there's more to education than just getting those grades. If he doesn't feel comfortable where he is, how is he going to achieve all this. I could have left him there, he did well, but it's the things he was writing, it's the brainwashing. But when I went out and met people and started to talk about things and get involved and start to talk about education and you know, history and child development, well, what is he reading? What is he taking in? Academically he's there. I don't look at that. It's other things, the confidence. All the things that really hurt me. You know, he doesn't have to know all the countries in Afrika, but it's something about the way he carries himself, but if I had a bit of knowledge and someone had listened to me, it would have made such a difference.

Amal's daughter Ebun ("gift") also attends the school. However, there have not been the same concerns for her daughter as for her son. Being involved at Queen Nzinga School for Amal is about being involved with mothers of like mind and being able to communicate and have a support network especially for developing child-rearing practices. At one time, Amal found herself hitting her son and imitating her parents' behavior when it was the very thing that she had rejected. After this realization, she became more involved with the school. Now Amal is doing what she wants to do for her own career—she is attending college to get her teaching degree. She can be called upon to do voluntary work for the school during the week when the center is open to cater to the needs of parents who have problems with the mainstream schooling of their children.

Enomwoyi ("One who has grace")

Enomwoyi is thirty-four years old and was born on the island of Grenada in the Caribbean. She is tall, slim, elegant, and her skin is smooth. Enomwoyi's face reveals a sadness and her manner is quiet and soft. She holds herself with great dignity and wears her hair in dreadlocks. She has one son of eleven years and two daughters, six and four years old. Her mother and father divorced and remarried, so she has two sisters by her mother, who is a caterer, and two sisters and a brother by her father, who is a bus driver. Enomwoyi was raised by her grandmother until she came to the United Kingdom at the age of eleven.

Growing up in Grenada with her grandmother was a happy part of Enomwoyi's life. Her grandmother, who was her mother's mother, was very kind to her and "spoiled" her. She grew up with a lot of cousins and sometimes she got into fights, but nothing serious and her grandmother would smack her, but not very hard. Sometimes she would visit her father's mother, who was also very nice to her. At the age of four, Enomwoyi started school.

It was very nice, I really enjoyed school back in the West Indies. Um teaching and so on was very good. Um it wasn't no fights or anything, no racism or anything, s'pose it was cos we were all Black there, everybody just get on with one another, lovingly.

Meanwhile in London, Enomwoyi's mother, who was living with her husband and two daughters, decided to send for Enomwoyi. Having been brought up by her grandmother whom she really loved, Enomwoyi was not too happy to leave Grenada. She had seen her mother occasionally but had never felt close to her. A quiet, shy, and graceful Enonmwoyi, at the age of eleven, caught her flight to London airport.

[W]hen I got to the airport in London, I cried a lot because I really didn't want to stay. It was snowing and I didn't know what snow was, I just saw the white thing on the floor. I didn't know what it was. Um, my mum came to meet me, we went back to the house to unpack everything.

At that time, Enomwoyi remembers everything seemed fine. However, soon after she began to realize that her mother's purpose for bringing her to England was to housekeep and look after her sisters, who were six and eight years old.

Enomwoyi attended the local secondary school and made friends easily. But she did not feel that she was able to understand the schoolwork very well.

I must admit I wasn't very bright because my mum she was just keep saying to people that I'm not very bright, I'm a dunce, I can't read properly and all them things, I dunno, just sort of, you keep hearing it so many times. I just sort of like accept it, you know, which I know I shouldn't have done. You know, in my heart, I know it's not true and I think that's why I'm like that.

Her favorite subjects at school were cooking, which she also did at home, typing, math, English, and sports, which she loved. Back home in Grenada, Enomwoyi was an excellent athlete and she continued to play netball for years after she left school. However, while still at school she did not take any examinations and therefore did not qualify in anything.

There were a few teacher there that wanted me to take the exam and said that I would do good in the exam, but, in myself, I didn't feel confident that I could have taken the exam. My mum wasn't interested, she never showed any, the right way, and help me out with any schoolwork or anything. At the time, I didn't even have time to do homework cos I was always cooking and ironing and things like that. By the time I finished all this, I'm really tired, um, just go to school and I just sit down in the class quietly, you know.

Life at school was not problematic for Enomwoyi. She made good friends who were both Black and white. In fact, she remembers that it was a white friend of hers who explained what menstruation was about when she first started her period at aged sixteen. She feels that school then was not racist in the way that is it now that her own children attend.

Life at home was an unhappy experience for Enomwoyi. Apart from her responsibilities to her family, she had also to deal with the advances of her stepfather, who was a sanitation worker.

[S]ometimes my mum would take my sisters and them to places and things and I'd be in the house ironing and things like that and um and my stepdad was, if I'm in the room he'd never knock, he'll just open the door and come in like even if I'm having a wash or anything. He would just open the door and come in and like, he would always come in and interfere with me, but I never told mum that cos I thought things like that would break up their marriage and she would call me a liar and things like that and I never did anything.

Eventually, Enomwoyi told her aunt and a cousin. Years later, her mother never accepted what her stepfather had done, and was angry that Enomwoyi had spoken to others about the situation. When they did speak with each other about those incidents, her mother accused her of lying. This really hurt Enomwoyi, who has always tried to understand her mother's dislike for her. She thought that perhaps it had something to do with her father. Perhaps her mother had been in love with her father and had not recovered from the separation. It may be that Enomwoyi reminded her mother of that union. Ironically, Enomwoyi does not look at all like her father—she looks exactly like her mother. She further reasoned that perhaps looking like a younger version of her mother made her angry. Whatever the reasons were for the relationships that took place in that home, eventually Enomwoyi moved out and went to stay with an aunt as soon as she could.

After leaving home around the age of eighteen she worked at catering and cleaning because she was not qualified to do anything else. She soon got her own flat and began to take night classes to learn how to type better. Around this time Enomwoyi met an insurance salesman who was from Jamaica. When Enomwoyi found out that she was pregnant, she informed him of this, and she never saw him again. Two of her cousins and her auntie helped her to raise her son Kamau ("quiet warrior"). While raising him, she worked full-time in the catering industry in London.

> I was living in the Southeast [London] and working down here [North London] and that means he [her son] had to get up very early in the morning , um, for me to get to work for 8 o'clock, um, which was, I feel really sort of guilty getting him up so early in the morning but I had to. I had to work for survival, I don't know how, I mean the money that we were getting on social [welfare], that was nothing. Bills, when winter comes everything, bills run sky high, couldn't afford anything, couldn't afford clothes at one stage. I had to go work to help us.

Luckily, Enomwoyi's cousin was buying a house and decided to allow Enomwoyi to move into the council house (a house owned by the local government—similar to a subsidized housing project) that she was leaving in North London.

She stayed there for five years, during which time she formed a new, more permanent relationship with a man from Guyana. He became the father of her two daughters Pili ("the second born") and Nwaoma ("a beautiful child"). They remained together for six years. He worked at the Post Office when they met and then he worked for the British Broadcasting Company (BBC). He was good to Enomwoyi at the beginning of the relationship, but then things changed.

> [H]e just wasn't helping me out, I'm doing everything, looking after the children, cooking, cleaning, everything, shopping,

everything, even when I come out of hospital I had to go and do the shopping. If I want to talk to him, you know, saying to him how I feel, he don't want to listen, he don't want to sit down and talk. So in the end I started getting really depressed. One evening I talked to him and he just started to laugh, and I said, "Don't be surprised one evening you come home and your clothes are outside."

That was exactly what Enomwoyi did. He found his clothes neatly packed outside and begged to come back in. She eventually let him in and while she was at work the next day, he changed the lock on the door. The council came at her request to break down the door. This time, Enomwoyi threw his clothes outside. The police were called when he tried to take the daughters and they made sure that he left peacefully. Since that day he has never paid anything to help toward his daughters' upkeep. Enomwoyi still stays in contact with his family and takes her daughters to family events, allowing their father to take them out occasionally when he calls to do so.

This event had an effect on the middle daughter, Pili, who for a while would not listen to her teacher at school. More recently, her work has improved. Just around the time that Kamau needed some extra help at school, she heard of Queen Nzinga School. Since it was a Saturday school and she was concerned about her children watching television on Saturday mornings, going to the school seemed like the perfect idea.

I enjoyed it, um, taking him and meeting parents there and talking to parents. Um, I got involved in the school because I like helping out. I really learn a lot from the school and he learn a lot from there as well. His mainstream wasn't giving him that extra bit of help and I feel that it really um boost him up a lot. Pili, when she started um, she, because Kamau was going there really like it because she knew she could mix with her own sort of culture and learn more about us Black people . . . which I learned a lot as well from there.

The school has definitely affected the children, according to Enomwoyi. The middle child looks forward to doing her homework.

The youngest one Nwaoma goes too and likes to just be with the other children. The older son has had problems with the mainstream school in the past, but he is happy at Queen Nzinga School.

> When children pick at him at the mainstream school, he gets into a tantrum and um throw things. He knows everybody at the Saturday school and I think because they're all one color, they get on a bit more.

However, he once had a problem with another Afrikan child bullying him in mainstream school, but they were able to make friends. Enomwoyi says that her son is a very friendly child and gets on with everybody. Both her son and daughter attend a Catholic school (non-fee-paying), which is disciplined and does not tolerate racism.

Enomwoyi has visited Grenada with her children three times. She took them there for six months when she went home to nurse her dying grandmother. Her future plans include building a house in Grenada and sending her children to school there. The children liked it very much. From her own experiences she believes that the schools are very good in Grenada.

> I think I'd be more happier down there because I've been there and I really enjoyed it, the atmosphere, the people are really friendly. It's hard, it's very hard down there but everybody is struggle. I mean if it means I have to struggle, I have to struggle, the same way they're struggling. If I'm struggling here then it's just the same thing if I'm gonna struggle down there. If I build my house from up here, then I don't see I should be struggling that much down there.

Enomwoyi sees herself as a powerful and strong woman to have survived as well as she has. No matter how painful life has been for her, she has been able to move on.

> I notice that I never cry. I know I want to but it's just hard for me to just start crying. There's a lot of pain inside. Probably, I could write a book.

Fujo ("She brings wholeness")

Fujo was born in Zimbabwe but lived much of her life in Zambia before returning to Zimbabwe. She left her home in Zimbabwe to come to the United Kingdom in 1975, when she was thirteen years old. She is around five feet two inches tall, slim with large penetrating eyes and a wide smile. Her dreadlocks are finely twisted and almost shoulder-length. Fujo is a Rastafarian, as is her husband, who was born in the United Kingdom but whose parents are from Grenada. They have three sons and Fugo has a daughter from her first marriage. Fugo is the eldest of two children. Her mother had nine miscarriages after Fugo was born and before her brother was born. Fugo's mother is a nurse and her father, a businessman, was one of sixteen children. Fugo's eldest daughter from her first marriage and her thirteen-year-old brother live with her mother in Zimbabwe.

Fugo has vivid recollections of growing up for a time in Zambia and going home to visit Zimbabwe, which was called Rhodesia then. The treatment she and her mother received on the journey across the border had a deep effect on Fugo, particularly in developing her political awareness. The border guards would search Fugo, and her mother. They were particularly interested in finding money on them.

> I'd get stripped searched and I mean that kind of thing made me realize that these people weren't quite right in the head. And the other thing that used to always strike me as quite weird until I grew up was that it was always Black people doing it. You know. But then you'd see the white person there. He's standing there and it never really dawned on me that he's watching the Black people and if they don't do what they have to do, they're out of a job. And most Black people at that time, what could they do if you've got a big family.

As a result of these experiences, Fugo said that she understood white supremacy from an early age. She remembers how concerned she was whenever she and her mother were stopped at the border:

> [M]y mother was left in, like we had a room like this and nobody there and the white man would come and question

and question, and my mother would answer all the questions. They would make us miss the train that we can't go where we're supposed to be going and they'll tell us we can go and it was night time.

Fugo is very close to her mother and believes that she is a powerful woman who went out and got what she wanted. She was the backbone of the family and worked all the time to support the family because there were times when her husband was unable to work.

This woman is immaculate. She knew my father was having affairs even up to just before he died, and she stayed with him.

Moreover, she would get beaten by her husband but did not tell any of her friends. Fugo asked her mother why she never left her father. Her mother told her that she believed that she would lose her son to him if she divorced him, and she was not prepared to do so after waiting so long to conceive this child.

Fujo remembered that when she arrived in England, her father made sexual advances to her. He did not pursue this when she rejected him, but she hated him for years as a result of this behavior. At the time, they had been close and she wanted nothing more than his approval of her. This act had a devastating effect on her because she was unable to tell her mother for a long time. In fact, when her father died recently, she felt very little for him. He did ask her mother for forgiveness and she forgave him. Fugo believes that she cannot carry on a vendetta against him and that she can forgive him in time. Some of his later erratic behavior she believes was related to the tumor in his brain that caused his death.

Fugo grew up within a close-knit family group. Her aunties used to tell her how clever she was and that she would grow up and become "somebody." In Zambia, where Fugo was schooled, she went to a convent school that was racially mixed.

I was never depressed back home at school. I mean, if I did well, I was told I did well, I actually got credit for it and there was no racism there. Possibly there was but I never saw it. In my school, we all played together, my teachers marked the work fairly, you know, if you were in trouble, you got into trouble, no matter who you were. May be it's just that set of people there.

She was boarded at a convent school in the United Kingdom where she learned the meaning of confrontational racism. Although, her feelings about the school are mixed because she enjoyed a lot of her experiences, she also had misgivings. When she first arrived at school, the nuns wanted her to take a test because they did not believe that she would be competent enough in speaking English to even attend the school.

Now when I looked at this test that they had given me, apparently it was for form 3, you know, and I had done something like that back home. It's like when I got 100 percent for both of them it was like, it was a shock to them, you know.

After that, however, Fugo often found herself receiving grades that she felt were inconsistent with her skills especially regarding English. For instance, she would receive A's in her English literature classes and E's in her English language classes. At the same time, working hard in class and getting her work correct created tensions for Fugo because she was then regarded as a teacher's pet by other students. As a result of peer pressure, she slowed down, didn't study, and hid her academic "cleverness."

Another cause of her concern related to her relationship with her father. He had high aspirations for Fugo and wanted her to become a doctor. Fugo had no interest in becoming a doctor. Her father was very strict and Fugo believed that the nuns at the school exploited this fact. It seemed to her that for any little incident the nuns would call her father on the phone.

[S]o when I went home for my weekends, I'd get a beating for something that I thought, even at the time, was very silly, where it could have been sorted out between the teachers or the mother superior and the pupil.

Although her father gave her beatings she did not regret this, in retrospect, she says that she was "glad" because she believes that children need strict discipline. However, there were times when she felt that she did not deserve them and that there were better ways of dealing with things. She, therefore, slaps but does not beat her children if they misbehave in public.

When Fugo left school she went to college to do her A-levels. She had an interest in studying law. However, her experience with a racist teacher, who gave her lower grades than she deserved in a physics examination, had a negative effect. Although charges were brought against him and she was able to prove that he had marked her incorrectly and consistently undermined her during classes, it was she who was advised to take another course. This type of treatment, coupled with the realization that studying law within the Eurocentric system would compromise her principles and values, led Fugo to feel very negative about what she should do with her schooling and her life in general.

Around this time, she was greatly influenced by an old school friend who had left school a year earlier and now had a child. Fugo visited her often and began to think that college was not for her and that having a child would be nice. During that time she had developed a relationship with a white man. She knew that if she had told her father she would be in serious trouble. Despite this threat, she got pregnant anyway.

Until her daughter was born, her relationship with the baby's father had been very good. As soon as Andaiye ("a daughter comes home") was born, he became violent. Fugo believes that he was probably jealous of the baby. Life was complicated for Fugo. During her pregnancy her passport ran out. She was sent notification to leave the country. Instead of leaving and returning home to her mother and father, who had gone back earlier to Zimbabwe, she decided to stay. She married the baby's father.

It quickly became clear that this marriage would not work. He was abusive and insulting to Fugo, particularly about the fact that she was from Afrika. Fugo often wonders why she married a white man. She believes that it had something to do with the relationship she had with her father. Her father often beat her mother.

I didn't want a Black man cos I thought, these Black people they just beat up their wives, but look what I ended up with, a white man. At the end of the day, when it comes to violence in relationships, Black men and white men are the same.

In fact, her husband was beaten by his father and Fugo believes that was the basis of his violence.

After they separated, they remained in contact because of their daughter. Fugo worked while raising her baby and saved enough money to take the baby's father, herself, and their child to Zimbabwe. He was very surprised to find out that Afrika was not a jungle, and that her family lived very well. This was one way that Fugo received some real satisfaction.

Her present husband, with whom she had three more children, two sons and a daughter, is a Rastafarian. He believes in Afrikan cultural values and has encouraged Fugo to respect and accept her Afrikanness. He visited Fugo's family and was welcomed in Zimbabwe.

I've taught my husband a lot of things and he has a lot of respect and that's why I'm still with him because, um, he was very natural and when he came there he wasn't pretending. I mean, back home, they would see it if he was pretending, but they really loved him. . . . Basically not many West Indian people who come from here and go up to Afrika would like to go through the ritual of Afrikan marriage. . . . He's taught me a lot of things, how to be humble and to keep my humbleness in this society and not think in the liberal sense of white [in other words, her husband encouraged her to retain Afrikan values].

However, her husband's family, who come from Grenada, particularly his mother, has not welcomed Fugo in the same way as her family has welcomed him. When Fugo first met her husband's mother, Fujo served her as she would serve elders back home. Instead of appreciating Fugo's humility, the mother invited her friends over when Fugo visited so that she would serve them too. Fugo felt exploited and rarely visits her mother-in-law now. Her children feel closer to their grandmother in Afrika than to their grandmother who lives down the road from them.

Fugo, who has followed her husband's faith, is a Rastafarian and is bringing her children up in the belief.

> I believe my son is quite a leader, he's the one who's 5. Um, what I usually do with my children, I don't force them into anything. If I'm reading Bible and they want to read with me, I read it to them. If I'm reading the Bible and they don't want to know, I don't read it to them. I have videos, I'm not forcing them, in a way I am forcing them. I don't put on a video and say, "Right, you lot, sit down." What I do is put things on like Farrakhan and Malcolm X and just leave the video running and they'll be running around and at some point in the day, they've got to come into that room, and they've got to sit down for five minutes. My son is very into Ayinde and he's 7.[3] I think seeing a little boy on the stage is inspiring. I'm just making them aware of who they are and what they are. Um, my son has dreadlocks and I make him aware of what dreadlocks are and what they mean and when he goes to school, nobody must tamper with his crown. I'm fussy . . . certain things they must not eat.

Fugo is attempting to provide her children with an understanding of who they are so that they may form ideas early about their goals and objectives in life. She sent her eldest daughter to Zimbabwe when she felt that she was getting too involved with trying to dance like "Salt n' Peppa" and not studying. Since Andaiye has lived in Afrika with her grandmother she has undergone some positive changes. Fugo and her husband have moved the other children to different schools several times because of what they were learning or not learning.

> One particular school my children were going to I never saw a map of Afrika, I never saw the people teaching my children about Afrika. So I went into the school and I said to the head teacher, "I cannot see any identification, how are my children going to identify themselves because they can't even see the map." I get involved fully with all my children's school because I want to know what they're doing.

As a result of her persistence with the school, changes were made to the curriculum in order to include information and images of Afrika. At the present time, Fugo is an administrator at Queen Nzinga School, where her three young children attend. She is also active in the politics of the local borough. Her plans for the future include going home to Zimbabwe with her family. She and her husband are building a house there and plan to live there.

I am a woman and I have been put on this earth to bring forth. These are not your children, you are just going to mind them for a time, because God has plans for them. You just bring forth them and let them go and direct them in the right way.

④

A Context for the U.S. Herstories

It is not possible to discuss the Afrikan ordeal in the Americas without reference to the conquest and holocaust of the First Nation (indigenous) peoples. As in the case of the his/herstory of Afrikan people, much has been done to obscure and distort that reality. Simultaneously, Afrikan people were violently taken to the Americas and First Nations people were violently expelled from their lands and annihilated. This his/herstorical reality was the political and economic basis for what we recognize as the Americas—North, South, and Central.

In the racialized socioeconomic order known as the Americas, the energies and resources of First Nations and Afrikan people are controlled. They are subject and contained populations. Segregation has played a major role in isolating these cultural groups, thereby limiting access to resources and their abilities to change their social conditions. This situation raises political and cultural questions concerning the rights of the autochthonous peoples. What does being an American or an Afrikan American mean while First Nations people are still contesting their lands all over the Americas? This question has a great bearing on the future of all people living in the United States. Any political decisions should reflect their presence and their voice. This chapter recognizes the indigenous story as a critical consideration in the schooling of the Afrikan person and therefore all persons.

As previously argued, Europeans, prior to their "discovery" of First Nations people and the Americas, had already developed the concept of the "race" differences between humans and a belief in their own superiority. It was continually evolving from an existing belief in differentiation among European ethnicities, like a kind of racialism, according to Robinson (1983). First Nations people were viewed as "Indians," resulting from Columbus's mistaken belief that he had "discovered" India. As Indian or Red people, as they came to be known, their subjugation was supported and justified by an ideological belief in their racial inferiority. As in the case of Afrikan people, the patriarchal aspects of European domination disastrously affected their largely matriarchal societies (see Diop 1959/1990; Carew 1994; Mohawk 1992). Similarly, as with Afrikan people and Europeans, a clash of cultures was in effect when Europeans met First Nations people.

The arrivals of Europeans in the Americas and Afrika—the Spanish in the Greater Antilles in 1492, and the Portuguese on the coast of West Afrika in 1435—were initially welcomed by the indigenous people in those locations. These his/herstoric moments were classic examples of the clash of cultures. In retrospect, the welcomes were most probably perceived by Europeans as the naiveté/stupidity of these peoples. Unknown to Afrikan and First Nations people, these contacts heralded the dawning of their enslavement and extermination. Perhaps, the religious and political upheavals, disease and famine taking place in Europe, provided some of the reasons for the "settlement" of Europeans all over the Americas. Again, as in the case of Afrika, there was a recognition by Europeans (Spanish) on their arrival in the Americas of life more splendid than that of Europe and a people more beautiful. Colon (Christopher Columbus), on his arrival in the Greater Antilles, marveled at the beauty, pacifism, and the way of life of the Taino women and men (Carew 1994). Another "discoverer," Cortes, made a similar observation when he entered the Aztec capital of Mexico, in 1519, which at that time included parts of Texas, Colorado and California. He was amazed when he saw their temples, pyramids, palaces, floating gardens (which were among the most advanced agricultural systems in the world), their aqueducts, zoos, and running baths. Cortes said he had not seen the like any where else (Van Sertima, lecture, London 1985). Pizarro's experience with the Incas of Peru in 1530 was the same. Within a short time these "discoverers" Colon, Cortes, and Pizarro, had set in motion the destruction of these people, their culture, and their civilization.

The Spanish, led by the Italian Colon, were the first to set the pattern of violent and genocidal behavior against First Nations people. Colon was personally responsible for the death and torture of innocent women and men. Within forty years of his arrival in Ghuanahani (Hispaniola), the population of 3 million was reduced to 300 people. Moreover, according to Carew, this story of genocide was also the story of the island peoples of Cuba, Puerto Rico, and Jamaica (Carew 1994, 261).

The main interest of these invaders was primarily to find gold and silver and to enslave the indigenous populations toward this end. Figures from Wolfe's (1982) work reveal that Nicaragua lost over 200,000 people to slave raiders in the early part of the 1500s. The Portuguese enslaved 40,000 in northeastern Brazil. In all, an additional 350,000 were captured and enslaved.

> In Mesoamerica and in the Andean areas, large-scale populations had supported complex tributary systems, such as the Aztec confederation and the Inca domain. In these areas the catastrophic population decline contributed to the fragmentation of existing polities. The pre-Hispanic population of Mesoamerica has been estimated at 25 million, that of the Inca domain as anywhere between 6 million . . . and 30 million. . . . In Mesoamerica the population count fell to a low point of 1.5 million by 1650. . . . The number of inhabitants of the Spanish audiencias Lima and Charcas . . . declined from 5 million to 300,000 in the 1780s and 1790s. (Wolfe 1982, 134)

The decline in the populations owing to enslavement, genocide, and diseases brought by Europeans was catastrophic. Carew (1994) cites an estimate of 68 million First Nations people who died in the holocaust (72). The transportation of captured and enslaved Afrikan people to the Americas was both in response to the demise of the indigenous populations and the continuous need for labor power. Thus, the massive reduction in the populations of the Americas paralleled that of Afrika from the 1600s. Although not precise, figures put forward by an unknown European scholar in Walter Rodney's (1982) work provide some indication of the stagnation in population growth in Afrika.

From 1650 to 1900, Europe's population quadrupled while in Afrika the population count remained the same every hundred years until 1900 when the growth was a meager 25 percent by comparison. These are the estimates in millions.

	1650	1750	1850	1900
Afrika	100	100	100	120
Europe	103	144	274	423
Asia	257	437	656	857

Source: Rodney 1982, 97

This population stagnation had disastrous affects upon Afrika and its development. Rodney's thesis on Afrika may be used to understand the American condition of its First Nations people in terms of the "arrested development" caused by European greed.

In the Americas, as well as in Afrika, Europeans—Belgian, Dutch, English, French, Italian, Portuguese, German, and Spanish (including the Swedes and Danes in the Caribbean)—worked out their separate nationalist strategies in their early claims on territories. All strategies involved the indiscriminate killing of indigenous people, in the name of Christianity, underpinned by the imagery and ideology of "Indian savagery." While Europeans fought each other for territorial ownership, they exploited both Afrikan and First Nations people in their attempts to gain control over lands. Promises were made and broken and the indigenous populations formed and broke alliances and federations for protection against the encroachment on their lands and their ability to survive. Countless treaties, deals, and laws were made and violated as Europeans consolidated their positions of domination as white supremacists while relinquishing their own nationalist differences. No matter what agreements indigenous people made with the white populations, the spoken and written word had no sacred meaning in European culture as it did in the indigenous culture. As a result, First Nations people found themselves victims of their own values and expectations. This condition may be viewed as a prime example of the manifestation of a cultural clash.

In the North American context, the premium was on indigenous land, not their labor energies because, ironically, a premium had been set on the labor energies of Afrikan people and European waged labor. With the focus on land, it meant that the lives of the indigenous people were inconsequential to the needs of Europeans. Moreover, the unharnessed energies of the First Nations people were perceived as a threat to European safety. Thus, a policy of genocide was actively implemented. As in the case of Afrikan people, indigenous resistance to European domination was continuous. Over time, in order to ensure peace and survive, some First Nations people took the assimilationist or acculturationist route. In reality, they fared no better than those who took the traditionalist route.

A case in point is that of the so-called "civilized nations," the Seminoles, Cherokees, Choctaws, Creeks, and Chickasaws who essentially became Europeanized. They became Christianized, intermarried with white women and men, and developed schools that taught English literacy (Wolfe 1982, 284–85). English or any other European writing was deemed superior to the indigenous writings, yet First Nations people like Afrikan people were *both* a literate and oral people. As early as the 1500s, Cardinal Ximenes, Grand Inquisitor of Spain, had ordered Bishop de Landa in Yucatan to burn First Nations books as the works of the Devil (Van Sertima 1992, 13).

These Europeanized First Nations people, complied with European standards, led sedentary lives, owned guns and cotton plantations, and enslaved Afrikan people (Wolfe 1982, 285). They even supported the Southern plantation owners during the Civil War. Ironically, becoming Europeanized or "civilized" did not grant these nations sovereignty. Even before the Civil War, "removal" from their homelands became law. It was envisioned by the government that dispossessing these nations would yield 25 million acres of land to European settlement. President Andrew Jackson was the man who brutally carried out the job of "removal" (Chinweizu 1975, 434).

Where Indian groups did not depart voluntarily, the army was sent in to enforce the removal order. Between 1820 and 1840,

three-fourths of the 125,000 Indians living east of the Mississippi came under government removal programs . . . between
one-fourth and one-third of all Southern Indians lost their
lives. (Wolfe 1982, 285)

This tragic lesson is one that we are all too familiar with especially in the contemporary neocolonial climate with Afrikan people
living in the United States, the Caribbean, the United Kingdom,
and on the continent of Afrika. No matter how "civilized," accul-
turated, or Europeanized any subject individual or group becomes,
"race" will determine the level of "inferiority" or the value of
humanity in a Europeanized world. Chinweizu (1975) believes
that the First Nations' civilizing or colonizing process was used as
a model for Afrika. This process requires the formation of a Christianized, Westernized elite that will associate itself with the
European elite, and allow access to the resources and energies of
the people. While this process may have been modeled on the
First Nations' experience, it is well to keep in mind that the
colonization of Afrikan people by Europeans on a continental scale
had actively begun from the time of the Portuguese's "discovery"
of West Afrika, prior even to Colon's arrival in the Caribbean.
Thus, one may surmise that Europeans did then as they continue
to do today, and shared their ideas on methods of domination
through the construction of such an elite so that any success in
one place could translate to another. At the same time, it would
be well to keep in mind the early conquests and colonization of
Afrika beginning with Kemet (Ancient Egypt) by the Persians,
Greeks, Romans, and Arabs. Initiated by the Persians around 525
B.C.E., these early invasions set a precedent for Europeans to understand their cultural links with Afrika in terms of modes of
conquest and appropriation.

    In this light, and much later, two major cultural groups, the
Afrikan and First Nations peoples, both of essentially matriarchal
origins, were subjugated simultaneously in Afrika and the Americas. The exploitation of the energies and resources of these women
and men were integral to the accumulation of wealth and therefore
the development of European capitalism. Thus, one may not speak
of the Afrikan enslavement, genocide, and colonization in the

Americas without recognition of or reference to the enslavement, genocide, and colonization of the indigenous peoples.

Furthermore, it is important to analyze the impact of European patriarchy upon these subjugated peoples. A deeper analysis of this nature will be used to understand the contemporary situation of the Afrikan mothers whom I interviewed. In this respect, it may be said that Afrikan women, as well as First Nations women, had a lot to lose, particularly in terms of the transition in status from that of the giver of life and the center of social organization to that of the inferior half of the male-female partnership in the European setting. Interestingly, and in the most bizarre way, the racialization of humanity that Europeans practice as a way of elevating their own female-male humanity, effectively placed both Afrikan women and men in a complementary relationship with each other. For, as Gloria Joseph (1981) argues, during enslavement, the dehumanization and brutality inflicted upon both Black women and men equalized their position as Afrikan people without regard to their sex (Joseph 1981, 94–95). From a documented account at the time, taken from Joseph's work, Moses Granby saw

> women who had sucking children suffered much from their breasts becoming full of milk, the infants being left at home; they therefore could not keep up with the other hands. I have seen the overseer beat them with raw hide so that the blood and milk flew mingled from their breasts. (Joseph 1981, 94)

Joseph goes on to say that

> [t]he rape of Black women and the lynching and castration of Black men are equally heinous in their nature. Today, the Black man carries scars from his slave experience as much as the Black woman carries her scars. We use no measuring stick for the oppression suffered by Blacks. (Joseph 1981, 94)

The point is that it was culturally expedient for European women and men to collaborate to racialize the social hierarchy. In an equally bizarre way the equal positioning of Afrikan women and men under white supremacy, equalized the position of white women and men through their partnership in domination and control. There can be no realistic separation between the behavior of European men and the support of their mothers, wives, daughters, sisters, and partners to this end. Inasmuch as the Afrikan woman's body was considered the domain of the white man, so the white woman had access to her body also. Ironically, the fathering of more enslaved persons through the white man, perpetuated the empowerment of white women over Black women and men. Thus, she had access to the bodies of both the Afrikan woman and man whom she could exploit and torture at will if she chose to do so.

Reflecting on the early white women's rights struggle, Angela Davis (1984) attempts to link its emergence with poor white working-class women who challenged their treatment from the factory floors during industrialization at least from the early 1800s. At the same time, she links this movement to the antislavery movement that involved women from the privileged classes. While Davis argues that in the case of both groups, white women likened their conditions to the plight of the enslaved Afrikan persons, in reality, this was not the case. European women were certainly subjugated to European men and ethnic or class distinctions determined the levels of brutality that the elite (men and women) meted out to the masses of their people. However, this treatment can in no way be considered to be the same as the sadistic treatment that Afrikan women and men experienced from both European women and men as a result of the cultural cohesiveness of Europeans. The history of white factory workers and their relationship to Black factory workers (Du Bois, 1935/1962); the herstory of white industrial female workers and their relationship to Afrikan female industrial workers (Giddings 1988); and the elite white women and their relationship to enslaved Afrikan people (Davis 1984) bears testimony to that.

The racism of white abolitionist women involved in the white women's rights movement was in itself a contradiction of their supposed beliefs. Elizabeth Cady Stanton, perhaps one of the most famous women of this movement, made clear the importance of European cultural unity before the struggle of all women's rights that she claimed to stand for. In a letter sent to the *New York Standard* in 1865, she said:

Although this may remain a question for politicians to wrangle over for five or ten years, the black man is still, in a political point of view, far above the educated white women of the country. The representative women of the nation have done their uttermost for the last thirty years to secure freedom for the negro; and as long as he was lowest in the scale of being, we were willing to press his claims; but now, as the celestial gate to civil rights is slowly moving on its hinges, it becomes a serious question whether we had better stand aside and see "Sambo" walk into the kingdom first.... "This is the negro's hour." Are we sure that he, once entrenched in all his inalienable rights, may not be an added power to hold us at bay? ... In fact, it is better to be the slave of an educated white man, than of a degraded ignorant black one ... (Davis 1984, 70)

Given the conceptual framework provided in this book, there are many contradictions apparent in this missive that will not be analyzed at this point. It is clear that these two contesting cultural groups, one for domination and the other for survival, should be seen in the light of their value systems, as well as the roles of women within those value systems.

However, in the present context, of Afrikan women and men living in white supremacist patriarchy, the effects of the imposition of European male-centered values upon Afrikan people living in both the United States and the United Kingdom cannot be marginalized. The words of the Afrikan women of the Combahee River Collective[1] ring so true in this respect as they also reflect their cultural unity among Afrikan people when they say:

Although we are feminists and Lesbians, we feel solidarity with progressive Black men and do not advocate the fractionalization that white women who are separatists demand. Our situation as Black people necessitates that we have solidarity around the fact of race, which white women of course do not need to have with white men, unless it is their negative solidarity as racial oppressors. We struggle together with Black men against racism, while we struggle with Black men about sexism (1986, 12)

These words reflect the powerful feelings of allegiance to their cultural group, which in turn signal the resistance to cultural domination that Afrikan women have practiced since their subjugation to Europeans. Like Stella Dadzie (1990), Paula Giddings (1988) presents examples of Afrikan women's resistance, in the form of the refusal to procreate and bear enslaved children through the use of abortion and contraceptives and open acts of bravery such as when, for example, Maria was burnt at the stake in 1681 for attempting to burn her owner's home and the unknown woman who was burned at the stake for participating in the killing of seven whites (Giddings 1988, 39–46).

A cultural analysis is useful in order to understand that the changing nature of the relationship between Afrikan people and Europeans in the United States reached an epochal moment during the Civil War between the competing industrial and plantocratic capitalists. This war led to the transition from Afrikan enslaved labor to "freed" labor (Du Bois 1935/1962). The consolidation of European power in the form of U.S. state organization provided the managerial context for insuring a new mode of control for the industrialization of Afrikan energies. This stage of capitalist development was for Afrikan people fraught with rampant white hostility emanating from the breakdown of the old plantocratic regime as well as from the construction of the new Northern regime largely instigated by these competing capitalists. Perhaps, fueled by the fear of retaliation for the years of torture and "inhumanity" suffered by Afrikan people, together with the fear of competition for waged work, white people went on a rampage. Hundreds and thousands of Afrikan women, children, and men were murdered (Davis 1981, 113). An observer of the time stated:

To kill a negro, they do not deem murder; to debauch a Negro woman, they do not think fornication; to take the property away from a Negro, they do not consider robbery. The people boast that when they get freedmen's affairs in their own hands, to use their own expression, "the niggers will catch hell" (Du Bois 1969, 136)

In particular, the poor uneducated whites, supported by police, courts, judges, and landowners, were able to act with impunity against Afrikan women and men. Du Bois cites many observations that testify to that fact. In the words of General Hatch:

The hatred toward the Negro as a freeman is intense among the low and brutal, who are the vast majority. Murders, shootings, whippings, robbing and brutal treatment of every kind are daily inflicted upon them. (Du Bois 1969, 144)

Another general also claimed that in the nine counties of Jackson District, one Afrikan man was killed every day and on one occasion he found seven butchered Afrikans on a forty-mile excursion. The Freedmen's Bureau for Mississippi claimed an average of 2–3 men killed per day. A governor of Mississippi believed that Afrikans would be exterminated (Du Bois 1969 141–42). The research by Ida B. Wells on the lynching murders of Afrikan women and men adds substance to these figures. Her study, based on official figures, showed an average of 100–200 lynching deaths per year. This would have been a conservative estimate, given that many lynchings were not documented. Ginzburg's (1988) more recent research documents lynchings recorded in newspapers from the 1880s right up until the 1960s.

In order to analyze the changing nature of the European-Afrikan relationship, particularly in the United States, it is important to look more broadly at the enactment of this relationship in other dominions. Diop's concept of cultural unity illuminates the way that Europeans worked together to construct a global racialized social order based upon murder and fear. In this light, the treatment of Afrika and her people appears to have been consistent among the competing European ethnicities. While the similarity in treating Afrikan people may be seen as a sign of the commonality in values held by Europeans, it is also reflects a general belief that Afrikan people were very much alike. This belief was so prevalent that it manifested in well-documented data that attempted to prove the cultural, genetic, psychological, and mental inferiority of Afrikan people through scientific racism. It is evident that a clash of cultural values and beliefs served to facilitate the ongoing conquest. At the same time, resistance to every level of debasement has been fundamental to the changing nature of the European-Afrikan relationship. However, the transition from enslaved labor to "freed" labor in the United States did not ultimately change the power relationship between Afrikan people and Europeans. The state, posing as a neutral entity, now mediated the control of Afrikan "free" energies. Any humanization of this relationship may be attributed to a European concession to Afrikan resistance. If Europeans could have kept Afrikan women and men enslaved forever, they would have done so. Clearly, and importantly, those European women and men who challenged this barbaric system were a minority and very likely suffered the consequences of any such challenges.

White supremacy is a cultural materialization of European origin. Its psychological manifestation, racism, helped to accomplish and justify the racialization of the world. In this light, racism may be viewed as a mental illness even by Western standards (Welsing 1991; Wright 1994; Hilliard 1987; Akbar 1991). At the same time, according to Fanon (1983), the undying attempts by the oppressed to liberate themselves from this condition manifest in dreams of freedom and dignity on a daily basis:

> [W]hen [s]he discovers that the oppressor can be killed, this discovery shakes [her]his social and psychological world to its foundation. Acting on that discovery demystifies the omnipotence of the oppressor and restores [her]his self-confidence and self-respect. (Bulhan 1985, 117)

When considering the psychological dynamics of such revolutionary practice, one is able to understand how this must have provided inspiration and strength to all Afrikans under European control everywhere.

Schooling as a Mode of Oppression

The "educated" Afrikan presented a danger to the stability of the established order for two primary reasons: the challenge to the ideological belief in the inferiority of the Afrikan and the empowerment gained from having access to the knowledge bodies and forms of written communication used by the oppressors. Several leaders of Afrikan resistance, such as General Gabriel, Denmark Vesey, and Nat Turner, were allowed to read. Their training had come through Christianity and the Bible that very likely inspired them to challenge the inhumanity of the regime in which their people were enslaved. Ironically, the same value system that the Bible espouses is grounded in the ancient spiritual systems of Afrika. One could surmise that Afrikan spirituality was then, and is now, a part of the cultural memory of Afrikan people. The Afrikan roots of New World religions have been well documented by scholars (Finch 1990; Rashidi 1992; Akbar 1994; Budge 1899; Ra Un Nefer Amen 1990).

At the end of the Civil War the breakdown of the plantocratic regime caused the uncertainty of how to manage landless, impoverished, and abused Afrikan women, children, and men. After the years of violent mental, spiritual, and physical abuse and neglect, the consequences and outcomes of this treatment were measured and analyzed as if they were somehow caused by the innate inferiority of Afrikan people. In other words, a subjugated and repressed people were looked upon as though they were the cause of their own degradation. Only the unrelenting threat of torture and death could create the subservient people that Europeans hoped for. In reality, Afrikan resistance to this treatment never waned and what Afrikan people really thought, in the main, was hidden.

The "outsider within" idea of Patricia Hill Collins (1990) speaks to the way of "knowing" that Afrikan people have. She attributes the manifestation of this act to Black women, in particular, as a means of surviving. Essentially, white supremacy created an Afrikan woman, man, and child who learned to act one way and think another. White supremacists feared that they could never know what was going on inside the Afrikan mind and thus could never have the complete control that they desired.

Given the prevailing situation, a major concern of the European elite was how to maintain control over the new circumstances of "freed" Afrikan people. The idea of "industrial schooling" as a method of control was developed by philanthropic foundations like the Rockefeller Foundation, the Rosenwald Fund, the Jeannes Fund, the Phelpes Stokes Fund, the Peabody Fund, and the Slater Fund. These funding bodies emerged from the rising new capitalists who were to play a key role in the creation of the General Education Board to control the education of Afrikan children in the production of waged "workers." The General Education Board would later influence the schooling of the mass of children through public schooling/education.

The industrial school rose to prominence toward the end of the nineteenth century with the Hampton Institute as the prototype. This led to the founding of the Tuskegee Institute. These institutions were excellent examples of the objectives of industrial schooling. The first president of the General Education Board and a trustee of the Tuskegee Institute in 1894 was William H. Baldwin. He represented the general beliefs of his colleagues and capitalist interests when he claimed that

> The potential economic value of the Negro population properly educated is infinite and incalculable. In the Negro is the opportunity of the South. Time has proven that he is best fitted to perform the heavy labor of the South. He will willingly fill the more menial positions, and so the heavy work, at less wages than the American white man or any foreign race which has yet come to our shores. This will permit the Southern white laborer to perform the more expert labor, and to leave the fields, the mines and the simpler trades for the Negro. (Anderson 1988, 14)

On the female side of this equation, Afrikan women would in the same sense carry out the same roles in relation to the menial tasks that women were seen as best "fitted." Ironically, these schools were to provide the training for Afrikan children to fill the roles that their parents and ancestors had carried out throughout the enslavement period. Prior to industrial schooling, Afrikan people had been deemed suitably skilled for the tasks they were forced to carry out. In reality, Afrikan women and men had been purchased from different parts of Afrika because of the specific skills that they could bring to the Americas (Holloway 1990).

The founder of the Hampton Institute, General Samuel K. Armstrong, held similar views to William H. Baldwin but emphasized the importance of uplift through instruction in the morality, health, and hygiene of Afrikans. This implied that Afrikan people needed to be instructed about morality, health, and hygiene as if their impoverished conditions had not been created by the racist social conditions but rather by their ignorance. Armstrong's star pupil, Booker T. Washington, himself a prime product and firm advocator of industrial schooling, was the founder of the Tuskegee Institute. He felt that given the existing conditions it was necessary for Afrikan people to prove themselves equal to Europeans through their industriousness (Anderson 1988, 155). This task must have seemed rather ironic since it was the industriousness of the Afrikan person that had made her such a successful "slave." It is clear that the idea of industrial schooling was to provide a way of preparing the Afrikan person for the role that s/he was expected to fulfill in new economic circumstances. It was believed that these schools would produce the new "educated," Europeanized, deculturalized, Afrikan worker who would take up her rightful position at the bottom of the racialized and race-gendered socioeconomic order without challenge, firm in the belief of her inferiority and inability to rise. These expectations were not unlike those of the British elite, when Afrikan peoples from the Caribbean and Afrika came to work and live in the United Kingdom from the late 1940s.

Assumptions about the educability of Afrikan people and their expected socioeconomic roles were shaped by the pseudo-scientific racism of the time. These ideas fed into educational policy that has remained in the control of the culturally dominant elite. The schooling of Afrikan people had been a major concern of European elites during the consolidation of their rule in the U.S., the Caribbean, and Afrika. Even prior to the development of industrial schooling in the United States, the first major European investigation into a "suitable education" for Afrikans was instigated by the British government in West Afrika. The then Royal Commissioner, R. Maddon, submitted a report to the British government in 1841 that stated in effect that Afrikan people could not be successfully intellectually educated. A suitable education would therefore involve training in mechanical and farming skills (Lyons 1970, 19).

By the early 1900s, British educational policy was strongly linked to the philanthropic foundations in the United States Ideas centered around a general policy regarding the Afrikan populations in the United States and British colonies in Afrika. In Britain, Michael Sadler published *Education of the Colored Race* in 1902, which may have been inspired, according to King (1971), by his relationship with Booker T. Washington. This work was to have an influence over the next thirty years on missionary and colonial policy concerning Afrika and Afrikan people. Sadler's work stated:

> The work which is going forward in the industrial and agricultural training schools for the colored race in the United States, is one of great significance. Lessons can be learned from it which are of value for those engaged in education in parts of the British Empire; for example, in West Africa and the West Indies, where there are large black populations. (Quoted in King 1980, 48)

Men like J. H. Oldham saw a need for Europeans to come together on this issue. He was a member of the Advisory Committee on Native Education in British Tropical Africa, had been secretary of the Committee of the World Missionary Conference, and a firm advocate of the Tuskegee concept. He was also an associate of T. Jesse Jones, the educational director of the Phelpes Stokes Fund. Jesse Jones traveled all over Afrika and inspired C. T. Loram, who was Natal's chief inspector of native education in charge of Bantu education in South Afrika. Jones wrote about "Negro" education in Afrika and carried out a survey on "Negro" education in the Southern states. According to King, the objective of the report, *Negro Education: A Study of Private and Higher Schools for Colored People in the United States, 1917,* was to determine the educational needs of Afrikans. In his assessment of Jones's work, King argues that this survey was biased in that Jones was a firm supporter of industrial education and set out to prove that this was the most suitable education for Afrikan people (King 1971, 33). It is clear that there were training plans being developed specifically related to Afrikan people wherever they were residing. The types of men involved in the industrial schooling project became "native"/"Negro" experts and their recommendations impacted upon the lives of Afrikan people all over the world.

At the same time, indigenous children were captured and forced to go to industrial boarding schools. The intention of the United States (European) government regarding First Nations and Afrikan people was the same. On the one hand, industrial boarding schools were meant to "civilize" or acculturate indigenous people into the

European mainstream in order to control the continual threat that they posed (Dove 1993). On the other hand, the objective of industrial schools for Afrikan people, both in Afrika in the United States, was to undermine cultural integrity in order to intensify the process of subjugation. Industrial schooling was not about developing skills in academic excellence, or disseminating knowledge. It was designed to produce essentially deculturalized First Nations and Afrikan peoples inculcated with ideas that denied their own humanity and worth, the byproduct of which was to be a menial laborer of some kind.

This method of schooling laid the foundation of the modern school system in the United States. From the 1920s until the 1960s millions of Afrikan people, seeking employment in the developing industrial Northern cities, migrated from the Southern plantations. Migratory patterns of a similar nature were taking place among Afrikan people during the 1940s who moved from Afrika and the Caribbean to Europe, especially to the United Kingdom. They were moving to change their economic circumstances. The "freedom" of Afrikan movement is more of an indicator of the need for cheap labor to support industrial development than that of humanitarian concerns on the part of Europeans.

However, the hard-won rights of Afrikan people against inhumanity must also be a critical consideration in this analysis. In the case of the migration from the American South, it would be fair to say that Afrikan women and men were not only moving away from chronically economically depressed areas but also from the severe psychological horrors and spiritual pain of living with a history of torture and subjugation where white racists like the Ku Klux Klan were free to kill indiscriminately. As the urban segregated "townships" in the North accommodated this movement, state repression through concentrated police brutality became a new visible force of oppression. Now, the mindset of the KKK could live legally and comfortably within the establishment as the force of police. By the 1960s, brutalities of the mind and body had reached an untenable level in urban life for Afrikan people.

The 1960s and the 1970s have had a major impact in directing the lives of the interviewees—whether they are aware of this or not. Most of the participants, however, acknowledge this fact. The importance of the historical moment of the 1960s in the 500 year resistance against the enslavement, colonization, and domination of Afrikan people is that it represents a period of explosion in the "belly of the beast," in the capital of world power—the urban and rural areas of the United States. The struggle for human rights reached an epochal moment as Afrikan countries and Caribbean countries gained their neo-colonial "independence."

The significance of the neocolonial situation should not be marginalized. As in the case of the "civilized" nations who became Europeanized and accepted the European value system, Afrikan people and others all over the world conceded to white supremacist conquest, at least as a strategy for survival. Thus, Afrikan people living in the United States began to speak of and to struggle for civil rights, that is, those rights ascribed to members of the United States state structure. In this way, the United States as a state organization was validated in the minds of those whose ancestors' blood had flowed in its making.

Figures like Fannie Lou Hamer, Angela Davis, the Honorable Elijah Muhammad, Malcolm X, and Martin Luther King, and countless others, rose as symbols of liberation in the United States. The period also saw the rise of the Black Power movement, and the Black Nationalist and Pan-Afrikanist ideologies. The emergence of these figures along with the proliferation of Black student organizations, the defiance of the Black Panthers, and the burning of the cities challenged the dominant culture, ideology, and politics of white supremacist social power relations.

At the same time, state violence against this resistance was sustained and carefully orchestrated in the shape of the FBI and its guerrilla tactics to break down the developing infrastructure within the Afrikan communities. There is strong evidence suggested by Ward Churchill and Jim Vander Wall's (1990) analysis of information relating to COINTELPRO.[2] In front of the world, key figures in the Panther organizations were assassinated along with Dr. King and Malcolm X while many others were subjected to character assassinations.

The schooling and education of Afrikan girls and boys became an important political issue. The 1954 Brown decision took on new meaning in relation to the breakdown of the Afrikan infrastructure by white supremacy. It was clear that out of segregated communities had risen powerful, educated leaders with ideas that threatened the stability of the status quo by challenging the principles of Western "democracy." The state-managed assassination of natural community leaders was accompanied by the acceleration toward desegregation. Desegregation at the time was understood as the hard-won victory of civil rights campaigners who had laid their lives on the line to demand the rights of Afrikan Americans to have access to the wealth of the nation that they had helped produce.

Out of this struggle, three definite movements can be identified. First, the movement by "Black" institutions to teach Afrikan people to become "equal" Americans. Second, the movement by white institutions to teach Afrikan people to become "Black" Americans and, third, the movement by "Black" or Afrikan-controlled institutions to teach Afrikan children to be Afrikans. The first two movements advocated the need to integrate into mainstream life through schooling. The third movement advocated the need to develop Afrikan-centered institutions in an effort toward nation building. The desegregation movement was enforced by the state as part of the process of infrastructural breakdown and control of the Afrikan population. It manifested in the employment of white teachers in Black public schools and the bussing of Afrikan students into white schools. As Marable (1983) argues, the traditionally run Black higher education institutions now became vulnerable to the imposition of white professors as part of the pay-off for state funding. Integration meant the transformation of Black institutions to white, threatening the ability of these institutions to serve the Afrikan community as they had done previously. At the same time, a brain drain occurred as Afrikan professors went or were forced to find employment on white campuses. Furthermore, many Black schools were closed down, leaving qualified principals and others unable to be employed in the same capacity and, thus, undermining the Black teaching profession.

The demand for Black studies or Black history courses was accommodated by white universities with the establishment of Africana and Afro/African American Studies programs and departments. Many of these programs began disappearing from educational institutions in the United States, as well as in the United Kingdom, by the mid-1970s (Marable 1983, 219; Dhondy 1982, 31–33). The building and developing of Afrikan-centered institutions in Afrikan communities was part of the material realization of the Black Nationalist and Pan-Afrikanist movement. These institutions were not based on the same ideology as traditional Black-run institutions, which followed the patterns of "education" in which excellent scholarship and academicians were created to produce Americans who were Black and able to compete in the market. Instead, these schools were about developing a new Afrikan person. They emphasized the cultural aspects of Afrikanity that were conducive to the healthy development of the minds, bodies, and souls of our children. In these institutions, scholarship and academic achievement are seen as important outcomes in the development of critical thinking. Although Black-run educational institutions that were not Afrikan-centered were not interested in integrating their schools, they were interested in developing well-adjusted Black Americans who could buy into Americanness. Their interests would direct the Afrikan struggle toward fighting for a position within the existing system, thereby legitimizing the American/European way of life. Ultimately, this action can be construed as another level of integration into the system. It may also be viewed as another mode of survival.

This chapter has provided an important context for understanding the environment within which the mothers' herstories took place. Their choice to send their children to culturally affirming schools is significant, particularly in the light of the attempt within the U.S. social structure to use schooling as a way to falsify Afrikan people's reality for the specific purpose of keeping Afrikan people ignorant of the true nature of the clash of cultures between European and Afrikan peoples. In this way, Afrikan energies can successfully be used to serve the interests of European domination.

⑤

The Herstories of Afrikan Mothers in the United States

Mothers Who Send Their Children to the Sankofa School

Camara ("One who teaches from experience")

Camara is thirty-nine years old. She is five feet one with natural hair and a gentle manner. She is the head teacher of Sankofa ("return to the past to take from it what is relevant for the future") school. Her two daughters, Sibusiso ("blessing") and Sihle ("beautiful") who are eighteen and nineteen years of age respectively, were raised by Camara alone.

Camara grew up in a small Afrikan community on the east coast of Canada as a fifth-generation Afrikan Canadian. There, she went to school and was taught by Afrikan teachers from the community. In retrospect, the best teachers that Camara ever had were from that community school. It was ironic that many of the teachers who came to this school were excellent teachers who were unable to get hired in the white community and ended up living in this Afrikan community. These teachers always had a positive way of teaching about Afrikan people even when using the public school curriculum.

111

In Camara's eyes, the community provided a support network for all its people.

> My grandfather would always say, "This is my mother's father and also my father's people, they all, my ancestors." [He] always instilled in us a pride in our community. I lived in a segregated community. It was not integrated until I was in grade nine. I would be about fourteen years old. That was the first time I was introduced to white culture.

During integration, Camara attended school in a white community. She learned about the stereotypical depictions of who she and her school friends were and the types of lives they led. However, she refused to consider herself poor or disadvantaged.

Most of the people in her community were self-employed through farming. Her grandfather had the largest farm in the area. He was a justice of the peace and the first Black councilor in the district. Camara's mother raised eight children. Camara was the third child of five sisters and two brothers. Her two brothers were older than she. She remembers how her mother, who was on the board of education, always wished that she had more schooling, fought to keep the community school open, and encouraged all her children to achieve in school. All eight children were raised essentially by Camara's mother.

> My father was always there [but] my mum was the backbone. . . . She was always there working . . . housework and raising us and taking care of Dad, always on committees, very, very active.

At seventy-five, despite diminishing health, Camara's mother is still involved, close to Camara, and often goes with her to important functions. When Camara entered high school in the white community, she suffered a culture shock. She was accompanied by twenty-five of her friends who graduated from her community school. It was during this experience that she became aware of how the schooling system evaluated children according to their race. In other words, Black children would compete against Black children and white against white, so that a Black child receiving a 90 percent grade would do less well than a white student receiving an 80 percent grade. Children were being streamed according to supposed levels of intelligence associated with their race. It was only when outside examiners marked the children without knowing who they were that the Black students found themselves moving up from failing grades to the top of their classes. When the Afrikan children and the European children were not graded according to race, students positions changed overall—European students did a lot worse.

As a result of the streaming process, many Afrikan pupils were put into grades lower than necessary, and some dropped out of school. Camara found this practice prevalent once she became a teacher. The racism encountered in this school took place on many levels, even among the students. From grade 10 until now, she became actively involved in championing the rights of Afrikan students, fighting racism, forming groups, getting funding, and raising scholarships.

I was always a rebel [laughing] from high school, doing something you know, that was, like if I felt an injustice was being done, I'd always say something, right from not getting into the cheerleaders team, why not? All the cheerleaders were blond-haired and blue-eyed. . . . So we formed our own team . . . of course in the 70s with the Black Panthers and movements and the Vietnam War, I'm a product of all that. I think the movement instilled the need to keep on going to fight for what I believed in.

During her university studies, Camara, who was married, found it difficult to study pharmacy, raise the children, and take care of a husband, who did not support her studies. The husband lost out. She took the children and changed her degree from pharmacy to Afrikan studies and then to education. While completing her master's degree, she traced her own family history, finding out that her people had fought on the side of the British during the American War of Independence and sailed to Canada. Interestingly, her community had historically provided a haven for Afrikans from the continent, from the Caribbean, and from the U.S. South. Her work is now a valuable contribution to the historical reconstruction of Afrikan and Canadian history.

Her decision to become a teacher, although predicated on difficulties in her marriage, led to her involvement in the public school system. She taught and created an Afrikan heritage program that was accepted by the board of education but not given to Camara as her subject area to teach. This move was viewed by Camara as part of the racism exhibited against Afrikan teachers. Especially, when, as in this case, the job was given to a European male, although she was needed to regularly lecture on the subject.

In terms of the racism inflicted upon children in the public school system, Camara has always been concerned about the treatment of Afrikan children. Her concern stems from the insights gained from her own schooling and her children's schooling. As a teacher, she played a major role in teaching Afrikan history to children, including her own. As a parent she found herself marching into schools in defense of her daughters and their ideas.

> I've always been opposed to what they taught. Going to my daughters' interviews, I walked in with an attitude and they could see me coming. . . . When they found out I was a teacher, it was like, ok, ok, so she does know what's going on. I hated them, and you know, when the tables were turned and I had parents coming to me, I'd say, "Listen to your child. You have to believe in your child." Unfortunately, a lot of us, a lot of Afrikans, believe in the teachers. No, I have no respect for teachers and yet here I am and I love teaching.

Camara's love of teaching ultimately led to her interest in running her own school.

By the time Camara applied for the head teaching post at Sankofa, she had run her own Afrikan heritage program as an afterschool program and a Saturday program for twelve years. Camara found teaching fulfilling and worthwhile:

> It was part of at least half way reaching my goal [of] doing something that I liked. So when I heard about the school open-

ing, I thought, "I'm going to try out for it." I feel that having a school such as this is very important for the community.

It seemed important to note whether Camara had received any negative feedback about taking this position. Camara observed that her mother was concerned and worried about her safety.

I guess it stems too from the fact the people are going to be watching and don't get yourself into anything and don't say anything that you shouldn't, that's going to jeopardize you.

Colleagues have also been worried about Camara leaving her public school job and all the benefits to teach in a school that holds no guarantees. This is a risk and she is well aware of it. Risks are not new to Camara; she is resourceful and brave. She does not see herself as strong, although everyone tells her that she is.

I'm tired of hearing it. My mum says that to me all the time. And I'm so weak, sometimes you just want to give it all up and say take it. A couple of years ago I was in this very bad relationship and I just made myself totally sick and I just became useless and landed up in the hospital, which was just great because at least I could just relax [laughing]. I remember the girls coming in and saying, "Mum, you're not supposed to be sick," and that really scared me and shocked me. They got me up again. And that was frightening in a way. They always said, "You're strong. You can do it."

Camara attributes much of her strength to her mother's strength and to her sisters' support. Her sisters have always been there for her, and like "wicked aunts" for her daughters. That inner strength, she feels came from the female side of the family. The strongest male that she could think of was her grandfather, who instilled the pride of being Afrikan in all her family.

Ayoluwa ("Joy of our people")

Ayoluwa is forty-six years old. She is tall and elegant and wears her long hair natural. She has played a key role in getting Sankofa school off the ground as a board member and parent. In her career outside motherhood, Ayoluwa has been a teacher's aide in an alternative school with mostly white children and has worked in the public school system as a remedial teacher teaching mainly Afrikan children. She has had three marriages and two sons and two daughters, three of whom she brought up on her own. Her fourth child, her daughter Aziza ("dignity") goes to Sankofa School. Ayoluwa's mother raised five daughters and one son on her own. She remembers her father, whom she saw sometimes, but her mother divorced just after her birth. She was very close to her mother and feels that her mother helped to create the inner strength necessary to cope with her own life.

> My mother was definitely a very strong Black woman and she did help me with my little ones growing up. If I had to work she would watch the children and all kinds of things. You know that, now that she's not here you just know how much you depend on her. I guess people know how much mothers really mean when you kind of come through it all and just look back and say, "God, how could I have even done it," you know.

Ayoluwa's mother migrated from the South but her relationship with her own mother and family in the South was severed over time.

Until the sixth grade, Ayoluwa went to a neighborhood school that was predominantly Black and where the majority of teachers were white. There were some white children in the school, but they were mentally challenged and were kept apart from the Afrikan children. In the sixth grade they were moved to a developing area— the "projects" (public housing). Her family was only one of five Black families in the whole area.

> It was tantamount to Afrikans being pulled out of Afrika and brought here. So I had a very bad reaction. I was physically sick . . . not having my friends and not being nurtured in my little street. We must have had sixty houses in the street. It was a community.

This move affected her grades badly. She went from being an A student to failing in her seventh- and eighth-grade subjects. After that, Ayoluwa chose to attend a mixed vocational school. The schools were turning out people to become employed in the factories, there was plenty of work, and Ayoluwa left school to work. Going on to further education never entered her mind; she was just interested in earning a living as soon as possible like everyone else.

I wanted to know when Ayoluwa became interested in nation building. She related to me that she saw that as her salvation after her first marriage and having children. In fact, it was in the Nation of Islam that she met her second husband. The Honorable Elijah Muhammad was her first inspiration and then Malcolm X. She became involved in meetings centered on the teachings. At this point, she married her first husband and moved to the West Coast. They debated about entering the Nation of Islam. He was against joining. She eventually joined, but she found confusion within and felt that she needed guidance. However, the teachings on diet, dress, and coming together as Afrikan people to build a nation still guide her today.

Because of the climate of the sixties and seventies, when it was time to place her three elder children in school, she chose an alternative school run by white radicals. No culturally affirming schools for Afrikan children were around at that time. She found some contradictions among the white radical movement:

> In the sixties and seventies, there were a lotta white youth out talking about overthrowing the government here in America but when everything fell they could always go back home to their parents.

However, the school provided an option that was suitable to her needs and, importantly, it was close by. She did not want her children to attend the local schools, which housed small gangs in the "hood." In part payment for the tuition fees, Ayoluwa worked as a teacher's aide, teaching basic reading, writing, math, yoga, and Black history. When the first child entered school, there were six children who were white. By the time that all three of her children were in the school, there were eighty pupils, 50 percent of whom were Black. At that time, realizing the need for more Black teachers, she struggled against the racism of teachers and parents who did not see the need.

Even after the birth of her fourth child, she continued to teach in this school. Eventually she left to teach remedial reading to Black students who were bused to a predominantly white public school. She found tremendous freedom to teach what she wanted to in this environment. They were predominantly boys and Ayoluwa was aware of the type of oppression affecting them.

We had a lotta of the Black youth able to begin to feel good about themselves, you know. I mean I worked with students who were in the eighth grade, sixteen, fifteen years old looking like they was about, you know, to be grown men. These are the youth where a lotta people have difficulty, a lot of maybe white people have difficulty. I am very comfortable with because I know what they are lacking. They are lacking the knowledge of who they are.

This experience really fed into the desire that she had held on to for years since joining the Nation of Islam—to run her own school. Essentially she realized that she may have been able to get access to these children but the school did not belong to Afrikan people. Therefore, when the first meetings were held to discuss opening this Afrikan-centered school, Ayoluwa willingly joined.

Obviously, Ayoluwa has no faith in public schooling; she sent none of her children. Even the free school for her first three children was not ideal, because she saw a lack of teaching in the cultural aspect of their self-identity. The model Sankofa School presents is, for Ayoluwa, ideal in the sense that it can be developed all over the community to serve everyone. She plays a supportive role to the head teacher, Camara, as a volunteer teacher's aide. She has a tremendous appreciation of and respect for Camara.

Ayoluwa attributes her strengths in succeeding in raising her family and in being where she is today with her mother, sisters, and brother:

I think that my struggle even with my relationships has been something that I have developed within my household with a lotta females and also the strength that my brother has. I'm stronger than many men. Somebody made up a song, "I am woman," well, I am man and woman [laughing].

Kumiwa ("Brave")

Kumiwa is certainly brave. She is forty-seven years old, stands five feet two inches, with medium light brown skin, and large beautiful eyes, single, and has raised three sons and a daughter on her own. Her daughter is the mother of the grandchild that she sends to Sankofa School. She has a key position on the board of directors, and is a social worker, educator, and a doctoral candidate. Her mother's family migrated from Alabama and her father's family from Missouri. Kumiwa was one of her mother's five children and was raised by her grandmother, father, and mother at different times during her childhood. Her father worked on the railroad, so the children were able to visit relatives in different cities around the country. Her mother was a seamstress, although she was also employed as a nurse.

Kumiwa was born and raised downtown in the busiest part of the city during the time when this area was "all bars with apartments over shops." Her mother left her father and took the three children to their grandmother's when she was around seven years old. She sent for the children later from Philadelphia, where she lived with the two children from her relationship with her new husband. They were very poor and eventually the three older children returned to their father. Kuwima trusted him; she had always thought of him as a kind of "savior" because he kept in contact with the children and sometimes sent money. She was therefore glad when she went to live with him.

Their father had a passion for education and paid for Kumiwa to go to Catholic school to get a good education. He was an active member of the Parent Teacher Association and kept a constant eye on Kumiwa's schoolwork. The school was 95 percent Black and she was comfortable with that. However, she was taught by white nuns, who were mean with a miserable attitude. Kumiwa attributes their attitude to the fact that they were nuns rather than to being white. The only nun that Kumiwa liked was kind to the children, but she eventually left the convent.

I wanted to go to public school with everyone else like all those other people, because it seemed like that's where all the cool people went. I was down there with these squares and I didn't like that.

Going to this school eventually turned out to be an unhappy time, as did staying with her father. His work on the railroad often took him away for days at a time. His strict attitude about school, his domineering, cruel ways, and an attempt to have sex with her at the age of fourteen years led Kumiwa into rejecting school, running away from home, living on the streets, and eventually being incarcerated in a girl's home. Later, when her father was suffering from cancer, Kumiwa and her sister tendered to him until his death.

At the girl's home, Kumiwa befriended lesbian women who later on played a pivotal role as friends and supporters when she led a street life and later on when she entered university. These women, some of whom were white, offered her an intellectual freedom in terms of understanding and respecting women in a way that she had not received earlier.

Kumiwa then returned to live with her mother, having really done nothing to deserve being incarcerated or receiving probation. Since she had taken the initiative to run away from her father to safety, it was she who was punished, not her father. Eventually, after returning to school, Kumiwa was unable to settle down. The freedom her mother allowed served to disorient her since the situation was the opposite of what she experienced with her father. By this time she had no interest in school.

I was drinking wine in the bathroom, shooting dice, you know, they put me out of school. And once they put me out of school and I started you know, just hanging out and stuff, eventually, I got pregnant and that's when I started having children. I hung out for a good while before I got pregnant. I was seventeen when I got pregnant.

When Kumiwa met the young man who became the father of her first two children, it was an abusive relationship. Kumiwa had him arrested and sent to prison as a result of his violence. During this time she lived at home with her mother, but when the second child arrived, her mother moved her out of her home into her own apartment where she went on welfare. Kumiwa gave birth to her third child. The father of the third child was employed and owned a car at the beginning of their relationship. Unfortunately, he began to sell drugs, became hooked on them and went to jail. She made attempts to get back into school to study, but being on welfare made it difficult because the rule was that you cannot go to school as an adult on welfare. She went back to get her high school diploma without informing the social services.

While Kumiwa was going to college, a "friend" who was minding her children while she was in class, abandoned the children and stole her welfare money and her belongings. This was devastating emotionally and financially. She later turned to the last child's father:

> I had jobs like waitress, domestic work, cashier, you know, just lowly cos I didn't have an education. Um and I was always getting either supplemental welfare of partial or all welfare at various times, so I wasn't economically independent ever. Umm, I got involved in prostitution and I pulled him, started going with him. And um he was what they, you know, my pimp, in the sense that he would get me out of jail.

Kumiwa saw prostitution as the first time she had money. She felt independent and was able to provide properly for her children. The level of dependence on welfare had been crippling. It had created a dependency that did not provide for her or her children's needs, but she was caught up in the downward cycle of poverty. The bills were forever unpaid, the gas, the lights, the telephone were forever being disconnected. Ironically, prostitution changed her life and for the first time she moved out of a depressing state of mind and being. However, things began to change after the youngest son was told at school that his mother's name was in the paper and that she was a prostitute. He asked her:

> Ma, was your name in the paper? I heard you was a prostitute. What is that? What is that, Mama? What's a prostitute?

Kumiwa said:

That's what I do to keep the bills paid and keep the clothes on your back, that's the job that I do. Yeah, that's what I am.

She explained that he was happy with that answer and that it wasn't a big deal to him, but she worried about him growing up to understand what prostitution is and perhaps not liking her. She was now pregnant with her daughter.

The father of this child joined the Nation of Islam while he was in a drug rehabilitation center. This was the most positive move for him, Kumiwa believed. In fact, she was the one who encouraged his introduction to the Nation of Islam through a minister friend of hers. Kumiwa began to go to the mosque. This had a major influence in providing her with the confidence to know that she could do something else. It was during this time that she gave up street life and decided to go to school.

Once she had made this decision, an employment opportunity arose. Almost immediately Kumiwa became involved in community social work by helping women and men coming out of prison get back into the community. This eventually led to other kinds of important work in the community with Black-based groups such as looking after battered women, working in the prison system, and then educating, studying, and researching in the university. She eventually found the man who she really loved and they bought a home together. Sadly, he died of AIDS, but she continues with her community work.

As an educator, social worker, and doctoral candidate, Kumiwa is clear on what she wants at this time in her life.

I want my granddaughter to understand the importance of education. I want her to have a sense of who she is or she can never really succeed. Going to the Masjid gave me that sense of self. My granddaughter as a Black person must have this. I was shocked one day when she said "I ain't no Afrikan," but now she is proud to be Afrikan. I know a girl like Mudiwa ["this one is truly loved"] could easily be destroyed in public school. As long as I can keep her in school, as long as they open, you know for her age group, she can go there. I'm gonna try. If I have to sell pussy, she gonna be in there.

Binta ("Beautiful daughter")

Binta is twenty-six years old, she is about five feet two, well built, with large eyes and a shy demeanor. She has one son aged five who attends Sankofa School. She lives with her mother in the house she was raised in as the middle child of five children, with two brothers and two sisters. Her mother raised the children alone; in fact, Binta's mother was herself raised by her grandmother (Binta's great-grandmother). While Binta was growing up, her mother worked at a local plant. Life was very hard and her family poor. She remembered that her mother never complained. They all lived together, Binta, her mother, and her great-grandmother. She often wished that she had clothes like her friends and when she reached sixteen she moved in with her father, who also worked at the plant, for a while.

Binta's father had six brothers and sisters. Their mother and father died when they were young so they brought themselves up. Her father became withdrawn and set in his ways. Binta relates this condition to his childhood experience. She never realized until much later how difficult it was for her mother to raise the family because she made things seem as if they were normal. Binta is herself a single parent and works in her mother's nursery and as a Head Start Program teacher for children aged three to four years old. She is still in contact with her father whom she has known all her life. I wanted to know about Binta's mother.

> Yes, my mom is Muslim. I'm a saved Christian. She encouraged me, that is my main inspiration. If I didn't have her, I don't know what I would do. Even though we have different backgrounds, I respect her and she respects me; we can still come together. Not too many people have inspired me to go after what I want besides her, that's why I stick by her so much. She teaches me and says, "Don't do like I did. Get in there and get your total understanding." I'm learning. She says, "I'm glad that you learnt because it took me so many years to learn whereas you learnt it in a lot less time."

It was Binta's mother who encouraged her to send her son Hakim ("wise") to the Sankofa School. Her mother has played a major role in helping Binta to raise him.

Binta was sent to an all-Black school that had Black teachers and was developed in the sixties as a Black-awareness school. She then went to Catholic schools, which were mixed, and finally to a public school that was also mixed. In Catholic school she found that all the white students would be put into the honors classes though they were in the same classrooms as the Black students, even if their grade averages were only two points higher. Binta, however, would be put in the regular class and told that she needed to adjust. On one occasion, when put into an honors math class, she was told after one week that she couldn't keep up. Her mother told the teachers that one week was not enough time to determine whether she could be an honors student. In the public school even the honors society organization had only two Black pupils in it, and when she tried to sign up, she was told that it was full. Binta continued to struggle to get into the honors classes because of her mother's encouragement.

Her mother helped her to realize that she remained in the regular classes only because she wanted to stay with her friends. Once she understood this, she was able to get into the honors classes and, as a result, her friends wanted to be in them as well. She tried to help them as much as possible.

So something athletic, entertaining or cooking, these were the things they would encourage us to do and it was like that was what they were telling us. That's all we could do, you know. You can be an athlete or an entertainer or a cook or sing.

Her favorite school was the all-Black community school, where she learned the Afrikan national anthem. She still goes back to visit this school because it was a great inspiration to her. Binta really became aware that the things she was being taught in school about Afrikan people were untrue because her mother always put the children in different Afrikan-centered cultural programs. At sixteen or seventeen years old she received lessons in Black history and became interested in doing her own research. She went to Kwanzaa festivals and noticed the confidence of the children. She had always wanted to be a doctor, a pediatrician. This goal was discouraged at school. She was told by her teacher that it was so difficult. She was asked if she knew that it would take four years of premed in college and then four years of medical school. This type of attitude greatly affected her confidence.

However, with the help of her mother, she became her own advisor and took the subjects that she felt would be most beneficial for going to college. Binta found just the same attitude and incorrect advice at college. She was finally put off the whole idea and turned to teaching. She is still in the process of getting a teaching degree, for it was put on hold when she became pregnant. However, her work with Head Start gave her the training to enable her to work in building up the self-esteem of young children. While teaching the children in her mother's nursery how to read and write, she teaches them about Afrika. She believes that children must gain the confidence to believe in themselves so that they will do what they want to do and not be put off the way she was.

Interestingly, Binta has always worked with children. She used to babysit when she was a child. She found that her own child was very conscious about racism from an early age. He would visit Maryland with his grandmother and when he came home, he would want to know why there are no Black people on television like in Maryland. Binta said she was shocked that he noticed such things. She explained that it happens because it's their culture but was concerned that he would hate white people. He began public school late because he spent three months in Germany.

In February of his first year he was learning about Black history month and his white teacher explained that there were some good Black people but never gave the children any background information. Therefore, the children remained unaware of their accomplishments. Binta discovered this while visiting the school with her child, she asked Hakim, "Who are the Black persons on the wall?" He could only identify the persons that she had taught him about at home.

"Well, why don't you know?" He said, "Well, my teacher didn't tell me. She just said that those was good Black people," you know, and I was like well, he really needs to know the things that are happening because of us and get a little bit more of his culture so that he can have that respectful and helpful understanding, you know, about where he came from and what he can do.

When Binta first heard about Sankofa she was skeptical, wondering whether he would be taught things that other schools don't teach, or whether the school would close down. Her mother encouraged her to send him because, she said, "He has a healthy curiosity." Her father, however, was not keen on the idea.

I was explaining it to my daddy and he was saying, "Nah, they gonna teach him how to hate white people and he's gonna be confused and everything" and I said, "What he's into now is confusion, you know. He said, "It didn't hurt you when you were growing up." I said, "It did because if I'd have known I would be a doctor now. I wouldn't have let anything discourage me because I would have had that self-esteem in me that was solid."

Since Hakim has been at the school, he always wants to read and do his homework. Camara allows him to work at his pace instead of holding him back as he was in the public school. Binta believes that Hakim is going to be a future leader and when he gets older he'll be teaching others. She wants him to be able to do something about the conditions for Afrikan people. Finding the money to send Hakim to Sankofa has been extremely difficult but her mother has helped by providing some financial support.

Ezigbo ("Beloved")

Ezigbo is forty-three years old. She is tall, slim, and elegant. She wears her hair covered, is married to a Muslim, and has three children, two girls and a boy. The eldest girl is twenty-one years old, the boy is fourteen, and the little girl of four, Abiba ("the beloved one"), attends Sankofa School. The eldest girl is from an earlier marriage.

Ezigbo grew up in the "projects," which she believes at that time relied on the extended family and respected elders. She was the third oldest of four sisters and two brothers in a two-parent family.

Ezigbo's father worked in a plant and the family was never hungry. They had food on the table and decent clothes. Neither of her parents finished high school, but they always pushed for the children to attend college. She went to a mixed school and never had an Afrikan American teacher. When Ezigbo was at school she really didn't try.

I was an average student. It's like if you're an Afrikan American you really got to excel on your own because there's not a lot of support. I remember lots of times I used to go to school and just go to the back of the classroom and do absolutely nothing. You know, just sleep sometimes. I used to cram at exam times. Back then I had a real good memory so I did fairly well. I used to do my homework. I was about an 85 student.

The only teacher that took a real interest in Ezigbo was her English teacher. As a result, she felt that she would like to become a teacher. However, during her school years she had an attitude, that, she remembers, developed at an early age. She described her attitude as quiet and rebellious. At the age of fifteen, she attended her first Black Muslim meeting.

It really grabbed me, because I just identified with going through that whole process, I just identified with a lot of the stuff. I mean, some of it I just left alone. I mean, my parents were having a fit, they, everybody was afraid of Black Muslims then. They were hating and killing and whatever people thought and I just latched on to it and I think in a lot of ways that was my salvation.

Everybody thought she was crazy but eventually they all came around because she didn't really change, she just didn't hang out.

Joining the Nation of Islam had a tremendous impact on her schooling because she was now getting a real education and realized the importance of doing things for herself.

It made me realize that even under the conditions that you're attending it made me look at the whole American structure and the fact that you have to function in it irrespective of what your ideology may be. I wasn't one of those people that was angry about the information I received about the atrocities that happened during slavery. It just made me more aware of the type of person I was actually dealing with, but I didn't vent out my anger, or hate white people kinda thing. It's like they use you so you learn how to use them. This is the way the system goes. So let it work for you not against you.

However, this education did not change her general feeling about school. She really didn't put much effort into it, although she was a "B" student.

After leaving school, Ezigbo entered university but dropped out and went to work. She worked as a secretary for about fifteen years in a community center that provided a tutoring program for children in the Afrikan community. During that time, she married and took a year off to have her first daughter. Then she had her second child, a son. After the birth of her son, she went back to the university but dropped out again. She was just not interested in the subject matter and so went back to work. This next job was with Vietnam War veterans in a counseling program and she worked there until the birth of Abiba, the daughter who attends Sankofa School.

The first daughter attended the community school that Binta went to. Although its focus was no longer the same since the school had to be integrated, Ezigbo felt that it still had some of the Afrikan cultural perspective. When her son came along, seven years later, it was much different, but she still felt that it was better than the alternatives. However, she has not been happy with what has happened to her son. I found out that the experience of her two older children has played a major role in Ezigbo's sending her youngest child to Sankofa.

I think mainly because I really understand the value of being able to have a child in a school where ultimately she learns about herself and her ancestry. It is very obvious to me, a lot of the problem we are having with our youth today is because they don't really know who they are, and it happens through the public school system because they don't really um work to help us know who we are. I've had two other children go through the public school system and I just know what it does to them.

Her son is labeled as a problem child, his grades range from the nineties to the sixties, and she is often at the school because she wants the teachers to feel that he has parents who care about him. He is the classic example of the child who fell through the cracks as far as Ezigbo is concerned. She also believes that our boys are at risk.

They don't really give you the same opportunity to feel like you're a part of this whole learning process, simply because of the educational materials that they use. Even from very, very small children the visual things that you're putting in your mind are Caucasian, all the time, so when the children can't identify, they become restless. Instead, they [teachers] start to label.

However, whenever he has an Afrikan American teacher, male or female, he does extremely well because the teacher takes the time to make him understand that he has to get it for himself.

When Ezigbo heard that Sankofa School would take four-year-olds, she decided that she would definitely send Abiba.

I just know the value of having someone that does not have the restraints that public school puts on them, and who is of your own ethnicity and really wants the best for you and they give their best to you.

Ezigbo felt that she wasted her time at school and does not want the same thing to happen to her daughter, especially since she has this opportunity that was unavailable to her other children. This is a financial sacrifice that she believes is well worth it. Ezigbo believes that the tuition does exclude other children because she knows of parents too poor to send their children. She thinks that the trust factor in the community regarding ourselves and divide-and-conquer racist tactics play a role in some of the other reasons that parents don't bring their children. Her own view is that we need to trust one another and not question our intentions so much. Because of this view, she visited the school, met the head teacher, and decided to send her child.

Dalmar ("Versatile")

Dalmar has been married for twelve years and has three daughters. She is thirty-three years old, tall, proud, and slim with short natural hair and smooth skin. Her husband owns a family business in the community. Her mother migrated from Alabama. She was one of ten children and came here when she was a year old. Her father's family came from South Carolina. He was one of twelve children. Both families migrated during the twenties to work in the plants. Her father worked in a plant all his life and her mother was a secretary. Dalmar has a younger sister and brother. Although links were kept with the family in the American South, and Dalmar even took her own family to visit, she said that her family in the North, once they had left, had no desire to return. She felt that perhaps the memories were too painful.

Dalmar's mother divorced when Dalmar was seven years old and brought up the children on her own.

> My mother . . . she's like really remarkable. She worked like from 8 to 5. She did all the cooking and the cleaning and the house was like immaculate. We didn't get into a lot of trouble like we've never been to jail or anything and we were like latch-key children. It didn't bother me 'cos I knew my mother was out working and she wasn't like goofing off.. We'd go over to my father's so we saw him every day so then we had my grandmother and grandfather and my aunts and uncles so we had like a good support system.

Dalmar went to an all-Black grammar school where the teachers were excellent. She found that they had high expectations of their students and let nothing pass unnoticed. For instance, bad grammar was corrected and work had to be of a high standard. Later she attended an all-Black high school that did not require the same high standard of work. She was an honors student, but she felt that in the general classes a lot less was expected of the students. She felt that the responsibility lay partly with the students as well as the teachers.

> We had kids, that were like twenty years old. I was a fresh-man taking algebra and I had seniors and juniors in my al-gebra class. What can you do with twenty-year-old kids? It's part racism and part the kids' fault. I don't know if they had problems at home or whatever or maybe they didn't get the basics, so they make trouble. I think it was partly low expec-tation and then partly the children.

She had high expectations of white students when she did get to a predominantly white college. This was her first experience with white people. It was a surprise to find that her schooling had stood her in good stead and she was able to compete. She was the first in her family to attend college. In some ways this was a disadvan-tage for Dalmar because she felt that there was little support to help her with her work. Since her mother did not have much money (although Dalmar received a scholarship to go to college), she could not afford the books. Furthermore, after a while she felt isolated among the white students and received bad advice from counselors, especially concerning how to go about achieving her goal of becom-ing a computer specialist. The whole affair had a detrimental effect on Dalmar, and she changed her major from computer science to business.

Dalmar was married while still at college. She stopped school to become a full-time mother. Her husband has been very supportive in helping her raise the children. Her husband's family business has helped to sustain them and she has been involved in it from time to time. Her husband has Muslims in his family and a brother who was once in the Nation of Islam. She has seen Minister Farrakhan several times and her husband has taped speeches. This has influenced her interest in self-help in the community and she sees it as essential that we Afrikans support and develop our own businesses. In this way she believes that the concerns of the community can be dealt with by the community. As far as she is concerned, desegregation sabotaged community development.

> It was as if communities were far more self-sufficient and then when the idea of desegregation came, in a sense a lot of those things were undermined cos there was like a kind of brain drain that happened.

Dalmar is a strong advocator of small businesses for developing the community especially since she is involved in one.

In terms of her children's education, Dalmar taught her first daughters to read and write before they went to school. Her eldest daughter and second daughter both went to Head Start before they went to school. Dalmar worked in Head Start herself and often subbed if teachers were away.

She encouraged her three children to attend Afrikan-centered affairs like Kwanzaa. They even attended a Saturday Afrikan-centered school that was around for a while. The children do not watch a lot of television and are encouraged to work at home. When the school started, Dalmar was having a problem with her second daughter, who was attending a public school that was mainly white. This daughter had been at the top of her class in Head Start.

> When she got to kindergarten, she went to like an integrated school and I think that she kinda got intimidated. It was to a point that she was white and she thought her father was white and like I was really concerned about this. The oldest one had expressed the same interest but I was able to talk to her and find out where she was coming from and it was ok but with Sakile ["peace and beauty"] it never got to be ok.

Dalmar could tell from her daughter's relationship with the teacher what to expect. In the second grade she had an Afrikan American teacher and she was fine. Now with the white teacher, Dalmar admitted that she doesn't know if it was just the teacher or her child's oversensitivity about image, but she began to do badly in her schoolwork and then attempted to hide it from her parents and teacher. As a result, the other children teased her, and she failed to understand what she had to do. She became overly sensitive to any criticism. When the teacher tried to talk to her, she felt that she was being singled out. Dalmar felt that this problem had something to do with her self-esteem.

She heard about Sankofa School, but she didn't feel that they could afford to send the child. However, she made inquiries and spoke to her husband and to trusted friends about how she felt. She was encouraged to read a book about the different learning styles of Black children. She then decided to look at the school, so she took her whole family along.

I was looking at the quality of work that the kids were doing and I could see the camaraderie with the kids and I liked the teacher. Well, you know, she had a lotta patience. With there only being a few students, I thought Sakile would get individualized attention that she needed. I made her go on a trial basis for three or four days and I made her write out to me, "Why you think I should pay money to send you to this school." She wrote [that] she would do much better [and that] she liked learning about Black people.

Since Sakile has been in this school, she is like a different person. Each morning she is up early and gets dressed and clean, makes her bed, and is ready to go well before time. In the past she never wanted to go to school. Her whole attitude has changed. She is doing better in math and the work is more difficult now. The child loves the other children.

I don't know if it was the atmosphere, you know camaraderie, but she really cares about the teacher. She was like a middle child and she was a baby for a long time, too. I think that was part of her problem. Now she is one of the older kids and so the younger kids look up to her.

Dalmar believes that it was a combination of a number of things that affected her daughter. Certainly, the daughter needed something to be done before the problem became more serious. Now she is happy because her daughter is happy.

Interestingly, Dalmar was thinking about starting her own school. This stemmed from her experience in teaching her own children as well as her views on self-help. She wishes that Sankofa wasn't tuition based, so that it would be more available to more children. I wanted to know then what other reasons prevent parents from choosing such a school.

A lotta people aren't committed to anything like that. A lotta people like the desegregation and all that and this surprises me because a lot of them came from all Black schools and did really, really well. And if it had been left to integration they wouldn't have gone to school in the first place.

In terms of her own strength, Dalmar feels that she hasn't been really tested, but she believes that she comes from "very strong stock," as she put it.

Ife ("Lover of art and culture")

Ife is forty-two years old. Her hair is usually worn braided, she is around five foot seven inches tall and has a gay, infectious laugh. She holds an important post in a university as director of a program. She has recently married her second husband and has just had a baby son. Her daughter Shami "(like the sun)," who attends Sankofa, is from a previous marriage. Ife and her younger sister were raised by their grandmother in Harlem. Ife's grandmother came from Mississippi and lived in Detroit before moving to New York. She left Mississippi in the middle of the night on a train and never went back. Her grandmother's brother was nearly lynched and she didn't like to remember the horrors of that life. She owned her own home in Detroit in the twenties. She sold her home before the "crash" and moved to New York. There she put her two daughters into Catholic school and worked as a nanny for a Jewish lady whose daughter thought of Ife's grandmother as her mother. Ife's grandmother was nearly forty when she had her first daughter and was in her late fifties when Ife was born. She was an educated woman, a product of the Hampton Institute and the Booker T. Washington philosophy.

Ife and her sister grew up in the same apartment as her mother and aunt. The Harlem that Ife grew up in was not like the present one. The neighborhood was like an extended family. Harlem was a place where Muslims and other clean and upright Afrikan people were working. It was a time when Malcolm X was making his presence felt and bringing the Nation of Islam to the masses. She grew up visiting the Masjid, Temple number 7. Her closest friend had converted to Islam. S.N.C.C. (Student Non-violent Coordinating Committee) and C.O.R.E. (Congress of Racial Equality) and Maulana Karenga's US organization were also around. Harlem was a cultural center, a type of Mecca, bringing together the West and the East of the country.

> My school was the ghetto school. Hughes was like the belly of the beast—60 percent Black, 40 percent Hispanic—on the lower East Side, 114th St. I went to junior high on 114th St., one of the roughest schools in New York City. I mean, people with attitudes. I was just a regular kid.

The first teacher to make an impact in Ife's life was a Black woman who involved parents in her work with the children by sending messages home about how the child was doing. Then later a male Spanish teacher who was also her homeroom teacher told her:

> I'm worried about you because I want you to know it's not good to be pretty and dumb.Your goals should be pretty and smart. You are spending your time trying to become dumb, but you're already pretty. I'm telling you now, as a Black girl, there's nothing you can do with being pretty.

This advice had a profound and tremendous impact on Ife because of the negative pressure she was facing over being popular or smart. After that, she was always at the top of her class. She did extremely well in science with the encouragement of an Afrikan science teacher who saw her potential and opened up that world to her. She won a four-year scholarship to the college of her choice. Instead of going to an all-Black university, she made what she believes was a terrible error in listening to her college counselor, an Arab lady who advised her to go to an integrated university. To this day, she regrets that decision. She later dropped out of university.

Being resourceful and talented, Ife became involved in the activism that she took from Harlem. She worked in the cultural revolution in art, dance, and theater. Outside and within the Nation of Islam she worked particularly hard to change the rules for women. Her interest in the Nation of Islam centered mostly on their Pan-Afrikanist ideas. Ife left the Nation of Islam on the death of the Honorable Elijah Muhammad, whom she believed to be a prophet.

When Ife's first child began to have problems in school, she was concerned because the public school that had informed her that her child was gifted and talented now claimed that her grades were going down. After investigating the situation, Ife felt that it was time to consider Sankofa School as a possibility. The father of her baby son felt that perhaps the child needed to adjust to the school and that a decision to pull her out of school would be too drastic. She consulted with the father of her daughter and he also believed that perhaps she was not being very wise in her decision. This brought Ife's integrity into question. She, after all, was the one who had virtually brought up the child on her own. Ife again looked at the facts. The child's grades were going down, this meant she wasn't learning anything, that she wasn't happy in the school, and that she didn't want to go to school.

Ife always helped her child with her homework and was aware of what was happening. Often her daughter brought home English work that had not been properly corrected.

I kept questioning myself, you know, may be it's her, you know, but things kept pointing to the fact that it's not just this teacher. No, it's not just the fact that Shami may need to be more disciplined. It's that environment. It has to be the school and the school has to take some responsibility.

Ife visited Sankofa and was very impressed by the head teacher, Camara. Camara appeared to be very disciplined and loving toward the children, she seemed committed to helping the children to learn, discover, and be the best that they can be. Ife felt that Camara could cater to the needs of her child, whom she felt was a demanding child.

After Shami had spent a day there, she said that she had received a lot of attention and anything that she needed to know she was helped with. However, Ife did not make the decision immediately. It took a month for her to make a commitment.

I have really ah, ah, had a whole lot of turmoil over this . . . a lotta frustration, because I strongly believe in the value of education. I believe in learning. I believe you have to be a critical thinker, that it's important to the survival of Afrikan Americans. They've taken my child's mind, a mind that was full of curiosity and basically admitted it had to be above average and now I've got a total mess.

After her daughter spent four years in the public school system, Ife was upset, but she saw it as a known negative and found herself hesitating about an unknown that may in fact be positive.

When I questioned her about this dilemma, she said she felt that it is a sad thing about Afrikan Americans that there is a hesitancy about supporting our own. We still think that in some way the white man can do it better. Ife believes that Camara is the best teacher that her child has ever had in the four years she has been at school. She decided that if the school closed down that it was better her daughter went for a short valuable time rather than not at all.

After her decision to send Shami, the teacher in the public school noticed a change in the last two weeks that Shami attended. She seems so happy, she confided to Ife. Ife thought, "She's happy leaving all you nuts." Ife's daughter played an important role in convincing her mother, father, and stepfather to let her attend the school because she listed all the things that she had missed learning in the month that it had taken them to decide.

Aisha ("Life")

Aisha is twenty-eight years old. She is married but barely sees her husband. She had two daughters with him, whom she has raised alone. She is a Ph.D. candidate in education and also has a law degree. Her grandmother raised her in St. Vincent, a small island in the Caribbean. She is tall, well-built, regal, and has close-cut natural short hair.

In St. Vincent Aisha grew up with her grandmother and the women of her village. The school building was a tent and they used a stick as a pencil and the earth to write on. Later they used a sheet of paper that was cut in four pieces so that it would last until the next day. Everyone's mother in the village was everyone else's mother. Everyone, including her uncles, took on the responsibility of looking after the children in the extended family. The men of the village did the heavy work. They hunted, worked on the plantation or in the factory. The women worked alongside the men and taught the girls to be women. She was taught how to weave baskets and hats, sew, cook, milk cows, and look after babies. This came in useful when she had her own children. Aisha did not know her father before the age of four of five years, but he lived outside the village. She also did not know her mother, who played no part in raising her but did send money so she could go to prep school later on. Her mother collected her from St. Vincent and Aisha's sister from Trinidad and took them to New York when she was ten years. When Aisha went to school in New York, she suffered.

> I went to a public school in Brooklyn. It was predominantly Black. There were a couple of Hispanics and very few Jews. Because the school that I went to was on the border of the Jewish community, 98 percent of the teachers were white and a large percent of them were Jewish.

Although her schools were mostly Black, she was picked on because she had an English accent and received good grades on her tests. She was beaten by the other children because she was from the Caribbean. She fought back.

> I remember when we first came up here, my mother used to make me wear that uniform because that's what schoolchildren did. The kids used to say I wasn't clean, I didn't change my clothes, so I'd get beat up after school. Then my mother would beat me for fighting.

Unfortunately, Aisha's mother believed that school would teach her just as it did in St. Vincent, so she never questioned what went on.

She punished Aisha for fighting because in St. Vincent everyone is punished for fighting, but her mother didn't understand the cultural differences and the struggle it took for her daughter to survive under these circumstances. Aisha did not get on with her mother and left home at sixteen.

Ironically, Aisha was greatly encouraged by some of the Jewish white teachers and formed crushes on three male teachers who very supportive of her work and her potential. Influenced by this, Aisha went to school to become a teacher. Her experience in teaching almost all white students was not pleasant. She was very annoyed at the attitude of the students she was teaching because she believed that they did not understand the real value of getting an education. This idea related very much to her own early schooling in St. Vincent.

> I almost had a nervous breakdown. It was difficult teaching people who didn't want to learn. I just couldn't do it. I could stand up there and do a song and dance. I could make up a rhyme in math. It just wasn't working because they just didn't want to do it. They just had it all. I walked to school and they drove up in BMWs.

Shortly after this experience, Aisha decided to leave teaching and take up law. By this time she had just had her first child, Adanma ("daughter of beauty"), who accompanied her everywhere. It was with reluctance that she placed the child in the university daycare center. Aisha said that she was bothered about her daughter being in daycare because she used to come home and tell her mother that she wanted to be blonde.

> I remember one day in law school, we were sitting down and talking to a professor who knew Adanma very well because Adanma had always gone to her classes. She was just playing and she said, "Mummy, I wish I was blonde" and I started to cry. "Why do you want to be blonde, Adanma?" She said, "Because it's pretty." So I went through the whole business about, you know [trembling and visibly upset] your hair being pretty, your skin being pretty, and all that. But no matter how I

would tell her that, she needed to see it. She's bombarded with children who are blonde and blue-eyed with ivory skin [in] cartoons [and] children's books. That's all she sees.

Incidents like this affected Aisha's decision when it was time to put Adanma into school. She believes that the public school system can provide the basics, but she was skeptical about leaving Adanma in the hands of the system. Her worries centered around placing her child in the hands of people whom she, Aisha, wouldn't know, not knowing the teacher's lesson plan, not knowing the diet or who is in the classroom.

I wanted her to develop a strong sense of character. To me in public school she was going to get a dose of somebody's neurosis.

When Aisha heard about Sankofa School, what was important to her was the environment and the extended family type of relationship that Adanma would receive between the head teacher, the parents of other children, and herself. This reminded her very much of her own upbringing. The respect for elders was also another important consideration.

To me, society is not getting any better in terms of dealing with racism. It's getting worse and I feel that the best way for me and my family to deal with it is to educate my daughter about it. You don't get that in public school. I don't want my child to grow up believing that it's not there.

However, Aisha's husband did not share the same enthusiasm. He was concerned that Adanma has to live in an integrated society and that she should learn to function in an integrated system. Aisha was quick to use her own upbringing as a challenge to the belief that there could be a problem interacting with her own people. She also pointed out to him that she felt that children today grow up empty and need to be able to help themselves before they can help others. After that, he was worried about the monetary aspect of supporting Adanma in the school. He was won over, according to Aisha, when he spoke to his daughter about what she had learned. It got to a point where Adanma was educating him about himself.

Not only was her husband originally against the school, but so were some of her friends who sent their children to prestigious private schools. Some felt that this was another of Aisha's political expressions like the choice to wear her hair natural. This was seen as a negative choice.

Aisha explained their attitude as the conscious acceptance that white is better, or established and therefore better. She found this reaction to her choice to be a lack of faith in her own intelligence and integrity as an educated woman. Obviously, making a choice of this kind, in the climate of suspicion, was a major stand and show of strength. Aisha believes that any strength that she has must be attributed to growing up among Afrikan women in St. Vincent who taught her everything she knows about being a woman.

Aidoo ("Arrived")

Aidoo is thirty-seven years old. She was one of nine children who were raised in the United States after coming from Puerto Rico in the late fifties when Aidoo was very young. She is petite, just under five feet tall, and has short natural hair. She speaks Spanish and English fluently. Aidoo is a Ph.D. candidate in education, teaches Spanish and has also been a journalist. She was married once, to an Afrikan American, and has a daughter of six whom she is raising alone. Aidoo was brought up by both her parents. Her mother, who had a primary school education, had eight children by the time she was twenty-eight. Aidoo did not and does not model herself after her mother. Her father is a Korean War veteran who is "educated," as she puts it, and speaks English.

Aidoo did not go to school in Puerto Rico before coming to the United States. On arrival, Aidoo could not speak English and this was a disadvantage. She found the environment very hostile as a result of her lack of English. Aidoo's father placed all of his children in private Catholic schools because he was dissatisfied with the public school system. These schools Aidoo described as being very nice. They provided her first experience with middle-class children who were predominantly white. While Aidoo was the only Puerto Rican girl in her class, she remembers there was a Black (Afrikan American) girl in fourth grade. It was not clear to me at this time whether the Black girl was Afrikan American or whether Aidoo considered herself to be Black. In fact, Aidoo felt that race was not a factor in her upbringing.

> Race wasn't a big thing when I was growing up. The fact of whether we were Black or white wasn't the issue. The issue was that we was a different culture, we spoke a different language. The Blacks and whites spoke English and they understood each other better. Many times there used to be a lotta problems sometimes associating with the Black kids. Black people were Black people and white people were white people. We were all Americans. We were different . . . we were immigrants. We had our own church, our own stores . . . we didn't mix too much at all. I didn't come across problems of myself perhaps as racially different until I got to college.

After going to college, Aidoo went to Florida to work as a teacher's aide for Head Start. She worked with multiple-handicapped children of all colors, most of whom came from impoverished backgrounds. They all had problems with their language and speech patterns. Later, she decided to go to a private women's Catholic college, which led to her entry into the university. She joined the international student clubs, feeling little identity with the Black clubs. She even became president of the Latina Student Association and became politically involved in trying to introduce more Latinas into administrative positions. As far as Aidoo was concerned, it was time for the institutions to begin to reflect the student body and to challenge the key positions held by the white middle class students.

Aidoo did not meet her husband, an Afrikan American and Black cultural nationalist, as she describes him, until she was around thirty, when they were both at the university. They met while she was a copy aid and he was a journalist for the same paper. When they chose to have Runako ("beauty") three years later, they were both concerned about the type of schooling she should have, given that she was as Aidoo said "a Black American and a Puerto Rican, with two different cultures." Although Aidoo is now separated from her husband, they both take care of the child's financial responsibilities and her welfare. His mother and sister also play a supportive role in caring for the child.

When the child was four, she attended a public kindergarten that Aidoo felt did not provide enough mental stimulation. Prior to that, she attended a Black nursery in the locality from the age of two years both on a part-time and full-time basis and became essentially school-ready. Her mother then found an innovative state program with a small classroom ratio and two Latina teachers with whom Aidoo was familiar. This seemed ideal. At least it was the best program with a sound educational curriculum that was not centered on Afrika or Puerto Rico.

Aidoo made several attempts at enrolling her daughter in what she thought would be suitable schools. However, it was extremely difficult. About one local kindergarten, Aidoo said,

I just didn't like the fact that she was in school, it was like almost reaching the thirty limit in the classroom and they were all boys. And a lotta them, you could look at the children, right away you could say so much about them, how they dress, how they look, and some of these kids look like they had some problems. And I just decided, that I just didn't want Runako to mix like that. And um she was bringing home material that I just thought . . . she was bringing home more in preschool than she did in kindergarten.

Finally, after a few more attempts at finding a better environment for her child, Aidoo came across the Sankofa School. It was this school that mirrored a lot of her preschool experiences. First, the school had just one teacher in a small environment. Secondly, the children were able to provide better role models for her daughter's behavior. As far as Aidoo was concerned, this was incidental and could have in fact happened at any school. Thus, in this child's case, the fact that the school is Afrikan-centered was not the main criterion for her placement. However, Aidoo felt that the pedagogy was good.

It is important that she is learning that, um, Afrikans have had accomplishments, also they've done many things and I, I mean essentially at some point in time, as the child begins to realize that they are Black and they're different and if they're not different, society puts them in a different category, then the school experiences will serve to only help them to understand things better, I, I [stuttering] do believe, and strengthen them.

Aidoo believes that the extended family environment helps her child feel secure and comfortable and most importantly, she is learning. In her social life, Runako goes ice skating with "upper-crust" children who are white and she also skis. Aidoo believes that it is important for her child to interact with all kinds of children that she normally wouldn't interact with, so she makes special provisions for getting her involved in many activities.

Aidoo feels that values, morals, and principles are very important for her child to learn. She has mixed feelings concerning the Nguzo Saba, the seven principles on which the Afrikan-centered schools are built. These are Umoja (unity), Kujichagulia (self-determination), Ujima (collective work and responsibility), Ujamaa (cooperative economics), Nia (purpose), Kuumba (creativity), and Imani (faith). She believes that the Nguzo Saba is very bourgeois, although she admits that it does have its merits.

Aidoo believes also that the whole Black nationalistic movement is bourgeois in that it does not deal with the class disparities that exist in the Black community. Her attitude is not surprising given her experiences at the university where she has had to deal with those she calls "Negroes." She found them to be "worse than racist." She describes them as "boulders" holding the fort, the modern-day overlords, who are very conscious of what they are doing. As far as Aidoo is concerned, she sees them as counter-revolutionaries. The class alliance between the "Black boulder" and the "white master" has for Aidoo brought into question the authenticity of the position of Afrocentrists and Afrikan-centered schools. However, she and the child's father are very supportive of the school to such an extent that Aidoo teaches Spanish to the children.

⑥

The Herstories of Mothers Who Do Not Send Their Children to Sankofa School

This chapter looks at the herstories of four mothers who decided not to send their children to Sankofa. While four herstories are a small example to use for this study, I believe that they are valuable as a resource for trying to analyze reasons for not using Afrikan-centered schools.

Jaha ("Dignity")

Jaha is thirty-two years old. She is beautiful, tall with a serious countenance and wears her hair braided. She works in the university in an education program for "minority" students most of whom are Afrikan. She has been married for seven years and has one stepson who is nine years old. Her great-grandmother on her mother's side was enslaved. As Jaha explained, her mother came from a "high-complexioned" family from the South and her father came from a "dark-complexioned" family from the North. Her mother was one of ten children and her father one of eight. They had three children, Jaha, her brother, and her sister. The marriage ended after ten years.

145

After the mother and father broke up, Jaha's mother's health deteriorated and she had a nervous breakdown. Jaha found herself with insurmountable responsibilities. She had to look after her brother, sister, and mother. After eight years, she left home and went to law school. Jaha's mother suffered another breakdown and Jaha blames herself in part for this. Her mother left her full-time employment and eventually their home was lost to foreclosure. All the family possessions were eventually lost as well. Jaha's mother and sister were reduced to living in shelters. Her brother was old enough to be independent by this time. At fifteen he had already been sexually abused and introduced to cocaine by a white Jewish male schoolteacher. Jaha blamed her father for not being there when her brother needed him. At this juncture Jaha refused to return to the family to take on any more responsibilities. She was determined to finish her schooling. In desperation she called her father and asked him to take her sister in, which he did. This was an ideal situation because her sister wanted to be with her father at this time.

While Jaha was taking care of the family, she attended high schools in Queens, New York. They were primarily mixed—mostly Latino, Jewish and Protestant. She was always the only Afrikan, or one of two, in her class. Prior to high school, she attended a junior high where the children were predominantly Afrikan. Here she received a lot of pressure from other students for being a "smarty pants." She remembers that in high school

I was very involved with the student government. I went to this high school on a Latin varians and had to take three years of language. I had the same teacher for three years, who was also the dean. My grades slowed from the 90s to the 85s. I was out sick and as a result had library books that I failed to return and received a fine of $9.00, which the dean insisted I pay or I would not receive my report and wouldn't go to college. On the day I was expected to pay, the president of the Student Advisory saw me crying and paid my fine.

Jaha believes that this threat to withhold her report was a racist act. Her family did not have that type of money. She believed that the dean, who was nasty in general, did not like to see her working in a leadership role particularly because she was Black.

When she finally left home and went to law school, she was quite unprepared for what she met.

> I was very unsophisticated, I was very unprepared for going to law school in terms of my, ah, naive thoughts of what it was going to be about. Not really paying attention to the structure. . . . You know, the whole gray suit structure when I'm there as a freedom fighter, you know, thinking I wanna learn how to advocate for the people. And when I got there I learned how to, ah win, not necessarily for the people and how you pervert and contort and I learned there was really no justice, just who had the fanciest more prepared lawyer. I learned in terms of mental health that there really is a big gap in terms of how to help those people because of the way that the history of the mental health law has evolved. The system has been put in place to maintain rich people's status.

The racism that she experienced there related very much to her attempts to address serious issues concerning Afrikans. In order to succeed, she found that she had to do things the way the system requires. As yet, she has not taken her bar examination but plans on doing so.

Presently, in her work in "minority education," she has programmatic responsibility for 220 students from seven high schools who are at risk of dropping out. They come to the program with academic and/or emotional problems. She employs three counselors and sixteen to eighteen student instructors who work with the students. The program places stress on developing ways of seeing the students as whole persons. Given her own background in education, she is very much involved in her stepson's schooling. She made the decision not to send her child to the Sankofa School.

In her son's five years of public schooling, he has had three Black women teachers, two of whom she believes have had a positive effect on him. One of the teachers was "terrible." According to Jaha, she was more concerned about how sexy she was than how she was able to communicate with the children. However, Jaha

says, the other two were "excellent." These teachers were very
involved with the child and the parents. The worst teacher he ever
had was in the second grade and she was white. Presently, he has
an excellent Jewish teacher who is probably the best in terms of
"teaching" according to Jaha.

The class is multicultural, predominantly Black and white, but
includes other ethnic groups. Her approach is also multicultural.
The son, Nkokheli ("he is a leader"), has done a lot of interesting
projects and academically his work is very good.

> My concerns about him are primarily behavioral. He has some
> experiences with his biological mother that have not been
> healthy and maybe a Black school could help him with that,
> maybe not. We are looking right now to having some help
> from experts. . . . This influences his willingness sometimes to
> do his work and it influences the way that he reacts to differ-
> ent social situations in school, which of course affects his school-
> work. Of course, those things go hand in hand.

Jaha believes that his teacher is very helpful in that she does not
share the concerns about her son's behavior with the entire school.
He has to be diagnosed by the committee dealing with handicapped
children, but the teacher is not trying to put him into a program.
The father and Jaha are looking for counseling preferably from an
Afrikan American.

Jaha believes that if his teacher was horrible, or the grades were
down, (they are As and Bs), then she perhaps would have sent the
child to Sankofa. However, she feels that he is well grounded at
home with Afrikan cultural affirmation. There is a library and he
likes to read. Jaha, in particular, makes sure that he is aware of his
history, participates in Kwanzaa, reads Black books, and has all his
activities well screened. He plays the piano and would like to get
into acting. As a fair-complexioned child, Jaha tries to make sure
that he does not feel superior as a result. Often, though, people talk
about how beautiful he is as if it is because of his complexion.

Ideally, she would have wished that he could go to a place like
Sankofa because she is not happy with some of the things that he
is being exposed to in public schooling.

I think that it is important for our young people to realize that it's possible for us to have our own society even if it's a school environment or business or any kind of social . . . organized environment. We know that we can party, we know that we can make music and we know that we can entertain, but it's important for them to know that we can have a business and we can be organized.

Jaha is essentially trying to groom her son to be a leader so that he can deal with white people on their level and not be intimidated by them. He performs brilliantly, as far as Jaha is concerned, and she believes that even at his age, he is progressive in his ideas.

Prior to the opening of Sankofa, Jaha was involved in a group that was interested in starting its own school. This group was a Christian-based group but their ideas did not materialize into the formation of a school. After attending two or three meetings for interested parents, she had formulated some ideas about the school's organization and its members. She also looked at the fact that her son would be the oldest child in the school and felt that he was immature in his relationship with his peers.

Another one of my concerns was that Nkokheli seemed to be very kinda cliquish. The people that were involved seemed not really to be a broad cross-section of Afrikan Americans in the community. It seemed to be like a group of semi, may be even progressive, pseudo, who maybe had an esoteric quality about them, which I think is good in terms of knowing all kinds of people, but I didn't know if I wanted my son to be that esoteric. I wanted him to be a little grounded as well. Cos I'm esoteric enough I think [laughing].

She believes he has enough spiritualism in his life, but it appeared to be more cultist than Christianized. An article in a local Afrikan community newspaper calling on priests and priestesses to come and support the school was not impressive to Jaha. At a meeting, a parent who could not afford the school's tuition, Jaha felt, was not properly handled. She felt that if the school cannot pay for students, then there must be a way of allowing the parent to buy into the school somehow.

When we talked about tuition and those kinda things, I still think we are living in the twentieth century. Yes, you know we had the one-room schoolhouse, but no one had to pay $2,800 for a one-room schoolhouse. The walls weren't even painted at the time, and it was a couple of days before school started. There was nothing there for me to buy into. Certainly, it would have been a sacrifice financially, so I couldn't sell it to my husband. I couldn't sell it to myself. We weren't in a position to put our son in a situation that we weren't sure of.

However, Jaha believes that if the school lasts, then she may still be interested.

Adaeze ("Princess")

Adaeze is thirty-three years old. She is married and has three children: two daughters and a son. She is a doctoral student in educational administration and a trained teacher for elementary schoolchildren. She is tall and slim with long hair and a lovely smile. Her husband is a professional man and they have been married since they met during their college days. Her mother and father came from Alabama. Her mother raised five children on her own and is also a community activist. Adaeze is one of two girls and three boys and is right in the middle. She was raised in this city, but left for five years when she attended Howard University with her husband.

Raising five children was probably difficult for her mother but she never really let her children see that. She gave them a very secure life. They dressed nicely, went to dance classes and the like, and had nice homes. Her mother helps with the children sometimes and her strength has been a great inspiration to Adaeze.

Adaeze went to public and private schools but most of her education took place in integrated schools except prior to the second grade when the school she attended was predominantly Afrikan. When her family moved to the west side she and her brothers and sister went to an all-white school where she was the only Black child. Then the busing began. The transition was difficult for Adaeze.

I was in third grade, but I didn't know anything about racism or things like that. I knew I was different. I guess I was used to my teachers [who] had always been white so it wasn't as if I hadn't ever been around white people, but I don't remember having a difficult time making adjustments. It wasn't until later on that one of the kids told me that one of the kids had said something about that "nigger," but I didn't know and it didn't bother me. My sister and brothers were at the same school. When the buses came, the white kids would say is that your brother or your sister?

It helped that the family was at the school and that Adaeze's mother was very involved with their schooling. However, Adaeze became more aware of racism when her mother met and formed a relationship with a male friend. This man was very "conscious" and was a major influence in all their lives in terms of their identity and giving direction to the whole family. He is still a very strong person who she feels matches her mother's strength in being able to take care of the family.

He was saying something about white people. Adaeze said

"What's wrong with them?" I'm not saying he's a racist, I said, "You're prejudiced. You just don't like white people." He said, "No, I don't have anything against white people. I just don't have anything for them" [laughing]. I'll never forget it. I thought, "That's interesting" and then through life's experience and having different things happen to me, made me realize that, you know, a lot of what he was saying hit home.

She began to notice the types of segregation taking place in the school. This brought her close to other Afrikan Americans. She graduated from a suburban school and then went to college. She got married at college. Adaeze went to the Hampton Institute and loved it because it was an all-Black college. It was one of the most exciting times of her life. It had a nurturing environment. Then later she went to Howard, following her husband. She had her first child at Howard during her last year, so it was a struggle to complete her work.

In terms of her children's own schooling, Adaeze was very interested in Sankofa School, especially with regard to her daughter's experiences. It was her mother, the community activist, who introduced her to the early meetings. One daughter goes to a predominantly white school where she is the only Afrikan child. Noni ("gift of God") is always saying:

> "Well, Mom, I don't really have many friends." And when I talk to the teacher, she says, "Well, a lotta times during playtime, she'll just get a book and read." That's ok to me [laughing]. That's fine as long as she's not in a corner somewhere crying. She's used to people approaching her. She wants kids to come up and say, "Noni, we want to be your friend." I say, "It doesn't work like that." She says, "They don't like me for this reason," you know, silly things that kids go through.

Adaeze's daughter was recently invited to a skating party and she was the only Afrikan child. While the children were eating together, one of the girls invited everyone to her house afterwards. The mother of the child told her to keep on eating. In other words, the mother did not want her daughter to invite the Afrikan child back to her home. Adaeze's daughter was fully aware that the mother had silenced the child because of her presence. Although she is very sensitive, she can accept these things, says her mother. The eldest daughter forces herself to be accepted and does not discuss it, whereas the second one accepts this as well as she can. Adaeze makes links with an Afrikan group that meets outside school on weekends. She feels that this helps to prevent any alienation that her children might feel.

Her views on the school are interesting because although she does not send her children she is involved as a founding member. When the school was opening, Adaeze believed that the school was not adequately prepared to open. Up until that time, she felt that everyone would be ready, including herself. By opening day, she decided no way was she going to place her child in the school:

This is just not grounded enough for me. Well, you know some could argue that, you know, back in those days, we learned out of barns and this and that, but this is not back in the day and in my eye . . . for three thousand dollars! It's just that we just need to be doing a little bit more.

Another serious consideration for her was that Noni had changed schools four times. The financial instability of the school and the low enrollment also played a part in her determination not to let her daughter attend. Furthermore, Adaeze was unhappy with the cut in pay that the head teacher had taken in accepting the position. She knew that Camara was not happy with this decision, and to her mind this made the school unstable in terms of the likelihood of continuing a second year. As far as Camara's credentials are concerned, Adaeze thinks that she is wonderful and just perfect for the children. Adaeze is pleased, however, that the school is still operating, although she is surprised. She would still consider putting her child in Sankofa, if it manages to stay afloat financially. Her main worry now is the contradictory nature of her position and involvement with the school. She wonders what message she is giving to other parents when she does not send her own child.

Nalo ("Much loved")

Nalo is forty-two years old. She has one son Yakubu ("he is blessed"), aged nine years, and is a single parent. She is very slim and petite, around five feet one inch tall with lovely skin and braided hair. She is a teacher who works in the public school system with an important role in educating teachers. Nalo is also a talented jazz singer, and sung professionally at one time. Both her parents came from the South: her mother from Georgia and her father from Virginia. Nalo's mother came from a big family who were farmers, ministers, and musicians. Two of her aunts and her mother were in a singing group when they were younger. Their father died when they were very young and their mother raised them alone. The three sisters traveled North, and there Nalo's mother met her father. Nalo's father had only one sister and they lost their father when they were young. Nalo and her older brother were the only children to her parents. Nalo spent a lot of time with her grandmother, who meant more to her than even her mother. She was considered by Nalo to be the "light of her life." Regular visits to the South kept Nalo in touch with her relatives.

For most of her life, Nalo grew up in the same house in the neighborhood. The neighborhood, once Italian and Jewish, is now Black. She attended a white neighborhood school.

> I had this marvelous teacher. She was the only Black teacher but she was just the loveliest thing. She always reminded me of Lena Horne. I don't know if that's why I thought that she was so sweet. She was very, very encouraging she would always push me, so to speak. She was probably the first person who really impacted [me] outside my house.

Nalo had her first confrontation with racism in the eighth grade. As a result of her singing, Nalo was very popular and her art teacher resented this. Nalo was aware of her teacher's resentment and recalled:

> It seemed like she was always on me because she didn't like the fact that I was doing well. I mean that's the way I assessed it then and that's the way I still do. I was always picked for assemblies to sing. I think that she didn't like it that the belle of the ball was Black. I remember her saying something to me one day about St. Patrick's Day about being in charge of the program. She came up to me at my locker and said I was a little Black girl and she didn't see how or why I was the one doing these things on St. Patrick's Day.

Later, Nalo was cast as the lead in a Julius Caesar play by her Latin teacher, who was straight from college. On a couple of occasions the young Latin teacher gave Nalo a lift home from school. The art teacher made a remark about her character because she had accepted lifts home from the teacher. To Nalo, her comment revealed the level of this teacher's vindictiveness. However, Nalo was very strong and did not allow the art teacher's attitude to break her spirit.

The sixties had a major impact on her life. She remembers the deaths of President Kennedy and Dr. Martin Luther King, which were traumatic for her. She went to a mixed university instead of Howard as she had wanted. Her parents were against the idea of Nalo going to an all-Black university, so she gave in to their wishes. On the campus she found that she was one of about 35 Black students out of a total of 4,000 students. The Afrikan students gravitated toward each other and then a "street brother," professor, doctor, and intellectual ("a male Angela Davis" according to Nalo) walked into the academy midway through Nalo's first semester. He designed a Black history course and his perspective and consciousness changed her whole life. She became secretary of the Black Student Union and led the takeover of a university building in order to make demands for the establishment of the Black history course. This move also made a difference to the university and the next admission of Black students.

After qualifying as a teacher, she hated the public school system and believed that her ideas could never be influential in what she considered by that time to be a racist school system. Disappointed, Nalo went to Washington, D.C. By 1976, Nalo had become a Muslim. The Black nationalism of the time directed her experiences. After living for a while in New York, she returned to Washington and got married. Later, she and her husband moved to Chicago and ran a children's home. It was there that her son Yakubu ("he is blessed") was born. During her marriage she worked hard at the relationship.

> I had tried to change who I was, changed my lifestyle, changed some of my beliefs, my opinions, totally gave up my rights as a woman, to be married. I thought there must be something wrong with me. I kept trying to do these things. I said I will not raise my son in a situation like that.

After a continuous struggle with the marriage she returned home with her son and began teaching in public school. Nalo taught in an early childhood center and developed an Afrikan-centered program to cater especially to the 75 percent of Afrikan children in the school from preschool to second grade. The program involved the inclusion of parents in the teaching of the origins of humankind and the history of Afrikans. She is very proud of this accomplishment and considers it to be a major one in her life. She knows that it touched all the children and the parents. This has helped very much in the education of her own son and the development of his identity. He is her partner and "sidekick." He has accompanied her to Afrika (Kemet and Ghana) and attended lectures all over the country.

> I always wanted to have a little boy to start a new breed of young Black men. I wanted my son to be the kind of Black man that I wrote about in my poems. One who would be the strength that a real good sister needed and would let a real good sister be the strength that he needed. That would get out here and make a real good contribution to us . . . that he would understand the link, the responsibility, the vibration of this whole thing that I have felt.

Nalo recognized that we need men, leaders, caring men, who do not marry in order to have someone do their laundry. She makes a conscious effort to make sure her son meets good strong Black men. Her emphasis on self-identity and Afrikan-centeredness and her experience as a parent and teacher have made an impact on the school.

Nalo was asked in the early phases of planning the school, whether she would be the head teacher. Although flattered, she was in the middle of reconstructing her life at the time, and was unable to commit herself to the responsibilities that the role would require. The later appointment of Camara was ideal as far as Nalo is concerned. She feels that Camara is perfect and has done everything that she would do as head teacher. Her reasons for not sending her son to the school really rest with her son. When the school began with four children, Yakubu was uncomfortable with being the oldest child and only one of two males, the younger one being only four. He still felt the same when the numbers rose to ten with two boys and eight girls. During the summer, he attended the program because boys, his age and older, attended. At this point, he is seriously considering the school because there are now twenty-five students, nine of whom are males.

In terms of Nalo's commitment to the struggle, a story that always gives her the strength to carry on is one that her grandmother told her many times about her own grandmother who was in slavery. Nalo's grandmother saw the slave master hit her own grandmother on the side of the head with a hoe and she never forgot. Neither has Nalo.

Mawasi ("In God's Hands")

Mawasi is thirty-four years old and married to an Afrikan from Nigeria. They have a son and a baby daughter. She is an administrator in the university and her husband helps to raise the children. She is tall, dignified, and statuesque with a calm persona. Mawasi laughs a lot. She coordinates a "minority" program that predominantly serves Afrikan students. Her mother is from North Carolina and her father from South Carolina. Both are from small rural townships in the South. Her mother's mother was a city girl and raised eleven girls and one boy, mostly alone because her husband was a sharecropper.

Mawasi is from a family of eight children, three girls and five boys. She was brought up in an Afrikan community one hour from New York City where her father, once a farmworker, became a plant foreman and her mother became a homemaker. They grew up in a six-bedroom apartment most of their lives. Although it was a struggle her father provided well for them and they "wanted for nothing." The mother and father have been together for over fifty years. Mawasi's mother was a strong influence in her life because she always encouraged her to become "educated" and have a career. She herself had wanted to teach but never fulfilled that ambition because of her career as a homemaker.

Mawasi went to an all-Black elementary school because of segregation and then she was bused after sixth grade to a mixed school. Even in her elementary school, she had mostly white teachers. However, she had a very positive experience at the Black school. There were some teachers who were Afrikan and community workers. This had a major impact in grounding her in her Blackness. One of the head teachers made a comment that she still remembers. If the pupils were making noise in the corridor of the school, he would come out, said Mawasi, and ask, "What are you doing out here?' White kids don't behave like that, they're worse."

He made us really appreciate being Black. My church did
weekly activities that involved being Afrikan American. In
our Bible studies there were times when we didn't discuss the
Bible but we learned Black history.

The church was involved in community programs during the
sixties and seventies, when racial issues were the major focus. Her
parents participated in community activities. If it was decided to
keep the children off school for a day, then her parents would take
a stand in support. She remembers that by ninth grade she had
refused to say the American Pledge of Allegiance.

After leaving school, Mawasi entered college and then came to
the university to major in English. While in the master's program,
she transferred to American studies because of her lack of interest
in white literature and in order to learn and teach about Afrikan
women writers.

Regarding her children's schooling, her son Azikwe ("healthy")
who is almost four, has attended the same white daycare center
since he was born.

I trust them. I have problems internally because they're white
but he's ok, he's well adjusted. The issues that I deal with
every day are problems involved in understanding who we
are, acknowledging, accepting it, living it. When I put him in
a setting where those who are teaching him are white, then
I wonder if I'm giving him the right messages.

Mawasi wants a quality education for her Azikwe but feels that she
can take her time in choosing because he is not yet of school age.
Mawasi has an input into the daycare and has taken time to teach
on occasion. She once took a day to teach the children about Afrika.
It is important, she believes, for her son to understand the important aspects about being an Afrikan, which he may not learn in the
daycare center. Mawasi seriously considered Sankofa because after
a visit with her son on an open day, he was very happy with the
school and decided that he wanted to go there. However, she decided not to send him. Something happened at that time that apparently changed her mind.

[S]ome of the kids were running around. The administrative assistant [Aisha], maybe it's because she didn't know him and he was just this little boy running around but he wasn't creating havoc. The way she treated him was like, "Get away from me." She was feeding the fish and he was asking her if he could help her and she was trying to get him to say "Please." And I watched because I wanted to see how he interacts with people when I'm not around. He didn't know I was watching. He eventually did say "please" and then she said, "Well, I'm finished now." I wonder what kind of role does that woman play in the school. Because he is a little Black boy, some people will respond to him like that. I know the teacher is good and I met her and I like the way she interacts with the kids, but I didn't like that experience.

Mawasi believes that her status affords her the luxury of choosing her community, unlike her family's experience while she was growing up. She feels that her family can now live in safe areas and that she can give her child a good life.

⑦

An Analysis of the Mothers' Experiences

Ipuwer laments the reversal of the social order when outsiders have destroyed the internal harmony and stability of ancient Egyptian society. He says: "Behold now how greatly the people have changed. The robber has become rich and the honorable person a thief. The foreigners have imposed new ways and created new relations and the righteous Egyptian of yesterday cannot be found anywhere."

—The Books of Contemplation

The use of the concept of culture as an analytical tool can show that there are significant ramifications for the conquered Afrikan family as an institution. As previously stated, the racialization of the world is a feature of European patriarchy. In a matriarchal society, humanity is not defined on the basis of race as a standard of human differentiation. In Kemet (ancient Egypt), for example, Maat, which is represented as a woman, is a divine principle of the creator. She stands for truth, justice, balance, honesty, righteousness, order and reciprocity among other things. Within the Kemetic spiritual system of beliefs, the

161

soul/heart must be judged before entering the afterlife. The life of the deceased is symbolically judged as it is weighed on the scale of Maat. The soul is weighed against the feather of truth.[1] A person is judged according to the way s/he has lived. This is true across the entire Afrikan continent. Ideas like this were known to have existed in written form from at least 4,500 B.C.E. Thus, the Eurocentric concept of race is not a consideration for defining human worth.

The matriarchal relationship between women and men is based on reciprocity and complementarity. The mother is perceived as the giver of life and the bearer of culture. The children are considered the wealth of society and therefore the basis of its continuation. One's behavior is judged by her/his value to the well-being of the society. Given these principal values of matriarchy, it is possible to view the continuing conquest of Afrikan people through institutional imposition as one that continues to erode traditional cultural values. In effect, this condition means that the relationship among women and men is compromised, thus the status and roles of the man and woman as family members is also compromised. Based on Afrikan-centered values and beliefs, Afrikan people in the United Kingdom and the United States are not living under idealized conditions. Therefore, we are analyzing the ways that we are influenced by as well as the ways that we are influencing alien values that are socially imposed.

Under patriarchy, the male is perceived as the warrior and physical threat to European social order, while the woman is the reproducer of future generations. In reality, the woman is considered an equal threat to the social order. Her treatment under white supremacy is more subtle. The preponderance of male incarceration, death, underemployment, unemployment, and involvement in negative entrepreneurship negatively affects her ability to reproduce the new social order. In effect, her movements are controlled by the treatment of the male. The management of male and female energies, thus, differ and fluctuate according to the socioeconomic interests of the culturally dominant group. The overrepresentation of males incarcerated and the overrepresentation of single mothers on welfare are prime examples of government-based policy decisions. The search for profit outside Western centers devalues the lives of Afrikan people detained in the West. The importance of the sanctity of Afrikan life diminishes as the need for Afrikan energies erodes. This is the racialized socioeconomic context for the Afrikan family in the United Kingdom and the United States.

Part I: The Afrikan Family: The Site of Oppression and Resistance

Frances Cress Welsing (1991) defines the Afrikan family institution under white supremacy as a "survival unit." She believes that the "family" is supposed to be

> a social institution that functions to support maximal development and protection of the young. However, under white supremacy, Blacks and other non-whites are not to be developed maximally; they are permitted to survive as functional inferiors, alienated from self and from their own kind. The non-white survival unit is not permitted to defend itself or its young. (p. 87)

These are important considerations for analyzing the interviewees' experiences as mothers. I have categorized the data under different subheadings to make it easier for the reader to follow my findings. I have also incorporated data from my 1990 London study on supplementary schools and the Ratteray and Shujaa (1987) study on independent schools.

Single Parenting

With regard to this study and the earlier London study (1990), the single parent factor is significant. During the London study, while carrying out a pilot study for the questionnaire, the first four mothers interviewed suggested that I should incorporate the category of single parent. They believed, as I do, that single-parent Afrikan families have a difficult time surviving under often untenable circumstances. Ideally, the joining of the parents brings together two families who take on responsibilities to help raise the children of their extended families. I believe that highlighting the single-parent status has added an important dimension to the work because it shows, in particular, the tenacity, integrity, dignity, and survivability of single parents and their children. Thus, instead of appearing as solely victims, single parents show how they are actively changing untenable conditions.

Of the twenty-one mothers that I interviewed, ten are single parents. They are the head teacher Camara, Kumiwa, Aidoo, Binta, and Nalo in the United States and Adoaha, Abebe, Amal, Diallo, and Enomwoyi in the United Kingdom. My interest in the single-parent factor began with the London study (1990) when I discovered that over half of the data came from single-parent women. There were 32 single parents out of 60 respondents. During that study, I gathered data from the Queen Nzinga School, which was established in 1985 by my friend Habibka ("sweet heart") and me. At that time we were single parents. Ten of the fifteen respondents from that school alone were single parents. Later on, after my arrival in the United States, I gave a secondary analysis of thirty-five interview transcripts from the Ratteray and Shujaa study (1987). Five of those parents were single. I was able to draw inferences from both of these studies as well as the present study. In the present study the incidence of intergenerational single-parent upbringing is also significant.

The Sankofa School Mothers (U.S.). There are examples of several generations of single parenting among the women in the study. In Kumiwa's family, she raised her children almost single-handedly and presently helps to raise her granddaughter, whose mother is also a single parent. She herself was raised by her grandmother, father, and mother at different times in her life. Another example is found in Binta's family. She is raising her son and lives with her mother, who raised her and her two brothers and sisters alone. Moreover, Binta's mother was raised by her grandmother. The head teacher Camara raised her daughters, who are now adults, from the ages of three and four years old. She is now a grandmother and is helping her younger daughter, who is also a single parent, to raise her son.

Ayoluwa raised three of her four children as a single parent and was one of five children raised alone by her mother. While Ayoluwa was a single parent, her mother helped her to raise her children. Dalmar, who is married, was raised along with her brother and sister by her mother. Ife and her mother and sister were raised by her grandmother. Aisha was raised by her grandmother in St. Vincent before her mother sent for her to come to the United States. Aisha's husband works in another city and she has raised her daughters without his emotional support for the major part of their lives. Aidoo and her husband live separately.

The Mothers Whose Children Do Not Attend Sankofa School (U.S.). Among the four parents who have decided not to use Sankofa, three have had single-parent experiences in their families. Jaha, who is not a single parent, was raised for sometime by her mother, after her father left and before her mother's nervous breakdown. Adaeze also lives with her husband. However, she was one of five children raised by her mother alone. Nalo is raising her son without her husband.

The Marcus Garvey School Mothers (U.K.). Adoaha has been a single parent for the last few years. She was raised by her mother in Grenada. Then she was adopted and raised by her aunt in Trinidad and the United Kingdom. Her aunt, whom she knew as her mother, never married. When Kesi's grandmother died in Jamaica, she and her sister were raised by their grandfather. At the earliest opportunity, Kesi's father sent for his daughters to come and live in the United Kingdom They were raised by a female friend of his who raised them alone as their mother. Diallo is a single parent. Nzinga is married. She was raised, first, by her grandmother in St. Kitts, and then her father in the United Kingdom.

The Queen Nzinga School Mothers (U.K.). Before coming to England, Enomwoyi was raised by her grandmother in Grenada. She was brought to the United Kingdom by her mother and lived with her two sisters and her mother's husband. Enomowoyi is a single parent who is raising three children. Her first child, a son, never knew his father, unlike her two daughters. Amal raised her son and daughter alone. Finally, Abebe chose to be a single mother when she made the decision to have her son.

It is evident in the intergenerational single-parent upbringings that the interviewees were not all raised by their biological mothers. Some were raised by their grandparents or, as Adoah's case, by an aunt or, as in Kesi's situation, by a friend of her father's. That is not to say that these situations were ideal for everyone because this was not the case. However, as Tedla (1995) explains, Afrikan traditional ways stress the responsibility for raising the children. It is/was literally a social responsibility and expectation. Thus, mothering

> transcends gender and blood relation. One's spouse, or sibling or even friend can be said to be one's mother if they have been kind and caring toward you. It is not unusual to hear at a person's funeral the spouse, the sibling(s) or friend(s) of the deceased crying loudly and saying that the deceased was their mother. In expressing the kindness and caring nature of a brother, a sister, a spouse, a friend, a father, it is said, "He is not just my brother/husband/father, he is my mother." "She is not just my sister/wife/friend, she is my mother." (p. 61)

As already indicated, the state of motherhood depicts the nature of the communal responsibilities involved in the raising of children and the caring of others. The capturing, enslavement, and colonization of Afrikan people from the fifteenth century shows that these "mothering" values and arrangements sustained Afrikan life then and now. Afrikan people frequently found themselves raising children who had been removed from their blood mothers for any number of reasons. This commitment to collective responsibility is a major feature of matriarchal values. Within those values, all members of society are responsible for the development of the children.

Single Parenting and Schooling the Children

Data from the London study (1990) included responses to a questionnaire that tried to ascertain the ideal school parents would send their children to if they had a choice. Of the sixty questionnaires completed, the data revealed that single parents comprised the highest percentage of parents who desired Black-run schools with a Black student population. Moreover, a significant number of single parents indicated that they were prepared to pay tuition so that supplementary schools could become full-time.

Interviews with twelve single parents showed that six of them traveled long distances for their children to attend supplementary schools. On Saturdays they either spent the whole day or half of the day at the schools working at the schools and attending parent meetings, or remained in the locality until the end of school time. Clearly, these parents are women who are committed to their children's education despite some of the obstacles associated with single parenting.

Four of these parents believed that their children were discriminated against in public school because they are Afrikan and from single-parent homes. They complained that teachers had low expectations of their children based on their single-parent status. The Ratteray and Shujaa (1987) transcripts revealed that two of the five single parents in the study who used Afrikan neighborhood schools said their children had extremely adverse experiences in the public school system.

One mother said that her son who, prior to going to an Afrikan-centered school, attended a predominantly white school, had "been shown to be academically gifted through testing and evaluation, and they were just trying to crucify him in public school." His work was frequently marked incorrect when the same answers were marked correct on other children's work. He was classified as having behavior problems and as a slow learner.

This mother found herself crying about her son every day while she was at work. She explained that her son was a child who, during second grade, had represented his school in the "Olympics of the Mind" competition, although many teachers objected. He carried the school to a second place overall finish in the competition. After he returned, he was not congratulated. As this mother put it, she was "born on the picket line" and thus, was prepared to fight for what she believed in. To resolve the situation, she placed her child in an Afrikan-centered school where she knows that he is loved unquestioningly.

The son of another mother in the Ratteray and Shujaa study had been categorized as "dumb" by the public school system. Unfortunately, according to the mother, even the child believed that he was dumb and couldn't learn. Public school officials who evaluated him believed that he needed "special ed" classes. He was moved by his mother into an independent Black educational institution. His mother makes great sacrifices to work overtime to pay for him to attend the school. However, she is happy because there is no stigma attached to him at the new school. His work has improved greatly.

A single parent who participated in the 1990 study in the United Kingdom found that her son's work was continually marked excellent and correct when it wasn't. This is quite the opposite of the first parent's experience described above. As a result, the son's work began to deteriorate. Working to maintain a mortgage made the mother very unhappy because she felt guilty about the situation. She blamed herself for being a single parent and leaving her son to take care of himself on occasions. This situation was, she believed, causing her son to do poorly. However, since sending him to a supplementary school, where he is respected and cared for, his academic work has improved dramatically. He is also a much happier child and she is overjoyed. However, she is still constrained by economic demands.

This is not to say that the experiences that these mothers reported is necessarily only the experience of single-parent children. These experiences may also be related to the fact that their children are boys. During the interviews, a number of mothers expressed concerns about the stigma attached to boy children and a fear for their safety. Beyond this data, my experience of working with parents serves to confirm the point that mothers with sons are not secure about what might happen to them. However, my data shows that the majority of children in this study have had negative experiences within the public school system regardless of their sex and parents' marital status. As I have already explicated in chapter 2, the responses of boys and girls to negative treatment may be entirely different. As Mac an Ghaill (1988) found in his study, girls fared better than boys against racism because of their covert attitudes as opposed to the overt attitudes of the boys. While racism toward the children is consistently practiced through their public school experiences, whether they are boys or girls, the ability of the single mothers to deal with this reality is severely handicapped by the fact that she alone and as a woman must face the problem of the school system's racism toward her children while sustaining a lifestyle that can provide for the needs of her children.

The nature of this work is to value the feelings and beliefs of the mothers. Recognizing the validity of the concerns of single mothers who know that their children are victimized because they are from single-parent families enables us to consider reasons for the trend in the numbers of young people from single-parent families who are shunted into "special schools."

Data, collected by the Inner London Education Authority (ILEA) Research and Statistics Branch (1988), shows that many children referred to the Educational Psychological Services in London and those who end up in "special units" for emotional and behavioral problems are from single-parent families. Unfortunately, ILEA no longer exists, and this data is dated. However, it has some relevance to this work, given the time of the first study in 1990. A 1988 ILEA report on characteristics of pupils in special schools and units reveals that as many as 32 percent of children live in single-parent families compared to 27 percent in mainstream schools. This shows an overrepresentation of students from single-parent families in special schools and units. However, these statistics were not broken down racially. Thus, no correlation was made between the over-representation of Afrikan boys and girls in these schools and their family status. It is important to note that, overall, the number of girls in these schools is minimal compared to the preponderance of boys. I believe that a future analysis of the numbers of children assigned to this category, accompanied by a racial breakdown, can provide an insight into the types of victimization that take place and to which parents have alluded.

In light of the single mothers' analyses, my own experiences of working with Black parent groups, support the notion that Afrikan children who were perceived to have problems in public/state schools were mainly from single-parent families. It was not generally the case that the children had not committed misdemeanors of one kind or another. However, it was the failure of teachers and the psychological services to look at the reasons underlying the behaviors, such as white teachers' racism or Afrikan teachers' deculturalization or unjust school policies regarding the treatment of these children compared to other racial groups and other family orientations.

While some single mothers believed that their children were discriminated against more than the children of two-parent families, it is important to take into account that within western patriarchy, there is a stigma attached to this type of family unit. The nuclear conjugal family is considered the archetype of family structures, with the male as the head of the household. Thus, any other family structure is viewed as dysfunctional. This belief has a great bearing on the treatment of Afrikan families that do not follow this model.

The work of Niara Sudarkasa (1996) brings to light family forms practiced by Afrikan people that are not based on the nuclear family model. In her discussion on matrilineal family models from West Afrika, where most Afrikan families living in the United States are descended, the emphasis was on the blood relatives of the children—that is, from the mother's line. Thus the stability of the family did not rely on the strength of marriage as in the nuclear family setting. The end of a marriage did not mean the destruction of the family. The families brought together by the marriage were still considered to have lifelong responsibilities to the children (1996, 82). Under white patrilineal supremacy, both the parents and the children of single-parent families are vulnerable to negative forces not only because the parents are attempting to do the work of several people, but also because of the treatment of children bearing the stigma. Moreover, in a typical European social system, financial conditions play a major role in facilitating the ability of single parents to cope. Such families may bear the brunt of the trauma. The survival of these families is related to the family's ability to deal with these conditions, often by any means necessary.

Importantly, these mothers exhibit concerns and interests about the schooling of their children that are influenced and shaped by their awareness of racism and its impact on their children's lives. This is not to say that other parents are not equally concerned. However, despite the multitude of responsibilities they incur as single parents, these mothers have chosen to put their children in environments that affirm their Afrikanity. In this light, use of these schools may be conceived of as a measure of their consciousness about the cultural needs of their children. It seems possible that the availability of culturally affirming schools has a bearing on their value, but it is well to remember that some mothers, particularly those based in the United Kingdom, travel miles outside their districts to place their children in these schools. Another important point is that these schools offer a family-based orientation that allows the parents and children to come together and form strong family bonds (in the broader sense of the Afrikan collective) that can enhance their lives.

Overall, the data show that the Afrikan family is always under threat regardless of class or single-parent status. The strength of the Afrikan mother, whether single or not, can, and has, herstorically provided a positive role model of courage, intelligence, support, integrity, endurance, responsibility, and commitment to surviving under extreme conditions (Dadzie 1990; Bryan, Dadzie, and Scafe 1988; Ladner 1971; Carby 1982). At the same time, the reality is that some mothers and fathers are unable to cope or must carry out roles outside those of parenting to sustain the family. If this happens, the grandparents may be called upon to take over responsibility for either the mother or the father. In this study, the grandmother has played a critical role. In any case, what I have tried to emphasize is the tenacity of women who, in a racist and sexist hostile environment, exhibit the strength that is fundamental to the survival of Afrikan people.

Male and Female Roles in the Family

The father has had a critical impact upon the family. Some fathers have played a less dominant role than would be expected in a patriarchal society and some have played a dominant role that might have been condoned. In either case, the father is not in an ideal situation; he, like the rest of the family, exists as a conquered person. The Eurocultural conditions that women and men face are different and complex. Aggressive characteristics are a feature of Western patriarchy and men are expected to exhibit them. Michael Bradley (1978) associates the emphasis on violent behavior with the Caucasian[2] need to survive during the Ice Age.

Frances Cress Welsing (1991) goes some way toward explaining how racist dynamics imposed upon the internal dynamics of the family, the survival unit, "negate Black manhood, as fundamentally expressed in the relationship between bread winning and true power potential." She goes on to state:

Even when high-level income is allowed, there is no true power in its ultimate sense—meaning to support, protect and defend the lives of one's self, one's wife and one's children. Under any serious system of oppression, this right is denied the oppressed male, and with its denial there is a concomitant and proportionate loss of respect for manhood in the oppressed population. This attitude begins first within the oppressed man himself and radiates to all other members of the survival unit. The resultant frustration of Black manhood potential—a pressure and grievance that cannot be redressed directly at its source under fear of death—forces behavior into dysfunctional, non-satisfying, circular, obsessive compulsive patterns in areas of people activity where greater degrees of maleness are permitted to be expressed (i.e., sex, sports and entertainment). (87)

Welsing is able to provide a context for understanding some of the many contradictions that the Afrikan man as father faces in navigating a society that has debased his humanity and manhood as provider and protector—even within a patriarchy.

The Sankofa School Mothers (U.S.). In the herstory of Camara, although she was raised by both her mother and father, it was her mother who was the strong person in the relationship. At the same time, her grandfather was the major role model who instilled pride about Afrikan people in her family. Her father worked seasonally on construction. In the winter there was no work for the men, so the men in the community stayed at home. However, work was available year round for the women. While the men were at home, they provided an important support system for their children.

As a parent, Camara chose to leave her husband and raise her daughters alone. He was never involved in their upbringing once they reached three and four years old.

Ayoluwa's mother raised her and her sisters and brothers singlehandedly. Ayoluwa had a deep love for her mother, and remembers the strength and support that she provided, especially when Ayoluwa also became a single mother. There were some occasions when Ayoluwa saw her father, but he played no substantial part in her upbringing, although memories of him are positive. Interestingly, her soul-mate is her best friend. While he is not the father of any of her children, he is a positive male model to her youngest daughter and her older sons and daughter. Ayoluwa is very happy in this relationship.

Like Ayoluwa's mother, Binta's mother played a powerful role in raising five children and providing emotional support and guidance. At the same time, Binta was always in communication with her father. He was continuously employed at the local plant during her upbringing. When she was sixteen, she went to live with him so that she could have more material things. The father of Binta's son plays no role in raising him. Bintas's mother helps to raise her son both financially and emotionally.

Dalmar's mother worked outside the home and raised the three children while her father provided some financial support. Her parents did not live together. Dalmar visited her father every day because he lived nearby and if her mother had not returned home from work, she and the others would stay with him until she returned. In effect, he played a supportive role in also caring for his children. Dalmar also mentions that her grandfather and uncles also played a critical role as part of her extended family. In Dalmar's marriage her husband plays a major role in raising their three girls.

Kumiwa's father worked on the railroad and sent money to his children. Sometimes he would visit the children. In fact, Kumiwa looked forward to the prospect of going to live with him because she thought that he was rich. She little knew the types of torture she would receive when he tried to force her to become an A student. Moreover, she had no idea that when she was fourteen, he would further misuse his power to compromise her girlhood. Fortunately, she was able to navigate her way out of the situation. Despite her father's behavior, when he was dying of cancer, Kumiwa and her sister looked after him. She never stopped loving him, but she never forgave him.

In her own family, the father of her first two sons was violent and became addicted to drugs. Kumiwa had him incarcerated for his violent behavior. The father of her third child, her only daughter, was quite affluent when she met him. He later became involved with dealing drugs, became hooked on heroin, and went to jail. Finally, the father of her fourth child, a son, joined the Nation of Islam while in drug rehabilitation; Kumiwa joined at the same time. Kumiwa helps her daughter to raise her granddaughter.

Aidoo's father, who was from Puerto Rico, was the more powerful parent in her life. She admired him and it was he who inspired her and provided for the family. Aidoo did not feel as close to her mother. Aidoo has chosen to be separated from her daughter's father. He sends money for his daughter and looks after her on some weekends on a regular basis. Her husband's mother sometimes cares for their daughter as well. Aidoo is satisfied with this situation.

Both of Ezigbo's parents were involved in her upbringing. Her father worked in a local plant and provided for the family. They had everything that they needed. Both her mother and father did not finish high school but pushed their children to go to college. Ezigbo is a practicing Muslim in the Nation of Islam and so is her present husband, who is the father of the youngest of her three children.

Ife did not know her father. She is married to her second husband. Her daughter from her previous marriage and her son from this marriage live in the same household. Her daughter is in contact with her father and Ife consults with him in making decisions about their daughter's future.

Aisha was aware of who her father was as she grew up, but he did not play a critical role in her upbringing. She grew up with her grandmother in St. Vincent until she was fourteen years old and then went to live with her mother in New York. While Aisha is not a single parent, in reality the father of her two daughters has not been around to play a full-time emotional role in their lives. He has been working to help support his family. Aisha has raised them virtually alone.

The Mothers Whose Children Do Not Attend Sankofa School (U.S.).   Mawasi grew up with her mother and her father. They were both powerful influences in her life. According to Mawasi, her father was a great provider for the family. The family struggled but never wanted for anything. However, it was her mother who inspired her and empowered her as a woman. The father of Mawasi's son and daughter is from Afrika and he plays a major "mothering" role in their upbringing particularly since Mawasi is working full-time as an administrator.

Nalo also came from a two-parent family. Her parents came from the Southern states and met in the city. Her father, whom she loved dearly, worked in a local plant. Her relationship with her son's father did not work out, so she took him out of that situation and raised him herself. Her father and mother have had a major role in his upbringing.

Jaha's parents had irreconcilable differences and eventually ended their relationship. She was not happy when her father left her mother because she was very close to him. She and her brother stayed with their mother, who slowly had a severe breakdown and eventually became homeless. Jaha's mother later recovered and was able to piece her life together. Jaha is a mother to her husband's son and loves him as her own.

Adaeze's mother raised five children on her own. Adaeze has three children with her husband, whom she has known since they attended university together. Her husband plays a major role as a provider to the family and her mother provides support and advice.

The Marcus Garvey School Mothers (U.K.). Adoaha did not know her father. After she left her mother and was adopted by her aunt, she left the Caribbean and came to live in the United Kingdom. Her children's father has played a major supportive role in their lives, especially in terms of their cultural awareness. She and he are very good friends, though they are now separated.

It was Kesi's father, who sent for her to come to the United Kingdom from Jamaica when she was six years old. He placed her in the care of his woman friend, who raised Kesi and her sister. He paid for their upkeep while they remained with their "mother." He did not provide emotional support. Rather, his role was to discipline her when he was called upon to do so by her mother. The relationship Kesi formed with her first son's father, who was Nigerian, did not materialize into anything worthwhile. She is very happy with her husband, who helped her to raise her first son, and his relationship with the children. When he returns from work (he goes away to work), Kesi goes out and leaves him with the children.

Nzinga was raised by her grandmother. Her father brought her over from St. Kitts to live in the United Kingdom when she was eleven years old. She lived alone with him and cooked and cleaned for him. He abused her consistently by beating her and raping her. Nzinga's first child, who was put up for adoption, was fathered by her own father. Now, Nzinga is happily married to a man who adores her and provides the emotional and financial support that she and her children need.

Both Diallo's mother and father played equally important roles in her family life. It was Diallo's mother who was the more powerful of the two parents, particularly in making important decisions. While Diallo's father was the less assertive of the two parents, he was always there and helped as a provider of emotional and financial support. Prior to Diallo's arrival in the United Kingdom, her grandfather had played a prominent and positive role in her life and she loved him for that. The father of Diallo's two sons, who is white and from St. Vincent, is in many ways culturally Afrikan. He is still in contact with them. Diallo has a good relationship with his family, whom she can call on for help.

The Queen Nzinga School Mothers (U.K.). After her return from Nigeria, Abebe's father won custody of his three children— Abebe, her sister and her brother. Angry with her father for his role in the separation of her parents, Abebe returned to her mother. His strict attitude about his children receiving an "education" was appreciated by Abebe, but that emphasis was not placed on her schooling because she grew up mainly with her European mother, her Nigerian stepfather, and their four sons. She found that she spent more time helping in the home than focusing on school. She visited and stayed in touch with her father even when he remarried and had another daughter. His death had a profound effect on her. As she remembered him for me, she forgave him for the things that she blamed him for. Although Abebe is a single mother, she is very happy with her son's father's role in his upbringing. Through his family, she believes that her son has the cultural grounding and support that he needs.

At the age of eleven years, Enomwoyi arrived in the United Kingdom. She came to live with her mother, stepfather, and two sisters after being raised by her grandmother. She had a good relationship with her father and sometimes saw him. She did not get on with her mother or stepfather. The tense relationship between Enomwoyi and her mother may well have been triggered by her stepfather's molestation of her and her inability to discuss this situation with her mother.

After a disastrous relationship with her first son's father, Enomwoyi raised her baby alone while she was very young. Her later marriage produced two children. She was forced to end her marriage because of her husband's lack of respect for her.

Amal, who was born in the United Kingdom, grew up with her Nigerian mother and her father, but from the age of two until she was five, she was fostered out to an elderly white couple. Her father was the head of the family. He was very strict about her schooling and often beat her for not doing as well as he wanted her to do at school. Eventually, after she left home, her parents separated. The herstory of Amal reveals that she did not have successful relationships with her children's fathers, one was of Caribbean descent and the other was from Nigeria. Both of these men exploited her naiveté and took no responsibility for their children.

Living in the United Kingdom was quite a different experience for Fugo, who arrived with her family from Zimbabwe when she was fourteen years old. Her father was the head of the family. Both her mother and father worked to finance the family. Although, Fugo's father had a powerful influence in her life, it was her mother that she admired. On her arrival to the United Kingdom, her father's sexual advances left a deep wound in Fugo. When he died, she believed that his illness had contributed to his abusive treatment of both Fugo and her mother in his later years . In her early years in Afrika she had been very close to her father. Fugo believes that, eventually, she will forgive him because she only wanted to love him. While Fugo is extremely happy with her second marriage to a man of Caribbean-descent, her first marriage to a white man was abusive. Her daughter from that marriage lives in Zimbabwe with Fugo's mother so that she will develop good values and be culturally grounded.

In the main, the fathers of both the interviewees and their children, whether they lived with their families or not, had a visible presence and played a supportive role in the upbringing of their children. In the U.S. there are examples of men like Ayoluwa's partner; Ife's two husbands; Aidoo's father and her daughter's father; Dalmar's father, grandfather, uncles, and husband; Ezigbo's father and husband; Mawasi's father and husband; Adaeze's husband; and in the United Kingdom, there are Nzinga's uncle and husband; Kesi's grandfather and husband; Adoaha's children's father; Fugo's husband; the father of Abebe's son; Diallo's grandfather, father, and sons' father—all have played, in some cases, outstanding roles in raising their children and bringing joy to their families and partners.

This is all the more amazing when, as Welsing (1991) argues, the patriarchal and classical role of manhood within white supremacy as the breadwinner and protector is one not easily afforded and in many cases almost impossible to achieve for the Afrikan man. In reality, as previously postulated, as a result of both racism and sexism, the Afrikan male and female are the least valued in terms of receiving equal pay or access to employment compared to Europeans. Obtaining money is of course critical to the survival of the family, particularly in urban areas. Ironically, while the Afrikan male is vastly under- and unemployed in urban areas, the Afrikan female is more employable because of the cheapness of her labor value as an Afrikan and a woman. These tensions underpin the structuring and arrangements within the "survival unit." I believe that the resourcefulness and integrity exhibited by Afrikan women and men in raising families within urban and rural war-zones is a measure of the belief that we have that the Afrikan family can and will survive European domination.

Problematic Family Relationships

However, it is important to mention that in this study there is evidence to show that there were some negative father and mother relationships. The mothers in the study felt that their experiences with negativity were critical to helping them to become the women that they are today. Four fathers, those of Nzinga from Marcus Garvey, Enomwoyi from Queen Nzinga, Fugo from Queen Nzinga, and Kumiwa from Sankofa, exploited their parental roles when they sexually propositioned young females in their care. While no penetration took place in the cases of Enomwoyi, Fugo, and Kumiwa, these transgressions on the part of the fathers and a stepfather had a major impact on their daughters' personal development. Nzinga suffered greatly from the trauma of giving birth to her father's daughter. She said of this circumstance:

I wasn't prepared for the fear and the emotional pain. . . . I felt no pain when I delivered the baby. . . . I have to be there for my children, there was nobody there for me when I needed somebody. . . . When I left home, I walked away with nothing, I was scared.

Enomwoyi's stepfather molested her. Her real father did not live with her and she felt that neither he nor her mother could help because of the trouble that it might cause. Eventually, Enomwoyi spoke to other relatives about the situation.

I sort of came out a little bit, you know. I think my mum must have heard about, um, but she never accepted that until I was older . . . she never sort of accepted that he's done it . . . even when I went down to the West Indies. We're still talking about it and she's still saying to me, "How could you tell people he's done those things to you . . . you're such a liar," you know . . . it hurts, it really deeply hurts.

Kumiwa recalls that her father had his own nice room in the attic:

Up there I was subjected to my father's wrath because of my math I didn't know my timetables I had to learn them or be dead . . . so I did learn them. . . . One time he was going to punish me for some infraction. . . . I was pleading with him that I would do anything. He said, "Anything?" I said, "Yes." He said, "Get up on the bed." I was petrified. I said I wanna eat. He wound up taking me to the Chinese restaurant.

They returned to his room and she sat over the food for what seemed like hours and he lay there waiting. Eventually, he went to work on the railways. That same night, Kumiwa crept downstairs and took some clothes and ran away. Her entry into street life had a great bearing on her life afterwards.

Fugo, from Zimbabwe, had just arrived in the United Kingdom to join her mother and father when her father propositioned her. She says of her experience:

It was very upsetting because it was the first day in this new country. From then on, I couldn't tell my mother, but I eventually told her. He died of a brain tumor. Towards the end, my mother said he actually asked her for her forgiveness and that's why I think I'll end up forgiving him.

Fujo believes that her abusive marriage to a European was largely linked to her disrespect for her father which she had projected onto all Afrikan men.

The United Kingdom was an environment that proved to be hostile to the development of the womanhood of Nzinga, Enomwoyi, and Fugo. Their earlier positive and culturally affirmative experiences with their families in their homelands may well have played a role in helping them survive the traumas that they later faced. In Kumiwa's case, life on the streets seemed to offer her a support system that her family could not provide. She ran away from her family life to live on the streets. However, much later, she was able to piece her life together and become a community activist and academic.

These stories serve to highlight the need to recognize how such abusive relationships can be condoned in a patriarchal and therefore racist society as part of the general milieu in which an Afrikan girl grows up and develops and in most cases becomes a mother. Such behavior could not be condoned within an Afrikan matriarchal value system. Analyzing the impact of alien values upon Afrikan people is critical to our survival. Thus, there is a need to address the devaluation of the status of womanhood, as well as racial oppression, because both have a destructive impact on the survival and well-being of Afrikan women, men, and children.

There are also examples of mothers who had difficulties coping. The natural mothers of Aisha, from the Sankofa School in the United States, and Enomwoyi from the Queen Nzinga School in the United Kingdom, and the foster mother of Kesi from the Marcus Garvey School in the United Kingdom, exhibited hostilities toward their daughters.

Aisha and Enomwoyi felt that their mothers' relationships with their stepfathers affected their relationships with their mothers. For instance, Enomwoyi looked so much like her mother that she felt that her mother was insecure with her presence. It may have been one reason why the stepfather propositioned Enomwoyi. Aisha left home while she was still technically a minor because the relationship with her mother was so tense.

Kesi believed that her "mother"'s relationship with her father had some bearing on how she was treated. She felt that she was being punished because she was so much like her father and he was living with another woman. The blood mothers of Kesi and Nzinga from the Marcus Garvey School left other family members to raise their children. In all these cases, the grandmothers played a pivotal role in raising them and the interviewees remembered them with great love and appreciation.

In the case of Adoaha from Marcus Garvey School, she was raised by her auntie, who became her mother. Her aunt offered to raise her because she could offer a secure future, financially. Adoaha never had a negative relationship with her blood mother and has always loved her mother. She has visited her in Grenada several times. She understood that her mother was very poor and wanted her to benefit from a life that she could never offer her.

As I asserted earlier, some fathers played a minimal role in the raising of their children, but in most cases interviewees knew their fathers in a positive way even if they did not live with them. Again, in most cases, the mothers or grandmothers were the most powerful and important influences in their upbringing. The herstories testify to the strength and deep love of their mothers, grandmothers, fathers, and grandfathers, as well as the respect and equal love they returned.

Mother and Son Relationships

My focus on mother and son relationships is not an attempt to undermine the bonds between the mothers and daughters but rather to highlight some of the concerns raised by mothers with sons. This is in keeping with the general discussion about male roles in patriarchal and racist western-oriented societies. All the mothers' concerns about their sons were significantly different from their worries about their daughters. There is something happening in these societies that is extremely dangerous to the integrity and survival of Afrikan males. Statistics verify the concern of the Afrikan male as an endangered species (Dove 1990, 43–44).

Some mothers were quite explicit about the way they see the situation. For instance, reflecting on the effects of racism on the young men she taught at a remedial program in a U.S. public school, Ayoluwa from Sankofa, who raised two sons, believes that the problem for young Afrikan youth in these programs lies with their lack of knowledge of self and the failure of white teachers to address their own racism in perceiving and treating these young men as threats. Diallo, from Marcus Garvey in the United Kingdom, was very articulate and emotional about raising her two sons under white supremacy:

> I see what our men have to go through. Years ago I used to slag Black men off thinking they're useless and they're thing, but it's not so. . . . A lot of them do try and they get knocked back and I don't want Muata to get knocked back . . . I'm scared because there are nasty people out there and I don't want my children to get hurt. Sometimes, I'm not glad that I've got boys, I dunno, it's weird, cos I know how Black women are. The white society are not scared of Black women as such, that's why they're giving us the jobs. I said to Muata and Solwazi, "You must go out and get, you have to do well. If they do one, two, you do two, three, four, you don't accept any less." That's what I'm trying to drum into them, because I'm scared of how things are going and sometimes I wish I had girl children.

Another mother who expressed her deep concerns is Ezigbo from the United States. She believes that the boys are at risk. She has one son who has suffered at school and she says of the schooling system in reference to Afrikan males:

> [T]hey don't really give you the same opportunity to feel like you're a part of this whole learning process, simply because of the educational materials that they use. Even from very, very small children the visual things that you're putting in your mind are Caucasian, all the time. So when the children can't identify, they become restless. Instead . . . they [teachers] start to label.

Kesi from Marcus Garvey School is another parent who expressed deep concern about raising sons in a racist and sexist society. She has two sons and one daughter. Commenting on her attempts to raise her sons she believes that

> raising daughters is much easier than raising sons. Not that girls have an easy life but there are protections in place because the woman is expected to need help, whereas the sons are supposed to be macho and strong in a man's world that is made for his benefit.

She is resentful because this is not true, especially for young Afrikan men.

In reality, these mothers do not know if their sons will live. As Adoaha from Marcus Garvey says,

> I have this fear for my boy. Every time my child goes out there I think, gosh, you know, will he come home, will he be alright. Because of the way the climate is. There's a couple of incidents that have happen to him where somebody like stole his hat and somebody punched him, and stuff like that, and it really, really worries me. At the end of the day I think, "Well, if he lives to be fifty, I'll be happy, put it that way." I don't know if it's a negative way of looking at things, but I've got like a fear in me for my children.

These are some of the expressions of mothers with sons and it ties in with the whole work of raising Afrikan males in a society that attempts to prevent them from achieving the classical European male position of power.

While, on the one hand, it is against matriarchal beliefs to produce males who wish to dominate females. On the other hand, in a patriarchal society, it is problematic when males, who are forbidden to carry out the perceived role of "men," are simultaneously debased. Moreover, the existence of many young Afrikan males living in Afrikan townships or urban areas is threatened by drugs and guns controlled by Europeans who profit from the entrepreneurship (in drug dealing) of young men who have little chance of using these skills in a more productive manner. This type of business, while viewed by many to be CIA instigated, is constructed as "illegal" (Lusane 1993). The involvement of Afrikan males in this business endangers the lives of all who live in the neighborhoods. The police can act with impunity to kill young Afrikan men whether they are involved or not. These are some of the very real concerns of the mothers in this study.

Cultural Conflicts

Diallo, who spent her early years in Antigua, felt that her parents, in particular her mother, did not give her the cultural grounding that would have helped her understand some of the negativity that she experienced as an Afrikan person living in the United Kingdom. This background, coupled with the debasement of Blackness, led to her decision to marry a white man.

Amal was raised in the United Kingdom, but her parents are Nigerian. She had difficulties reconciling the contradictions between the values in her home and the values outside. She felt that her parents did not provide her with enough information about who they were and why they believed the things they believed. She understood much later how difficult it was for her parents to live in the United Kingdom with the expectations that they had from colonial Afrika. Her parents insistence on good grades at school became a destructive force in her life. Her parents seemed unable to understand the pressures that she and her sister experienced growing up as Afrikan women, in an environment hostile to their Afrikanness and femaleness.

Fugo, from Zimbabwe, suffered from the same syndrome. Her parents, particularly her father, demanded that she get excellent grades without appearing to understand the trauma of being an Afrikan girl attending all-white schools in the United Kingdom.

Kumiwa who lived in the United States, had a particularly difficult time with her grades. She did not place the value on them that her father did. Her experience with white nuns at a Catholic school failed to help her develop a clear understanding of the value of "education." Not surprisingly, she was experiencing, like the others, schooling, and this had a detrimental affect upon her life.

The emphasis that the parents put on their daughter's receiving good grades is understandable. For Amal and Fugo, whose parents were from colonial Afrika, British schooling was highly regarded. It was perceived as a way that Afrikan people, both males and females, could take control of their lands as neocolonials (at that time, becoming neo-colonial represented becoming independent). I am not trying to imply that Afrikans set out to become neo-colonials. The neo-colonialist analysis is a post-colonial assessment of what, in fact, did happen. The experience for Afrikan girls in the United Kingdom, however, was that it was only important for white males to achieve. Thus, Afrikan girls with such aspirations were like outcasts because under the racialized European patriarchy such ideas could not be conceived of. For Kumiwa, given her own family background, the achievement of good grades was not accompanied by a vision of possibilities. Such ideas did not become apparent to Kuwima until much later in life.

Ironically, Amal, Fugo, and Kumiwa dropped out of school and got pregnant. In part, it was a protest against the values that their parents had placed on school achievement and the realities of their school experiences.

It is ironic that Kumiwa, Amal, and Fugo have set extremely high standards academically for their children, or grandchild in Kumiwa's case. This may be perceived as in some way following the aspirations of their fathers but in a way that is enabling to the children through culturally affirming education. Certainly, once Kumiwa got off the streets, she was able to start on the road to another life, which led to her entry into higher education and her present community expertise as well as her ability to understand the effects of European oppression on Afrikan people. Amal always concentrated on her children's studies and is presently training at college to become a teacher. However, she has studied the her/ history of her people as part of her personal development. Her experiences have laid a groundwork for understanding the cultural nature of what is happening to Afrikan children in the public school system. Fugo is actively involved with her children's schoolwork and is also self-taught about her history as an Afrikan person. In other words, these mothers maintained a belief that gaining academic skills has an important place, even though they dropped out of the schooling system early. At the same time, they are totally aware of the hazards involved in the schooling process for Afrikan children.

Nzinga from St. Kitts and Enomwoyi from Grenada were expected to put household chores ahead of their academic achievement. In Abebe's situation, although her father was Nigerian and placed schooling above everything, when she lived with her mother, who was European, and her stepfather, who was Nigerian, she was expected to stay at home and help raise her siblings. Now as parents, Nzinga, Enomwoyi, and Abebe have high expectations of their children and are involved actively in facilitating their children's success in both the state and Afrikan independent schools. In Abebe's case, she ended her relationship with a European man, whom she loved, because she would not allow her son to be subjected to racist abuse from his family. Nzinga teaches in Marcus Garvey School, which her children attend, as well as working as a cook in a public school. Enomwoyi stays all day Saturday with her children at Queen Nzinga and works there during the week to help run the parent group and support parents who need advice for their children who are attending state/public schools. Abebe works as a librarian in Queen Nzinga School and teaches part-time in her son's state school. Of course, it is clear that all the interviewees have extremely high expectations that their children will do well academically as well as become well-rounded persons who understand their Afrikanness and cultural groundings. Perhaps it is more surprising when women who have had difficult and sometimes painful lives become powerful educators and intellectuals who hold visions for their children even beyond those held for them.

Part 2: Mothers and Schooling

U.S. Mothers

Many of these interviewees have a proficient level of skills and degrees gained from schooling. There were many university-educated parents involved in the creation of Sankofa School. I believe that this can be traced to the founding members. The early meetings, that were open to interested community members, were initiated by Dr. Nzegwu, who ran her own culturally affirming daycare center. Two of the major strategists who subsequently became involved in the actualization of the school hold Ph.Ds. Each started her own full-time Afrikan-centered school over eighteen years ago in other cities. This is very relevant because at the time of this study they both taught at the local university. Through their courses and networking they were able to recruit interested parties from the university population.

For example, I studied under one of these professors and became a founding member of the Sankofa School as a result of my background with supplementary schools in the United Kingdom and the nature of my graduate research. Moreover, their association with another professor from another local college led to Camara applying for the position of head teacher. Aisha, Ife, Kumiwa, and Aidoo, who use Sankofa, were linked to the university population as either graduate students or tutors and administrators like Mawasi, Jaha, and Adaeze, who do not use Sankofa. Nalo who does not use Sankofa and is a public school teacher, belongs to the same Black teachers organization as one of the professors. Ironically, Adaeze and Nalo played a significant role in supporting Sankofa in its early stages.

Binta, Ayoluwa, Dalmar, and Ezigbo do not attend the university or work in it in any capacity. Binta is training to become a nursery school teacher, Dalmar has a degree in business, Ayoluwa is self-taught and has been teaching for years, and Ezigbo is a consultant in herbalism.

Another interesting and significant factor in the United States group is that everyone but Ezigbo has taught children other than her own. Binta, Dalmar, and Aidoo were trained through Head Start. At the time of the interviews, Binta was teaching at her mother's nursery using an Afrikan-centered approach. Aidoo was teaching Spanish at Sankofa. Ayoluwa had taught as a teacher's aid in alternative schools, did remedial teaching with Afrikan students in the public school system, and was teaching yoga at Sankofa.

Of those mothers who do not use Sankofa, Adaeze and Nalo are public school teachers. Jaha and Mawasi are university administrators who teach and counsel Afrikan students in "minority programs." Ife, who uses Sankofa, is also a "minority program" administrator.

Aisha and Adaeze are the only two teachers who have not taught predominantly Afrikan students. Aisha's experience with college students was so negative that she gave up teaching. Her experience of growing up in St. Vincent with little material wealth and learning how to read and write without pencils and paper, coupled with her thirst for knowledge, shaped her view that the students did not value "education." I would add that from her description of the students' behaviors and attitudes, it is possible that these white students did not respect her as a young Afrikan female teacher. This treatment is nothing new for Afrikan teachers in white institutions either in the United Kingdom or in the United States

Interestingly, only Ayoluwa, Ezigbo, and Binta do not have degrees. Ezigbo and Binta linked the racism of their school experiences to their decisions not to continue with higher education. While most of the United States interviewees have degrees, only one of the United Kingdom group of mothers has a degree or the equivalent in psychiatric nursing. As earlier explicated, this situation is I believe reflective of the role of the professors who helped found Sankofa and their influence on recruiting university-based mothers. There is no evidence to suggest that such a high percentage of degreed persons normally have their children attend Afrikan-centered schools generally.

Although the high incidence of university-educated and teacher-trained women can be traced to the university professors' involvement in the formation of Sankoa, we may also view the academic backgrounds of these parents as a measure of the achievements of the women and their struggles and their economic status. Perhaps we can link these achievements in most cases to the struggles and sacrifices of their parents who believed like most Afrikan people that succeeding in school would help to create an easier life. The mothers or female caretakers of all the interviewees, except for Ife's grandmother, who went to the Hampton Institute, did not have a university education. At the same time, it is important to note that for those who grew up in the city, before the closing of the mines and the subsequent economic depression, there was the belief and possibility that the daughters of the miners would go to school and achieve greater things than their parents. Perhaps this is every parent's dream. It is much more difficult for Afrikan parents under white supremacy to believe in and achieve such dreams.

U.K. Mothers

Perhaps the raw racism within the state/public schools in the U.K. was so powerful that it prevented most of the mothers in this study from going on to or completing higher education. In general, far fewer Afrikan people go on to university than their white counterparts. Speaking from my own experiences of dealing with the rampant overt and covert racism and sexism in the British school system, the abuse was such that I was almost forty years old before I could see the possible benefit of going back to school. It is clear from the interviews with Nzinga, Kesi, Amal, and Fugo that the memories of their racist experiences are as vivid as mine. I must add the experiences of Binta, Camara, and Ezigbo from the U.S. group to that list. I believe that the aversion of the U.K. mothers to school and the racism that abounded there related very much to the fact that they lived in white areas and attended white schools, unlike the majority of the U.S. parents in this study. Similarly, Camara, Binta, and Ezigbo went to mixed, predominantly white schools when they experienced this racism.

For Fugo, Nzinga, Enomwoyi, Kesi, Diallo, and Adoaha, the negative experiences of white schools was a stark contrast with their experiences of living in Afrika and the Caribbean. I believe to some extent they suffered from a cultural shock during the early part of their experiences in the United Kingdom. Although Amal was born in the United Kingdom, she visited Nigeria and was able to make a comparison between the types of schooling. In Nigeria, she believed that the materials that the children used were not as blatantly racist as she had been used to in the United Kingdom. The general racist treatment of these mothers by teachers and students as well as the derogation of Afrikan women, men, and children in the curriculum played a major role in shaping their feelings about their choices not to remain in or return to school.

As earlier explicated, the fathers' pressure on Fugo and Amal to gain high grades very likely added to their dislike of school. In fact, I do not believe that the racism of European domination that invalidates the Afrikan ability to gain skills can be separated from these fathers' insistence that their daughters succeed in becoming professionals. At the same time, as men from Afrika, their decisions about their daughters' schooling reflected plans that their daughters would probably live in Afrika as professionals.

Enomwoyi enjoyed her schooling in the Caribbean. She was the only parent who does not recall being exposed to personal racism when she attended school in the United Kingdom. However, she believes that her children experience racism in their schooling.

Enomwoyi's feeling that there was little racism when she attended white school may well have related to her concentration on her stepfather's molestation and her mother's insistence on prioritizing her role in housekeeping and taking care of her sisters. In this context, school may well have been a welcome relief. Although Enomwoyi left school with no qualifications, her skills in catering and sewing helped her to remain constantly employed.

In Nzinga's situation, despite her father's behavior and her home life, she hated her treatment at school. Ironically, it was her father who sometimes sprung to her defense against racist teachers. However, he was like the fathers of Amal, Kumiwa, and Fugo in that they had a blind faith in the teachers' evaluations of their daughters. As they have all expressed, this situation put unreasonable pressures on them. After walking out on her father, Nzinga attended college and studied for a diploma. Shortly before completing her diploma, she left because of the way her tutor treated her ideas. This did not deter her; she was able to gain office skills and become easily employable.

By the time Kesi had left school she had no qualifications but started in an office job gaining skills that enabled her to work with computers. Amal left school with a few CSEs. As most people are aware, the Certificate of Education (CSE) means very little in the world of skilled employment. The CSEs merely show a level of attainment within a subject area. However, these examination passes can provide a basis for qualifying to take General Certificates of Education (GCEs) at Ordinary level (O-level) and then Advanced level (A-level) examinations. Taking A-level examinations can then qualify one for going to university and taking a degree. The standard of A-level is the equivalent of first-year work in a university. One may complete school without any examination certificates, one's qualification for leaving is age. One may leave school at the age of sixteen.

Fugo reached A-level status and dropped out of college before completing her A-level examinations. Diallo gained a few CSEs. She worked at all kinds of jobs. She eventually joined a women's training center and became a carpenter. Adoaha, who found school in the United Kingdom to be much less demanding academically than in Trinidad, became a fully trained psychiatric nurse but never returned after her first year of practice.

Nzinga, Adoah, and Diallo are educators at the Marcus Garvey School. They are self-taught. They have learned about Afrikan history and culture through their support of the school and their children. The mothers have known each other for a few years and have grown together and support each other outside the school. Kesi's children also attend the school, but she does not teach in it. Both Kesi and Nzinga work full-time in the state school that their children attend. They are "dinner ladies" in the school dining-hall so that they may watch over their children during the hours that their children attend the state/public school. Both of these mothers are qualified for more skilled and better paying employment but have sacrificed this opportunity in order to guard their children and in Nzinga's case, other Afrikan children.

At Queen Nzinga School, Enomwoyi, Amal, Fugo, and Abebe attend the school all day Saturday and play critical roles in the running of the school and the Black parent organization that it is affiliated with. Amal is presently pursuing a teaching degree in order to teach in the school. Abebe is studying for a teaching degree in the Montessori method, as well learning how to teach children with dyslexia. In this way she is able to work in the state school her son attends. She helps her son and other Afrikan children who have dyslexia. Furthermore, she hopes to use these skills to teach at Queen Nzinga School, which her son attends on Saturdays. She is presently the librarian at Queen Nzinga School. Abebe, who missed a lot of school to help raise her siblings, left school with few CSEs. However, she gained office skills in her employment and eventually ran her own accounting agency, earning over $35,000 per year. Fugo is the chairperson of the parent group and Enomwoyi works as an administrator at the Queen Nzinga School.

While none of the mothers in the U.K. group has a degree, except Adoaha, all the mothers have and are playing a powerful role in their children's education. They are self-taught in that through their own determination they have acquired skills and educated themselves to a proficient level that enables them to challenge the public school system and support culturally affirming schools in some capacity.

It may be relevant to add that entry into higher education and the university for Afrikan people is difficult owing to the different his/herstories of Afrikan people in the United Kingdom. It is only since the late 1940s that Afrikan people in predominantly large numbers from the Caribbean and Afrika have entered into the United Kingdom. This is not to deny the Afrikan presence in the United Kingdom for centuries, rather it is to emphasize that the social changes that involve the presence of Afrikan people with positions of status and even a substantial middle class is negligible compared to the United States. After centuries of the Afrikan presence in North America, Afrikan people have achieved a measure of success within imposed segregation to develop a substantial middle class and independent Black institutions, as well as gain access to white institutions through affirmative action policies.

As mentioned earlier, supplementary schools are virtually run on a voluntary basis so that if parents pay anything it is minimal. For this reason, mothers are generally a lot less well off than their counterparts in the United States, who normally pay tuition fees in order to maintain these institutions on a full-time basis. It may be the case that the academic success of the number of parents in the U.S. group reflects their involvement in higher-paying jobs that require more credentials. At the same time, as already mentioned, many of these parents came out of a university setting because of the influence of professors who, in helping Sankofa develop, had at the same time recruited university-based mothers to use the school. However, if another study was designed to incorporate the present set of mothers using Sankofa in the United States, I know that they are a lot less academically skilled. As in the case of the United Kingdom mothers, this would certainly not indicate their level of intellectuality. I believe that the mothers who held degrees were no more conscious of racism than those without them. In fact, the four mothers who do not send their children to Sankofa, Mawasi, Nalo, Adaeze, and Jaha have degrees and are employed in well-paid professional jobs.

Reasons for Sending the Children to Culturally Affirming Schools

In the London study (1990) all the parents sent their children to supplementary schools because they were dissatisfied with the public school system's inherent racism. However, not all the schools that were in that study were culturally affirming. In this study, those parents who send their children to the culturally affirming schools both in the United States and the United Kingdom have all been very concerned about the effects of racism in all its forms upon their children. Some parents have been proactive and some reactive. This largely depended upon their level of awareness about the pervasiveness and complexity of racism and/or the availability of culturally affirming schools.

Racism and Schooling the Children

It is clear from the interviews that most of the mothers believed that their children had experienced racism of some kind during their public/state school experiences. Some of these experiences related to overt racism. For example, from the United States, Ife, Binta, and Camara were aware of the negative treatment of their children. Parents from the United Kingdom, Nzinga, Kesi, Ezigbo, and Abebe, were also aware of teachers' undermining their children's integrity and academic potential. These parents were all actively involved with their children in the public/state school system and were aware of what was happening to their children in the classroom setting. However, Camara, Binta, Abebe, and Nzinga were active in challenging teachers' behavior and/or the curriculum, not only for their children but also for all Afrikan children. Mothers like Dalmar, Aisha from the United States, and Amal from the United Kingdom recognized a serious problem when their children exhibited symptoms of wanting to be, or thinking that they were white. Amal's son developed an aversion to being near the presence of other Afrikan children as a result of attending a white school full-time. Aisha's daughter became very upset when she realized that she was not white. The mothers located the source of the problem to be the schooling system and the reflection of whiteness as normal or superior. These occurrences led the interviewees to put their children almost immediately in culturally affirming schools. In Dalmar's case, although only her middle daughter was exhibiting obvious signs, she took a proactive stance and also put her youngest daughter in the school at the age of four years. In order to pay the tuition, she worked in the school to offset the payments.

Diallo from Marcus Garvey, on her own admission, became conscious of her "Blackness" and the history of her people later on in her life. Ironically, white lesbian women had led her to the discovery of her own Afrikanity. Until that time, she was not consciously aware of the effects of racism on herself or her sons. For a time, when Diallo was younger, she can remember that she believed that she was white. This was a way of tackling blatant racism. It becomes clear to young Afrikan children that being white offers privileges. Ignoring one's Blackness is to make invisible one's supposed inhumanity. Diallo's increasing awareness of her "Blackness" was contextualized by her developing knowledge of the positive and humane qualities of Afrikan people. This realization led to her decision to send her sons to Marcus Garvey School. She became involved in the school and began making demands in the public/ state school system.

Other parents, like the U.S. parents Ayoluwa, Kumiwa, Aidoo, and Nalo and the United Kingdom parents, Adoaha and Fugo were proactive in dealing with school racism. They had an overall understanding of the need for their children to receive information about their cultural history prior to their children attending public/state school. For instance, Ayoluwa had always been actively involved in alternative schools. She jumped at the chance to initiate, develop, and use an Afrikan-centered school for her youngest child. In fact, she was a pivotal force because of her experience and conviction that the public school system is no good for Afrikan children. Her experience of attending and working in public school to try and repair some of its victims, had made Ayoluwa very conscious of the condition of Afrikan children.

Kumiwa became increasingly aware of some of the sociopsycho dynamics of racism because of her involvement in the Nation of Islam and later in her social work. Again, like Ayoluwa, she was a pivotal person in the early development of Sankofa School. She sent her granddaughter to Sankofa School without allowing her to ever attend a public school.

As a doctoral student, Aidoo, who identifies herself as Puerto Rican and not Afrikan because of her very light skin and her political conditioning, was concerned about her child, who was born in America and looks very Afrikan. While Nalo never used Sankofa, she was very conscious, as a public school teacher, of the racism within the school system. Adoaha became involved with Marcus Garvey through her husband and his family, who started the school thirty years earlier. By the time Fugo had birthed her last three children, she was a Rastafarian. She was by now politically aware and conscious of the effects of racism on all Afrikan people. She sent her children to Queen Nzinga School while they were very young. Enomwoyi's son, in particular, was picked on by white children at school and began falling behind in his schoolwork. Her decision to send him to Queen Nzinga School was based on her son's needing help with his schoolwork. She took him along with his sisters to the school on Saturdays. In reality, her awareness of the pervasiveness of racism really began after she became involved in the school, met other parents, and saw the changes in her children.

Adaeze, Jaha, and Mawazi, who do not send their children to Sankofa School, did not believe that racism played a substantial role in their children's schooling experiences in the way that the other parents did. All the other parents were concerned about the impact of racism on their children through teachers, curriculum, and other students.

As earlier explicated, a significant finding in the 1990 London study showed that the impact of racism was the major influence in the decision to send their children to supplementary schools. Using racism as a context, I categorized some reasons that parents gave for sending children to these schools. These categories are not in any specific order. I found that parents wanted:

1. Teacher support and help
2. Cultural awareness
3. Black/Afrikan history
4. A better learning environment
5. A Black/Afrikan perspective
6. Positive role models
7. Relationships with other Black/Afrikan children.

In the Ratteray and Shujaa study (1987), similar categories were also identified with the addition of concerns about self-concept and self-image. In the present study, these categories are useful for identifying reasons that the parents chose to use culturally affirming schools. I believe that their dissatisfaction with state/public schooling is based either on their own experiences, the experiences of their older children, the experiences of those children that attend the school, or even the experiences of Afrikan children in the community.

It is as a result of these in-depth interviews that I am able to draw this conclusion. However, it might be fairly obvious that this is the case for all the mothers, but it is through in-depth interviews with them that one can make these associations. The point is that when a parent is approached with a question of this kind, that is, "Why do you send your child to this school?," the parent may not have the time to analyze the number of variables that have influenced that decision. I have categorized the reasons that the interviewees gave for sending their children to this school and then related them to their own experiences in a series of brief summaries. I have not defined the terms that they have used because to an extend I believe that we all have at least some understanding of what these terms mean outside the academic context.

The Sankofa School Mothers (U.S.). When Kumiwa became involved in the development of the school, she wanted her granddaughter to attend in order to develop her self-concept. I believe that she based this idea on her own experiences with teaching Afrikan children in after school programs as well as her own life struggle as an Afrikan woman who was without direction.

Aidoo desires a good pedagogy, a secure environment, and good role models. She based these desires, I believe, on her knowledge as a teacher and concern as a parent.

Aisha wants her daughter to develop a positive self-concept because of the child's desire to be white. Aisha was aware that, culturally, her early life experience in St. Vincent had helped in the development of her own self-concept. This school provides the type of environment that mirrors that experience. Binta wants the school to provide Black history and self-esteem for her son. She realizes the importance of these needs based on her own school experiences.

Ezigbo desired cultural affirmation and the development of self-concept and self-identity for her daughter, especially given her son's experience and her own early schooling, where, as she put it, she just "drifted through."

Ayoluwa believes that Black history and self-esteem are crucial for the healthy development of an Afrikan child. She realized the practical application of this while raising her own children and providing remedial teaching for Afrikan children in the public school system.

Dalmar needs the development of self-esteem and self-identity for her child, who she felt was confused, had become withdrawn, and believed that she was white. She felt that going to a white school had been too intimidating for her daughter, given her own grounding in Black schools.

Ife required a school environment conducive for her child's growth toward becoming a critical thinker. It was obvious that the "gifted and talented" school had failed to provide that environment. Because of her own school background growing up in Harlem, she sees that a culturally affirming environment is the key.

The reasons for sending the children to the school relate to their expectations as well as their experiences as users of the school. Ironically, a major aspect of Afrikan-centered schools not mentioned, but perhaps the most important reason why most of the parents chose the school, is the cultural affirmation provided by the school. This feeds into the development of self-esteem and self-concept. The importance of cultural affirmation to these mothers is implied by their expectations of what the school can provide, since they are aware that the school introduces Afrikan-centered cultural values and beliefs through the principles and philosophies of the school. Most of the parents want their children to be aware of themselves as Afrikan people.

The Marcus Garvey School Mothers (U.K.).   Adoaha has been involved in a culturally affirming school since her children were born and her husband was educated in the one that his father started over thirty years ago. Reasons for her children attending range from promoting self-love, understanding Afrikan and Caribbean history, being among Afrikan children, developing a Black perspective, and having a cultural background, to understanding one's identity and being among and learning about positive role models.

Nzinga wants her children to experience a positive environment, know their history, develop a love of self, be culturally grounded, and understand their identity. Nzinga grew up in St. Kitts with all of the above. The cultural shock of coming to the United Kingdom enabled her to understand the depth of racist and sexist debasement and the importance of a culturally affirming school to her children's lives.

Diallo sends her children to a culturally affirming school so that they can be in a positive environment, understand their true history, be proud of their Blackness, and see and read about positive role models. Once Diallo became conscious of herself and her relationship to Afrikan people, she was angry that she had been so unaware. Therefore, she wants her children to be grounded so that they can be aware and proud of themselves at an early age.

Kesi is adamant that her sons should know Black history, be in a positive environment, and have a cultural foundation. She was failed by the school system and has witnessed the same thing happening to her sons.

The Queen Nzinga School Mothers (U.K.). Abebe wants her son to be culturally grounded within an environment that can sustain this need. At the same time, she wants him to understand Afrikan and Caribbean history. Visiting Afrika as both a child and adult has made Abebe conscious of the attempt to Europeanize Afrika as well as Afrikan people.

When Amal's son exhibited signs of not wanting to be with or communicate with Afrikan children, she sent him and his younger sister to Queen Nzinga School so that they could be in a positive environment with other Afrikan children, develop a positive self-concept, have a cultural base, learn about their identity, and have a teacher and parent support network. Her decision was influenced by her own painful struggles in school.

Enomwoyi wants her son and daughters to be culturally grounded and have the teacher's support. This relates to her love of Grenada and desire for her children to achieve academically because she did not and because she felt disadvantaged as a result.

Fugo is planning to return to Afrika. In the meantime, she wants her children to develop a positive self-concept, know their history, know about Afrika, and learn in a positive environment. Her Catholic school upbringing has translated into a Rastafarian spiritual belief that provides the basis for teaching her children to respect themselves as Afrikan people.

Interestingly, the children of Nzinga, Kesi, Adoaha, Diallo, Fugo, Enomwoyi, and Amal have all visited their mother's homeland or in the case of Abebe, the father's. Thus, while the schools operate in a part-time capacity to ground their children culturally, their visits have helped them to experience another reality outside the United Kingdom. In this way, it has cemented their belief in and understanding of their Afrikanity. According to the mothers, for all the children, the experience has been wonderful especially with their guidance. Importantly, Fugo is building a house in Zimbabwe and Enomwoyi plans to build a home in Grenada. Abebe wants to take her son to Nigeria and she wishes to teach and live there.

It is clear that the mothers' links to their homelands offer an important dimension to the culturally affirming school experiences of their children. The visits to their parents' homelands enables them to understand their Afrikaness in less constrained environments than those of the United Kingdom and the United States. For instance, Sankofa School is situated in a city where the Afrikan population is underemployed and no longer affluent. The typical stress of living under direct white supremacy is obvious. For parents who use Sankofa, the desire to visit an Afrikan country may be a difficult undertaking when home has been in a city in the United States for several generations. Thus, while the schools in the United Kingdom are, for the moment, only part-time, the link to a home outside the United Kingdom compensates for this to some degree.

In the U.S. mothers' group, Aisha is from St. Vincent in the Caribbean and, like the United Kingdom mothers, was greatly influenced by her cultural grounding to register her child in the Afrikan-centered school. Interestingly, Ayoluwa, although she was born and raised in the States, has also visited Afrika, which confirmed many of her ideas. However, as a child, she has the vivid recollection of moving out of her Afrikan community into the projects. At that time, the projects were new and her family was one of only five Afrikan families in the neighborhood. She described this change in her life as,

> tantamount to Afrikans being pulled out of Afrika and brought here. So I had a very bad reaction. I was physically sick . . . not having my friends and not being nurtured in my little street.

From then on, her grades deteriorated. From this vivid description, it is possible to see how parents born into a western-oriented setting, while living in an Afrikan community, were shielded from the raw sting of white supremacy but became exposed to it on entry into mixed schools. In other words, a cultural grounding exists in Afrikan communities and the decision to use culturally affirming schools may be related also to that social reality.

Consciousness-Raising Influences

While recognizing that schools of this kind have been evolving since before the 1960s, the impact of that period on the parents is recognized by some of them. For instance, the influence of the Honorable Elijah Muhammad and the Nation of Islam in the lives of the United States women is startling. Ezigbo is a Muslim and was converted at the age of fifteen. Her family objected to her decision, but grew to accept it. Kumiwa was brought into the Mosque through the father of her fourth and last child when she was twenty-four years old. The baby's father was in rehabilitation and Kumiwa sent the minister, her friend, to help him. Subsequently, he joined the Nation and so did she. This decision helped her to believe in herself and was one of the major turning points that led her to abandon street life. Ife also joined the Nation of Islam and was a follower of the Honorable Elijah Muhammad for a while. She was greatly affected by this experience and she still admires him for what he did for Afrikan people.

Ayoluwa joined the Nation of Islam and was married to a member of the Nation. She still practices disciplines from eating habits to behavior that she learned. Binta's mother is a member of the Nation of Islam and encourages and helps financially to send her grandson to the school. Nalo is also a Muslim. Finally, Dalmar's brother-in-law is a Muslim and has an influence on their family's thinking. She has attended some meetings at which major orators have appeared.

It is interesting that Kumiwa, Ife, and Ayoluwa were not happy with the sexism in the Nation of Islam when they were involved. Ife and Ayoluwa actively attempted to change the situation by making demands for women. All, regardless, took with them the value of understanding the structural nature of white racism or anti-Black racism and anti-Afrikan racism that contextualized their experiences. The significance of a Black nationalist influence in these women's ideas may also be indicative of the impact that the Black Power movement and the independent struggles in Afrika had in the lives of Afrikan people living in America. Perhaps most Afrikan women and men who have been touched by these ideas have family who have been involved in one way or another.

The influence of the Black Muslims among the U.S. group, I believe, can be attributed to the parents' beliefs in the principles and values of the Sankofa School, which advocates the idea of self-determination, self-respect, and self-defense as fundamental to the building of a nation. The idea of nation-building, however, is not religiously influenced. The idea of Afrikan people working together to fight against the destruction of Afrikan civilization may have drawn together people of like mind regardless of religion. These observations suggest that this school may continue to draw parents with similar ideas.

In the United Kingdom, I found that the influence of the Nation of Islam and its religious aspects had been relatively weak, but recently has grown significantly. While it has not had an obvious impact on any of the U.K. mothers, Rastafarianism and Afrikan independence struggles probably have. The Black nationalist ideology is one that is recognized there as well as in the Caribbean and Afrika. While only Fugo, from Zimbabwe, spoke of herself as a Rastafarian, Enomwoyi and Amal, from Nigeria, wear dreadlocks, cover their heads, and believe that their children should go to culturally affirmative schools. Moreover, during my observations of the school that their children attend, over time, a number of teachers were dreadlocked as were the children and all carried themselves with the dignity of Rastafarians. Associated with the wearing of dreadlocks is a lifestyle that is essentially Afrikan and that has survived in the Caribbean. Certainly, the support of culturally affirming schools is reflective of Rastafarian beliefs. This is not surprising when one considers that the largest Afrikan group in the United Kingdom is from the Caribbean, although, more recently Afrikan people from the continent have entered the United Kingdom in greater numbers. An interesting phenomenon that has occurred is the mixing of Afrikan peoples and the influence of the Caribbean languages upon the young. Thus, you will find Afrikan as well as so-called mixed race (Afrikan and European) girls and boys and women and men who speak as though they and their families are from the Caribbean. In fact, as I earlier asserted, supplementary schools generally have come out of the Caribbean experience and in the main are directed and run by Caribbean people.

Within this milieu, young Afrikan people grow up influenced by the Caribbean story. In public school, little is known of Afrika beyond understanding it as the continent where Afrikan people were captured and enslaved, or, a place of starving people who do not know how to rule themselves. The Caribbean has had a focal point in terms of locating the origins of the influx of formerly enslaved Afrikan people or former British West Indies subjects. Constructed knowledge of this kind has been painful to the young child raised in Britain as it has been for their counterparts in the United States. The capturing and enslavement of Afrikan people bears the mark of shame. Young people have difficulty understanding why their ancestors allowed this to happen. Using the clash of cultures concept, it becomes apparent that might does not always represent right. Moreover, given the cultural distinctions between matriarchal and patriarchal values, it becomes clear that matriarchal morality is one that cannot condone the demise of an innocent people.

Importantly, the Caribbean presence has been a powerful force in voicing its opinion on urban streets when Afrikan youth have made political demands to the powers that be. Even within matriarchal values, the right to defend oneself in war has always been morally correct. Moreover, the influence of the Rastafarian belief system and values has been possibly as powerful in essence as the Black Muslim movement in the United States, especially concerning the role of white supremacy and the concept of Babylon and its destructive effect upon the potential of Afrikan people to become self-determining. However, this does not negate the influence of independence movements in Afrika. While not highlighted within the public school curriculum, like Rastafarianism, the knowledge of these movements enters the hearts and minds of Afrikan people in many different ways.

The Rastafarian story is the story of resistance. It is firmly grounded in the his/herstory of Afrikan resistance to European domination in the Caribbean, which began with the Maroons.[3] Horace Campbell (1987) concisely locates the origin of the Rastafarian movement in the Maroon resistance. Its effect upon Afrikan people in the United Kingdom has possibly been underrated. However, when one understands the critical role that cultural memory has played in the survival of Afrikan women and men, it begins to make sense. My own involvement in the Rastafarian movement in the United Kingdom directed me on the road to understanding that it is possible as an ordinary person to reconstruct the stories of our people as well as envisage a self-determining future for Afrikan people. Like the Nation of Islam, the Rastafarian beliefs are able to reach and appeal to the hearts of those most disenfranchised by white society.

Culturally Affirmative Schools as Opposed to Black Schools

Three ideological camps can be located within independent Black institutions: (1) the integrationist, (2) the culturally affirmative, and (3) the religious. The integrationists believe that they can find a place in the existing social order and compete on some egalitarian basis if they persevere. These Black-run institutions are trying to develop Black Americans or Black people in the United Kingdom or Black Britons, who are proficient in reading, writing, and arithmetic, have a positive self-concept, who will be brilliant and can lead and teach in a society where only the color of the leadership needs to change. However, the society would still be based on the same exploitative oppressive cultural determinants.

The culturally affirmative schools, which include the Afrikan-centered schools, are as independent as the Black-run integrationist institutions. Where they differ, is that although culturally affirmative schools wish to cultivate a new Afrikan who will be brilliant and can lead and teach, s/he is expected to be culturally aware of the world situation concerning Afrikan people. She must be able to align herself with the development of a new global vision of what is necessary to deconstruct the continual plight of Afrikan people under white supremacy. In other words, the culturally centered Afrikan graduate is expected to have a vision of possibilities about an Afrikan future outside the framework of the European paradigm.

Finally, there is evidence to show that a culturally affirming perspective is possible in the religious independent schools in the case of the Christian schools and the Black Muslim schools. Certainly, in the case of the Black Muslim position on self-determination for Afrikan people it is a central theme. Religious schools, however, may be European-centered if they follow Western beliefs and traditions. Historically, both the Christian and Islamic traditions of spirituality are alien reflections of the Afrikan indigenous spiritual models that preceeded them. These descriptions are brief and not rigid, rather they provide a summary of ideological positions. In fact, they may overlap to some degree.

Importantly, whatever the ideological bases of the independent Black/Afrikan school settings, parents may have different reasons for using the schools. For instance, some parents who send their children to culturally affirmative or Nation of Islam schools wish their children to become proficient academically and become part of the establishment.

For a profound understanding of parental choice and standing with regard to their children's schooling, Mwalimu Shujaa (1994, 17) provides an excellent analytical conceptual model that provides insight in this area. The model shows how decisions are influenced by the interplay between a society's structural conditions and members' achievement, expectations, and perceptions about the quality of their lives.

In the Ratteray and Shujaa study and my London study the schools included represent these three types. Thus, it is possible to see from the parents' concerns with racism and satisfaction with the schools that they use that these schools all provide similar environments. They carry out the necessary and equal functions of providing a safe haven with the love, care, and respect that these children need for their spiritual, mental, and physical well-being. However, the parents' expectations can differ in any of these schools and this difference can be located in some of the interviews.

In the Ratteray and Shujaa study, one parent uses a Black institution because he sees the environment as ideal for a Black child. It mirrors his experience at Moorehouse College and gives his child self-assurance. He is aware that, as a result of racism, when a Black child comes into a white environment it will change him.

> You see a Black kid that may not be groomed properly, whereas in a Black environment he's going to get that love and tender love and care that he needs, whereas in a white school that kid could very well be labeled as a kid with a problem, learning disabilities, because nobody wants to take the time to get close to him.

Another parent had sent his child to an Afrikan-centered school prior to the school that the child was in at the time of the study.

> It had become too Black. I didn't want my child asking why a white man had killed Martin Luther King. I don't think they can understand that in school or why we were treated as a slave. Yes, I know it's a part of our heritage. It happened a long time ago, it's part of our history. But we don't want to talk about too much of the past. We would like to talk more about the child's future. Where they're going from now.

This parent objected to celebrating only "Black" holidays and wearing dashikis. He saw these practices as being racially motivated and causing hate. He is obviously satisfied that although this school is a Black institution it is not Afrikan-centered or too Black. Yet he prefers the Black school to a white school because he understands his child's need to have a non-abusive environment.

Conversely, at an Afrikan-centered school in the Ratteray and Shujaa study, the parent is happy that her child is not pushed by the teacher, who gives the children individual attention and allows the children to master skills. She is pleased that her child knows about Afrika, geography, and famous Black people whom she didn't know about and is also learning about. The parent is unsure of whether her child should be around other cultures, but finds that the child is self-assured, friendly, and gets on well with other children.

I will try to show why some parents become insecure with the idea of using an Afrikan-centered school by analyzing the answers provided by the women in the present study who chose not to use Sankofa. I set up a frame of reference in which to understand how the social pressures and the accompanying mental state caused by racism creates confusion and contradictions in the minds of Afrikan people who live in the West. This framework is based on a composite of the ideas of three Afrikan activists—two psychiatrists and one psychologist. I use Frances Cress Welsing, Frantz Fanon, and Na'im Akbar to provide an understanding of the psychology of racist oppression that influences our ideas, behaviors, and attitudes, particularly with regard to the conditions of Afrikans and ways of changing them. My objective in creating this framework is to locate the interviewees with regard to their commitment to Afrikan-centered schools.

Importantly, there were only four parents who do not use the school in the United States. I met these mothers because of their interest in playing a role in the founding of the Sankofa School. Three of the mothers are involved in the university and the fourth mother teaches in the public school system. All four mothers were thinking about sending their children to Sankofa, but they eventually decided against sending their children. I did not contact other parents in the United Kingdom who did not use culturally-affirmative schools. Thus, while, these parents only represent a small percentage of nonusers of culturally affirming schools, I believe that their perspectives help us to understand other parents who are caught up in similar dilemmas.

Reasons for Not Sending Children to Sankofa School (U.S.)

Frances Cress Welsing (1991) defines Black defensive logic as one based on the fear of death at the hands of the white supremacist collective. This is a repressed fear that cannot be admitted by the adult Afrikan population. As a result of covering the fear, there emerges a sick protective logic that fosters the belief that there is no longer a problem with white supremacy. The patterns of defensive logic emphasize that existing problems largely stem from Afrikan people. This is reflective of self-hate (pp. 156–57). A high level of fear generates what Cress Welsing calls circular thought. This is a pattern of thought that moves away from problem perception and also diverts attention from problem solving into generating more fear. If one understands that the brain is a computer that is an instrument of problem solving, then circular thought is like the short-circuiting of logic networks. Ideally, problem perception and problem solution should be approached and managed in a linear manner, step by step (p. 153).

Frantz Fanon argues that: "Under conditions of prolonged oppression there are three modes of psychological defense and identity development. The first involves a pattern of compromise, the second flight and the third fight" (Bulhan 1985, 193). Finally, Na'im Akbar (1991) sees the lack of respect for Afrikan leadership as one of the most destructive influences that has emerged from the enslavement of Afrikan people. The devaluation of such leadership is associated with the systematic removal of any prospective natural leader through isolation, ridicule, or death. Instead, a leader who is authorized or accepted by the establishment is preferred. Because of the history of punishment and oppression, natural leaders are seen as a threat to the acquiescence of the oppressed community by both the oppressed and the oppressor. This situation has conditioned Afrikan people to fear and be disrespectful or suspicious of real leaders (pp. 15–17).

Together these concepts present a model that can explain how one can repress an awareness of the historical perpetuation of oppression through fear to such an extent that the oppressed person is psychologically prevented from comprehending the nature of the oppressive power relations. Therefore, attempts to reveal the true nature of the situation and to work toward change are thwarted by minds conditioned to blame and hate ourselves. This is done partly as a way of warding off the pain of seeing truth, and therefore, the knowledge of the necessary risk incurred by the need to build a movement toward real change. The levels of the realization of the true conditions provide a guide to where the mothers in my study are in relation to their decisions to send or not send their children to the Afrikan-centered school.

I call this model "the trust factor." I add to this model the idea that part of the reason for the lack of respect for ourselves is the belief that has been perpetrated in the dominant culture that we are less than human and that our culture is backward. Thus, to be an Afrikan is to be a savage. The myth is part of that oppression. That is why to believe in an Afrikan-centered or culturally affirming school is the beginning of believing in our own credibility as humans no matter where we exist. For instance, not all parents who send their children to culturally affirming schools understand the true meaning of the school. However, they may see some worth in the care and nurturing of self-awareness that these schools provide. This is in itself a radical move when choice is taken into account.

Not all parents who send their children to other Black-run educational institutions want their children to become part of the status quo. Like culturally affirming schools, these schools provide the environment in which Afrikan children can be nurtured and protected against the racism of white or public schools. Again, parents who send their children to public school certainly do not want their children to fail academically, and may hope their children will become revolutionary leaders.

What in-depth interviews can do is make connections between experiences and the way parents think and act. Interviews of this kind can show what parents' expectations of the schools are, how well parents accept what these schools stand for, and the level of their commitment to change. Aidoo is an example of a person who does not assign priority to the goals of the Sankofa School. The prime objective in sending her child was not related to the Afrikan-centered aspect of the school. She did agree that it had some relevance. However, she did not identify herself as a Black woman until the end of our interview. Throughout she thought of herself as a Puerto Rican. Many Puerto Ricans do not distinguish themselves on the grounds of race or color. Yet Puerto Rican society is not homogeneous; the white Spanish descended class owns the land stolen from the Taino, First Nations, people and rules the Afrikan persons and descendants who are the poorest. Aidoo was particularly hostile toward the seven principles of the school—the Nguzo Saba. She defined the Nguzo Saba as bourgeois. To my mind she is caught up in the European ideology of class and is unable to understand the racist dynamics affecting Afrikan people's lives, including her child's and her own. I do not deny the importance of the class dynamics of Western institutions. However, my work is an attempt to raise the consciousness of those whose focus on class reduces everything to the economics of the situation. Throughout our interview, she stated that she was proud to be an American, first. Aidoo represents an example of a person who uses the school without understanding its radical potential. However, it is a radical move to use a school of this type. It means that Aidoo trusts Afrikan people with her child's education. She is happy with the school and it is hoped that, like the rest of us, she will grow with the school.

Mawasi does not send her child to the school. Her reasons are confused. She admits this herself. Her son has been brought up since birth in a white day care center that had a major influence on his most formative years. As a career woman she has been unable to monitor the actions of the nursery staff or his growth in their company. As she says,

I trust them, I have problems internally because they're white but he's ok, he's well adjusted.

What is interesting is that the major reason Mawasi presented for not sending her son to attend the school in the United States is that Aisha, who was the assistant administrator at Sankofa, reprimanded her son for running around and did not allow him to feed the fish when he didn't say "please." As a witness to this incident, Mawasi said, "I don't know how people treat my child when I'm not around." She implied that Aisha was prejudiced because her child is a man child. Mawasi was aware that this woman was not a teacher yet she based her decision on not sending her child to this school on this person's actions. She admits that she likes Camara, the head teacher, and is aware that her son would like to attend the school. At the same time Mawasi is confident that her son has had suitable provision and treatment at the hands of white nursery attendants without her supervision. The trust factor model suggests that her confusion involves circular thought in reasoning out why she is not sending her child to the school. This may be related to a fear of making a commitment to the school because of what it implies in terms of culture and identity. It also shows a lack of trust in putting her child in the hands of her own people who she knows to be responsible, committed activists for the community.

Adaeze adjusted well to all-white suburban schools when she was a child. This may have a bearing on why she believes that her child is managing well in the same situation even when her child complains that she has no friends and is sensitive about racist abuse that she frequently encounters. The child's complaints are seen as "silly things that kids go through." Reasons put forward for not sending this daughter relate to the cosmetic condition of the schoolroom for the fee of close to $3,000. The lack of financial support and the fear that the school would only last for one year were other factors.

First, education and learning are not determined by the condition of the classroom as any teacher knows. It was understood that the school was tuition-based and that things would be very difficult at the beginning because these schools have a history at their birth of serving only a small number of children. I believe that Adaeze's desire to run her own school with her friend Jaha was based more on the lines of her own experience of attending the Hampton Institute and Howard University. I think that the idea of being an Afrikan rather than an American first is where the difference lies. In this light one can understand the trust in the white school, even though not ideal for the child, is preferable to what this school offers. A white school, after all, will promote the idea that we are all Americans and that this status comes before any other, while in reality, the his/herstory of the Americas shows us something completely different.

Jaha is interested in her son becoming a leader. She believes that he is doing well in a predominantly white school, although he does have so-called "behavioral" problems. The behavioral problems are not viewed as race-related. Since he achieves A and B grades, she does not see the need to send him to the school. Overall, and apart from the behavioral problems, the child is perceived as doing well. Thus, academic achievement becomes prioritized and emotional balance is less important.

Jaha likes the idea of Black schools. She wished that her son could go to a school like ours, but not ours because the walls were not painted two days before the school was expected to open. Our treatment of a parent that did not have the financial ability to send her child to the school was incorrect. The parent's concerns were not correctly addressed by one of the school representatives on an open day discussion about the school according to Jaha. Kumiwa, the parent who attempted to address the parent's concern, told the parent that until we can get scholarships we could not support her child but that if she really tried to get the money something might come up. Jaha saw this answer and the general feeling that she received as an indication of the esoteric and cultist nature of the school.

To my mind this feeling can be related to a fear in trusting our ideas and a lack of respect and credibility given to the school and those involved. Jaha, like Adaeze, was interested in starting her own school. I believe that Jaha has ideas about creating an American who is Black rather than an Afrikan person and that is where the problem lies. In that case this is another example of a rejection of our Afrikanity and a support for assimilation into the status quo. Of course, when one looks at the trust factor involved, it is easy to understand.

Nalo is quite a different case than the others. It was never clear why a person like Nalo did not send her son to the school. When I interviewed her, I could not fathom why. Her history of activism, her plans for her son to be a leader, and the fact that she has traveled to Kemet and taken her son with her did not fit into what I expected of a person who was not prepared to invest in the school. Although Nalo is in this category, it is as a result of the time when I conducted the interviews. When I finally asked her why she had not sent her son, she was surprised that I was not aware. She informed me that she had left the decision to her son because she allows him to make some important decisions. His reason related to the classroom composition. He preferred to have boys of his own age in the group. This seemed understandable.

I believe that this child is a potential leader and that his mother has provided him with the ability to understand himself as an Afrikan first, despite the fact that he has gone to public school. His early childhood days were obviously influenced by the Afrikan-centered curriculum that his mother developed for preschoolers. However, Nalo not only did not put her son in the school but removed herself from the board of directors. Early on in the development of the school, Nalo had been asked by the board if she would be the head teacher, she declined because of her financial situation. She later played a pivotal role on the board, but eventually left, I believe, when she could no longer justify being involved and not sending her son. Even though this case is unique, I still believe that the trust factor model holds true.

I believe that some of the concerns about Sankofa had some substance. I would say that it is true to say that we did not have the school room prepared until the day of opening and the other classrooms were painted a week later. One of the disadvantages of running a school with little finance is that the organizational aspects rely on people who are working full-time, have family commitments, and may be involved in many community activities. This is the case at the birth of any of these schools. The point is that it is an investment of time and belief. It is easy to understand how this state of affairs appears to people who work in white-run bureaucracies that are heavily financed and therefore appear to run efficiently. We are trying to build a community school in the community with limited resources in an old, well-used community center so that we can attract the people who live locally.

The fear of trusting Afrikan people is prevalent and understandable, given the history of oppression and how negatively we have been affected by it as a people. In this light, I believe that the choice of these parents not to send children to this U.S. school is symptomatic of the deep and devastating effects of racism. The result is fear of and lack of trust in the ability of Afrikan people to produce children who are academically and culturally proficient.

I have argued that the choice to send children to culturally affirmative schooling is part of the his/herstory of resistance against racism, which includes the deculturalization process so necessary for integration. Integration means European domination and control over the energies and resources of Afrikan women, men, and children. In other words, the Afrikan person must compromise a self-determining future to the dictates of European control. Moreover, Afrikan people are to believe that Europeans as the conquerors/patriarchs know what is best.

I have been critical of the parents who have chosen not to send their children to the school in an effort to try to understand why. My respect for them is not diminished by their inability to support the development of Sankofa. I believe that in time, the schooling of their children will carry new revelations as their realization of the impact of white supremacy on their children and the problem of deculturalization on their consciousness becomes apparent. This is certainly the case for all the mothers in the study. In the U.K. Diallo and Amal specifically sent their children to white schools as did Ife, Dalmar and Ayoluwa in the U.S. They believed that their children would benefit from the experience. Becoming aware is a process and it happens in its own time. In other words, the process of self-transformation is ongoing and while it is true that these mothers did not support the school, I believe that they have the capacity to change those ideas, based upon their realizations. The reason for writing this book is to help that process along for mothers who are interested in making sense of what is happening to their children, families, themselves, and Afrikan people, in general.

The interviews show that the mothers' choices to send their children to the school are based on a level of understanding won by living in and trying to survive in white patriarchal racist society. The majority of the parents are very conscious of the racism, sexism, and classism that they, their families, and in particular their children have experienced. They have all been very selective in making their decisions. Given the location and financial constraints on the school, parents are committed because they believe in what the school stands for and importantly what the school can provide for their children.

The parents in the two studies by me and the one by Ratteray & Shujaa have made a commitment to Black/Afrikan run institutions because they do not want their children to suffer in the public/state school situation whether the schools are predominantly Black or white. All the schools in the studies foster environments that are loving and caring and provide support for the children and parents. The history of all these schools is a history of Afrikan people taking control of their own schools. These independent schools differ from Black-run schools that are owned and controlled by the state. They are committed to caring for the children of the Afrikan population. They have evolved in response to the needs of parents who want to know that their children are in safe environments and learning the necessary academic skills. At the same time, in the United States, the rise of Afrikan-centered public schools in Afrikan neighborhoods that have been taken over by faculty who are committed to providing culturally affirming schools to their school populations is another development that will have to be looked at by Afrikan families in light of their consciousness and inability to support tuition-based schools. This may be a possibility in the United Kingdom since there are numbers of Afrikan populated schools in major urban areas.

In reference to the data in the study, although I say that these schools provide a service to parents who are concerned about the racism that may prevent their children from doing well at school emotionally, spiritually, and academically, I do not believe that the parents who use these schools are the only parents who are concerned about how racism impacts upon themselves or their children. The money factor plays a major role in preventing many more parents from using schools like the tuition-based Sankofa School in the United States. This is unfortunate. However, some may think that these schools are bourgeois because they are private. If one is steeped in Marxist class theory, then one would know that building a small Afrikan institution in the center of a poor Black community with minimal resources hardly constitutes either the actions of or the power of the bourgeois class. Paying tuition is the cost of trying to be independent from government sources of funding. In the case of independent Afrikan-centered schools, the aim is to provide scholarships by selling the idea of how the community will benefit by using such schools, so that community money will eventually support the school in order that all children will be able to attend. This involves a long process of educating the public.

As I have stated earlier, in London the majority of parents do not send their children to supplementary schools, which are free or charge minimal fees. To my mind, even if Afrikan-centered schools were free, there would still be the same suspicion and fear of Afrikan people running their own schools that there is in London. In fact, those four parents who chose not to use the Afrikan-centered school were professional people and more able to pay the tuition than other parents. In the London situation, the fear of using the schools is primarily based on the stigma attached to these schools. To use these schools is a radical, even revolutionary move. From the interviews, I ascertained that the parents who use these schools have made a radical move and are conscious of this. The more culturally affirming or Afrikan-centered the school is, the more radical the move. When one is aware of what the schools stand for, then one can understand their revolutionary potential.

Finally, it is my belief, based on the interviews, that the mothers have chosen these schools as a result of the level of their understanding concerning the Afrikan struggle against European domination and the need for Afrikan people to become aware of their Afrikanity as a basis for developing a vision for a new future for Afrikan women, men, and children.

⑧

Afrikan Intellectualism as a Basis for Institution Building

Be not arrogant because of your knowledge. Take counsel with the ignorant as well as with the wise. For the limits of knowledge in any field have never been set and no one has ever reached them. Wisdom is rarer than emeralds, and yet is found among the women who gather at the grindstones.

—*The Book of Ptah-Hotep*, 2,500 B.C.E.

There is a relationship between the mothers' personal transformations and their comprehensions of the importance of culturally affirmative education for their children. In other words, I believe that the mothers' understandings of the need for their children to receive culturally relevant knowledge are based upon their own realizations of the value of their Afrikaness. In all cases, I believe that this belief is rooted in and validated by the experience of having lived in or visited Afrikan communities whether they are in Afrika, the Caribbean, the United States, or the United Kingdom. Given the ongoing attempt to debase everything pertaining to Afrika and Afrikan people, these realizations are major accomplishments.

How is it possible for these women to see outside the story of the debased Afrika? By using Diop's (1959/1990) concept of cultural unity, it is possible to conceive that there is a connection between their consciousness and the cultural memory of Afrikan people from antiquity to the present day. In other words, the truth about the humanity of Afrikan people has never been erased from the collective cultural memory, no matter what forms of deculturalization have taken place. In effect, the transmission of culturally relevant knowledge is at its most potent within Afrikan communities despite attempts to destroy its institutional base.

Dona Richards (1980), now Marimba Ani, deals competently with this point:

> Various theorists maintain that the trauma of slavery severed all ties between us and our ancestors; culturally as well as physically. If that were the case indeed it would have meant "death" for us as a people, given the African understanding of the meaning of life. . . . Yet another irony is that while we persist in denying our heritage, it is that very Africanity that allows us to survive in the spiritual wasteland of America. . . . Ethos, like culture, is understood to refer to shared group reaction and group response. The African-Diasporic ethos refers to our unique spirit and spiritual being. It is a result of our shared cultural history and is derived from Africa. (p. 1)

In line with this thinking, the idea that Afrikan people should control the knowledge that their children receive and that the knowledge should be culturally informed, comes out of a rich his/ herstory of Afrikan struggle. I believe, for example, that Afrikan mothers who send their children to culturally affirmative schools in the United States and the United Kingdom are generally women who recognize the attempt to control the thinking and behavior of Afrikan people. This study has attempted to bring into focus the link between the mothers' becoming culturally focused and the education of their children. While these women come from diverse backgrounds, with a variety of survival experiences, those who use culturally affirming schools, are all extremely sensitive to the types of racist, anti-Afrikan/Black treatment that Afrikan children receive in the urban schools they attend. Levels of awareness about the perceived appropriate treatment that their children should receive is linked to an evaluation or analysis based on their own experiences. Standards of treatment that these parents deem befitting of their children are based on Afrikan values rather than European ones. Their Afrikan morality has guided their understanding of what is just. This is not new; these mothers have retained ideas that can be traced back to Afrika despite Europeans' continuing attempts to devalue and deny Afrikan humanity.

Within the resistance movement against European domination/white supremacy, there has always been an attempt to transmit Afrikan-centered/Afrocentric ideas; this is the way Afrikan people have survived. The belief in Afrikan humanity and integrity has been constant among Afrikan people, although contested by others. Logically, and in reality, ideas of Afrikan/Black nationalism or unity may be traced to the capturing and enslavement of the first Afrikan woman and man by Europeans (Hart 1986). These ideas have influenced both the building and supporting of these schools.

Division as a Method of Conquest

There has been a systematic and systemic effort to separate Afrikan peoples. This is an important strategy for destroying cultural unity. One method has been the creation and use of nation-states in Afrika to construct political and economic distinctions that provide a basis for separate interests. In this way, Ghanaians find little in common with Kenyans or Eritreans or Afrikan Americans or U.K. Blacks (Afrikans) or Afrikan Caribbeans and vice versa. Thus, common interests of European involvement in their political economies are subsumed by national concerns for survival as nation-states. Despite this state of affairs, all the mothers in the United Kingdom made it known that they were aware of divisions, created by European strategies of control through conflict, between Afrikan people from the Caribbean and those from the continent. Similarly, at least two of the mothers from the U.S. group voiced their concerns. Ife, for instance, experienced pro-racist or anti-Afrikan behavior among Afrikan children when she attended school in New York, during the time that Malcolm X was speaking to the people. She commented on this condition:

> I remember a young girl from Guyana. . . . They just hated this child . . . cut off her hair. . . . I mean, you know, we can be real vicious. . . . I saw some brutal stuff, but . . . it wasn't the drug thing, the brutality came a lotta times from us, not knowing who we are and hating the child that seemed to be too white or Mulatto or mixed. There was a lotta that good hair, bad hair, light skin, dark skin going on . . . light eyes, hazel eyes against brown eyes . . . wanna bes and jigaboos. It was a direct result from not knowing who we were.

Aisha from St. Vincent personally experienced this type of behavior from her own people when she came to live in Queens, New York, at the age of ten, over twenty years ago.

> Not only did I have to deal with the hostility of being a foreigner, but I had to deal with the hostility of being a Black foreigner. The kids were not nice. . . . They didn't like West Indians too much. . . . The way I talked. . . . Things like getting 100 percent on a test, I wasn't supposed to do.

Abebe, from the U.K. group, was born of a Nigerian father and a European mother. Her son's father is of Caribbean-descent. She remembers that in her own upbringing her father and stepfather were anti–West Indian, while she has West Indian friends who were anti-Afrikan.

> I think it's the way British society has made Black people turn on each other here.

None of the mothers, at the time of the interviews, supported such divisions and all believed in the unity of all Afrikan peoples. One may view their support of cultural unity as having been influenced by Afrikan/Black nationalist thinking.

As explicated in chapter 6 there is evidence to show that in the United States and the United Kingdom, the Black Power movement from the Nation of Islam to Rastafarianism and the Afrikan independence struggles have influenced the thinking of these mothers. It is a fact that resistance against white supremacy his/herstorically has influenced the thinking and behavior of Afrikan people, particularly those who support and work toward self-determining objectives. As a result of my investigation, I view these women as the vanguard in both the development and use of Afrikan-based institutions. They are not only consciously aware of attempts to create divisions among Afrikan people, but they are also aware of the ongoing endeavor to defame the her/history of Afrikan people. Moreover, they are critically cognizant of the negative and devastating impact this miseducation has on their children's lives. Therefore, I believe that these women are a critical part of the intellectualism of Afrikan people that has and will sustain Afrikan survival.

The Afrikan Intellectual in Crisis

The idea that there is a crisis in the thinking of the Afrikan person is not a new issue. As Carruthers (1994) argued, even before Cruse's book, *The Crisis of the Negro Intellectual*, thinkers and activists like Woodson, Blyden, Delaney, and others had grappled with and addressed this issue. It has been a particularly difficult issue to deal with since the attempt to deculturalize Afrikan people and impose alien morals and values has been an ongoing enterprise from the earliest invasions of the continent. Today, we are a people who have undergone and are undergoing a process of cultural alienation, described by Frantz Fanon (1961/1983) as being severed from one's cultural history and, therefore, identity. If we understand that identity is a core component in understanding our humanity, then it is clear that our problem is severe. It is the case that our cultural identity is one that has been constructed and manipulated by Europeans. In Cruse's estimation, the Negro intellectuals had no cultural allegiance to their people because they had become absorbed in their own interests as a Europeanized class of people. They had lost sight of their responsibilities to the people. His preference for cultural leadership lay with the "artist" as one who truly manifests the Afrikan aesthetic.

Cruse's understanding of culture was nevertheless narrow because he had a limited knowledge of Afrikan culture and history. In terms of cultural leadership, what of the priest/priestess in traditional Afrikan spiritual systems or leaders of traditional forms of governance, social structures, business standards, educational systems, personhood training, and so on? I believe that he held some antipathy toward Afrika. He, too, like the "intellectuals" he critiqued, was infected mentally by the European debasement of Afrika. This condition affected his ideas about a solution to the problem. For instance, in his reflections on the failure of the United States to pay or give due credit to Negro artists, he expresses the belief that any "advanced nation that has allowed its inner cultural expressions to be so debased and corrupted, deserves nothing less than governmental investigation, correction and control" (p. 111). In effect, the integration of the Black middle class into white society, about which he was concerned, is no less problematic and assimilationist than seeking a solution to this dilemma that calls for it to be addressed by the very social structure that created it.

The idea that the western world is advanced is particularly questionable when looking at its moral standing. From the vantage point of this work, all women are potential culture bearers of one type of culture or another and, therefore, potential leaders and bearers of leaders. Moreover, we know that culture is transmitted intergenerationally; manifests institutionally in all areas of existence, and affects the way we think, behave, and build a future. None of us, then, escapes what Ani (1994) has identified as the Yurugu virus, that is, the Europeanization of our minds. In light of this ailment, it is critical to our survival that we should become Afrocentric in our thinking, Afrikan-centered in our activism and behavior, and re-Afrikanized[1] as the ultimate goal toward developing a vision for the future. In the main, particularly in the West, we are none of these. This may be considered a measure of the success of cultural alienation.

How does cultural alienation impact on the intellectual? Is the role of the Afrikan intellectual the same as that of the European intellectual? If we use Diop's cradle theory as a basis for evaluating the significance of cultural distinctions among people, it becomes evident that the definition and role of the intellectual in European culture may not be the same in Afrikan culture. In both cultures, the intellectual can affect ideology and social change; however, the European intellectual is a privileged person, generally male, who stands apart from the masses. This was Cruse's contention when he moved the onus for intellectual leadership from the academic to the artist. Given the nature of the cultural war, the crisis may be seen as one that is focused on the allegiance of the Afrikan intellectual/educator to either the restoration of global Afrikan integrity or to the European agenda. The crisis is global, it does not matter whether s/he is based in Afrika or in the West. Since the whole world is influenced by western institutional development, it seems reasonable to assume that the most powerful intellectuals are westernized and employed in sustaining western control in one guise or another.

Defining the nature of the relationship that has been constructed between Europeans and other cultural groups is imperative if we are to become better able to determine the extent to which the process of western schooling may or may not be beneficial to the well-being of Afrikan women, men, and children. In other words, the schooled Afrikan intellectual is one who has the best chance of becoming deculturalized, Europeanized, or specifically de-Afrikanized. It is clear that without knowledge of the objectives of European schooling, one is not educated (Shujaa 1994). In this respect, Carter G. Woodson (1933) suggests that the longer a student attends school the less likely s/he is to become useful to her/his people (p. 2). Moreover, Woodson further explicates that

> [W]hen you control a man's thinking you do not have to worry about his actions. . . . He will find his "proper place" and will stay in it. You do not have to send him to the back door, he will cut one out for his special benefit. (p. xiii)

Thus, when we speak of an Afrikan intelligentsia, we speak of an intelligentsia that not only becomes conscious of the European control of its thought processes, but also can make a connection between that realization and the intellectualism of the people. Thus, as Woodson suggests, going to school may make one less educated particularly with regard to the real needs of one's people.

Certainly, the majority of the mothers in the study, particularly those who send their children to culturally affirming schools, perceive state/public schooling in this light. They also recognize that severance from one's cultural story is a critical factor in the problems that we face under European domination. I believe that these mothers qualify as intellectuals based not on their degrees but on their support of culturally affirming schools.

According to Akoto (1992), an educator is one who must not only be involved in the study of culture, but must be engaged in a concrete and ongoing way with advancing the cultural and/or political interests of Afrikan people. S/he is entrusted with the task of inculcating the essential values of that culture and thereby guaranteeing its continuation (p. 99). Using the Afrikan-based concept of education enables one to more fully understand who the educator is.

> The concept of learning in traditional African life cannot be separated from communal responsibility. Indigenous education is a lifelong process that engages everyone, as teachers and learners. The corps of teachers is composed of young and old, males and females alike. As soon as one is old enough to show a younger sibling how to do or make something, one begins one's career as a teacher, which continues until one's death. Since learning involves acquiring skills, and understanding what constitutes fullness of life, it becomes the responsibility of the entire community to make sure that every person learns and masters what s/he should know. For it is through learning and communal participation that one also comes to understand the meaning of personhood and what it takes to become a person. (Tedla 1995, 141)

What becomes apparent from this description is that an educator is always going through a process of personal transformation. S/he has a responsibility to continuing her own growth as well as the growth of those she is entrusted to teach. All this is placed within the context of her mission to transmit the skills that can support the continuation of her culture.

If we are to become re-Afrikanized or freed from the European determination of social reality then the problem for schooled Afrikan intellectuals or educators is their ability to critique the dominant culture's impact on their thinking regarding the Afrikan condition. In Carruthers's view, the miseducation of the Black intellectual or the diseducation of the Black masses through European-centered knowledge constructs is a method of control (p. 45). Thus, the intellectual who supports Afrikan liberation should be culturally linked (on a spiritual level) to, rather than estranged from, Afrikan people. For it is the thought that influences the direction of the activism.

As early as 1952, in *Black Skin, White Masks,* Fanon looked at the psychological impact of the colonizer's construction of a Black identity upon the Black psyche in both Europe and Afrika. By 1961, in *Wretched of the Earth,* Fanon had theorized that cultural alienation was a problem for nationalist struggles in Afrika. The question of allegiance to either the colonizer or the masses of one's own people, for the colonized or de-Afrikanized intellectual, rests with her ability to critically examine her own thinking. This same state of affairs exists for Afrikan intellectuals in the United States and the United Kingdom, where Afrikan people suffer from the legacy of deculturalization, colonization, and neocolonialism and the majority of Afrikan people live, without control over their resources and energies, in townships or cities.

The pain that one suffers in the process of cultural alienation was alluded to by W. E. B. Du Bois, who used the concept of double consciousness, the idea that there are contradictory constructions of identity within the Afrikan psyche. Because of the cultural war, the Afrikan is forced to look at herself through the eyes of the European. What Du Bois was trying to explain was linked to the cultural contradiction that westernized Afrikan people face. The debasement of Afrika has prevented Afrikan people from validating themselves as culturally Afrikan. Who would want to associate herself with a culture and people that have been constructed and identified as primitive, backward, barbarian, and with little to offer in a modern western world? This was as much a problem for Du Bois at the beginning of the twentieth century as it is for us at the end of the century. For Du Bois, schooled as a European, his attempt to forge an Afrikan mindset for himself and others was beset with trauma. Within his mind, a cultural war was going on.

Like Du Bois, Amal from Queen Nzinga School suffered because of a lack of knowledge about her cultural background. She describes the same cultural contradiction that she faced growing up in the United Kingdom. Her words are as eloquent and as illuminating as those of Du Bois when she claims:

> When I was at school there were a few Black children . . . some from the Caribbean, some from Nigeria. I never identify cos I thought that's reaffirming that we have something in common. I'd get out of the room. . . . I look back and I think how come I wanted to be white, how come I wanted to be something that I wasn't? I spent half a lifetime (wanting to be white). People used to say, "Look, they're monkeys, they're swinging from trees, look at them with the bone in their nose." . . . It was terrible, but because I was their friend they didn't mean me, so I tried to separate myself from my family. . . . I led a double life.

The trauma of cultural alienation is one that is felt by millions of Afrikan girls and boys on a daily basis. Its effect upon our lives can be debilitating, especially if access to the truth about ourselves is not easily available. Du Bois's decision to live in Ghana seems to be a clear indication of the developing awareness of his Afrikanity that led to such an expression of cultural allegiance toward the end of his life. The internal struggle between the cultural selves reflects the external clash of cultures that underpins the identity of the conqueror and the conquered. Who shall we align ourselves with? What we choose internally will affect our behavior externally. If we are to be or become Afrikan, then we must rediscover, redefine ourselves and re-Afrikanize. This is the basis for social change.

This process of transformation has been conceptualized by Fanon as a three-phase model of consciousness that signifies the awakening of the colonized. He used the Afrikan writer or intellectual as an example. In the first phase, she assimilates her ideas with those of the colonizer's country. During the second phase, she is disturbed by the process of colonization and identifies a past self within the colonial constructs. Finally, she identifies herself with her people and realizes her role as the "awakener" through her writing as an activist (1983, 179). Now her connection with a self that exists outside the colonial construct but within her cultural group identification guides her to use her skills in the interests of her own people. It is during the third phase that she is perhaps becoming educated.

Further, I would say that the Afrikan intellectual should not be defined only in terms of her academic skills, for there are some among us who can neither read nor write very well but have maintained profound knowledge about the needs of Afrikan people. Thus, it is important to recognize the intellectualism of a people as inclusive of all people who are able to maintain and transmit their belief in Afrikan humanity despite attempts to debase Afrika and her people.

It follows then that resistance to cultural alienation and intellectual control lies in the ability of Afrikan people to retain, regain, and reproduce a culturally affirming Afrikan-centered epistemology. While it is difficult for Western-trained educators to critique their intellectual development, that is, to understand how Eurocentric methodologies and concepts have affected their ability to value Afrikan humanity, the onus for transforming the world has never rested solely with the schooled intellectual. After all, many Afrikan women, children, and men have died in the struggle with a clear analysis of the situation without ever having been considered intellectuals.

For example, Fryer (1988) writes that after a particularly massive uprising in Jamaica during the time of Afrikan enslavement, of the one hundred executed, one man was chained to an iron stake sitting down. Was he an intellectual according to the European determination or not? It seems feasible to assume that as a captured Afrikan person he was very likely not. When his feet were set on fire,

[h]e uttered not a groan, and saw his legs reduced to ashes with the utmost firmness and composure; after which, one of his arms by some means getting loose, he snatched a brand from the fire was consuming him, and flung it in the face of his executioner. (p. 89)

He was a man, however, who maintained the greatest dignity and composure in this moment of torment after having been actively involved in creating social change that would influence the lives of Afrikan people forever. Thus, in keeping with an Afrocentric perspective, intellectualism should be evaluated by the ability to realize the importance of respecting Afrikan humanity and making that connection with its cultural roots. In that respect, such intellectualism may manifest in many ways.

Intellectualism as a Level of Consciousness

This book attempts to express the validity of these mothers' thoughts on social reality. These thoughts are critical to their attempts to teach their children their Afrikan origins as a basis for social change.

Reflecting on the state of Afrikan people, Ayoluwa, who uses the Sankofa School, says:

> For all Afrikan children around the world . . . we are faced with the same downpressor giving us his arrogant way as the only way. . . . That is not the only way, and I think that we see daily the effects of there being only one way . . . this particular European way of thinking.

Ezigbo views the situation in a similar way and sends her child to Sankofa school because

> I really understand the value of being able to have a child in a school where ultimately she learns about herself and her ancestry. It is very obvious to me, a lot of the problems we are having with our youth today is because they don't really know who they are and it happens through the public school system because they don't really work to help us know who we are. . . . I've had two other children go through the public school system and I just know what it does to them.

With reference to the need to send her daughter to Sankofa, and in the same vein, Aisha says:

> To me society is not getting any better in terms of dealing with racism. . . . [I]t's getting worse and I feel that the best

way for me and my family to deal with it is to educate my daughter about it. You don't get that in public school. I don't want my child to grow up believing that it's not there.

Again, there is a similarity in thought about the conditions of Afrikan people with regard to culturally affirming schools. Abebe, whose child attends Queen Nzinga School, says:

An awareness of Black people in Britain will arise out of the work that people like those at the [culturally affirming] schools do. They're [the parents] not aware, they're really ignorant about what is going on in school, what is going on with their children. . . . My way of changing things is through educating to the extent that they know what history is true and what is false and where they come from and who they are and where they can go. Until they know that they're just going to be part of this institution, with a few exceptions. . . . I have four brothers and each one of them has been in and out of prison. It makes me feel really sad because I can see their struggle. Until they direct it somewhere they're just going to struggle, carry on struggling.

Reflecting upon the circumstances of Afrikan people living under European control and the attempt to inculcate us with European values and beliefs, Adoah, whose children attend the Marcus Garvey School, comments:

It's such a struggle in this society. I mean, I've seen kids who dis their parents and dis their culture and have nothing to do with Black people and that is totally sad. Even people who go to university, you know. Although these people go to do Caribbean studies, most of them are totally fucked up. I don't want my kids to ever be ashamed of who they are and where they've come from.

These women are, like most mothers, are the first educators in their children's lives. As such, they are bearers of culture but have chosen to be the bearers of Afrikan culture. To effectively carry out this role, they have retained or regained a respect for themselves as Afrikan people. They are laying the foundation for their children to understand and define their own humanity outside the images and stories constructed by Europeans.

It is clear from the herstories that what qualifies these mothers as intellectuals is not necessarily the fact that some hold degrees. In most cases, these degrees are more representative of the mothers' academic skills, economic status, and ability to sustain racist treatment during the schooling process, rather than of the mothers' cultural awareness. This point is not made to negate the ability of Afrikan people to use the university to build knowledge about Afrikan people. However, western universities, as culturally based institutions, are naturally biased toward reflecting the theoretical and conceptual academic interests of Europeans. This condition is offset by the ability of Afrikan thinkers to understand the effect of Eurocentric paradigms on their thought processes. Any attempt in westernized universities toward rescuing and reconstructing the Afrikan story in the interests of freeing the Afrikan mind from the bondage of European thinking is orchestrated by Afrikan people who have a commitment to social change. The struggle in the academy represents the victory of the struggle in the streets.

It is evident that not all Afrikan persons who have a commitment to social change are taking a route that is grounded in an Afrikan worldview. Following this line of reasoning, then, the construction of a vision of a future should be based upon the same ancient and traditional values that are conducive to the well-being of Afrikan people. If this is the case, then it is possible to view the mothers in the studies who send their children to Afrikan-centered schools as part of an Afrikan intelligentsia who recognize that they and their children need to know their connection to Afrika. Moreover, it is possible to view these mothers as intellectuals who are learning and growing at the same time that they are teaching. Their work may be seen within the traditions of ancient Afrikan activism.

This is not to say that one cannot be educated while attending European- controlled schools, but one is not necessarily uneducated because one does not go to school. For Afrikan people, European-controlled schools, whether Black or white, have herstorically never been the sole site for the emergence of the Afrikan intellectual—

female or male. The preservation of the cultural memory of a people takes place within and without the academic world that is presently under the dominion of the West. The Afrikan cultural memory has been the basis for challenging, critiquing, and resisting European domination. Most importantly, I would go so far as to say that Afrikan mothers through time, from antiquity to now, have been the backbone of the preservation of the cultural memory and therefore the backbone of resistance. After all, how could an Afrikan mother believe that the child that she has carried in her womb is less of a human than any of the children of the dominant group who debase her. The fact is that she does not. It is plausible that the mother's level of consciousness about her child's humanity lays the revolutionary foundation for challenging the European story of Afrikan debasement and reconstructing the truth.

Afrikan Allegiance

The values of traditional and indigenous education have laid a foundation for the pedagogy of full-time Afrikan-centered schools (Akoto 1990). Prior to European and Arab invasions of Afrika, educational systems produced intellectuals and intellectualism grounded in the spiritual and philosophical beliefs that enabled the continual reproduction of value systems. Since then, the intellectual and intellectualism have been compromised by conquest and the imposition of differing cultural interests. However, it is the awareness of the significance of culture as a critical connection for liberation that leads to an Afrikan-centered or Afrocentric perspective and the development of these schools as a source of intellectual development. In this way intellectualism for Afrikan people, if it is about survival and re-Afrikanization, must be antithetical to present conditions and therefore revolutionary. This belief is transferred intergenerationally through the intellectualism and the activism of the people. Thus, although the role of academic intellectuals is critical for building knowledge bodies and for developing theoretical and conceptual models and activism, their work must be grounded in the cultural experiences of Afrikan people in order for them to be considered true educators and intellectuals. Moreover, they must have an allegiance to Afrikan people predicated upon a vision of the future outside that conceived by the oppressor. Afrikan mothers and fathers who send their children to culturally affirming schools have begun the process of education for their children because generally they are aware of the distinctions between schooling for subjugation and education for liberation. In this way, they are a critical component of Afrikan intellectualism.

Nzinga from Marcus Garvey School in the United Kingdom and Kumiwa from Sankofa in the United States are wonderful examples of intellectuals who combine thinking and activism in the public/ state school arena. For Nzinga, her upbringing in St. Kitts gave her a cultural foundation that helped her to survive incredible odds against becoming a guide for the betterment of others. She survived to challenge the agonizing racism of mainstream schooling in the United Kingdom on behalf of all Afrikan children. She survived her sexual debasement and torture and used that experience to direct her life in a positive manner. Kumiwa's long road to self-realization was painful and torturous, yet she succeeded in elevating herself mentally and physically from conditions that so many Afrikan women, men, and children are forced to face every day. The examples of Nzinga and Kumiwa as survivors in a world of limited choices, especially for Afrikan women, are a continuing testimony to the integrity and genius of Afrikan people.

Nzinga works as a dinner lady (school cook) in order to protect her daughter, sons, and other Afrikan children. Sending her children to the Marcus Garvey School in London has helped Nzinga as well as her children to learn about the accomplishments of Afrikan people. At the same time, it has provided her with a network of people that she can rely on to support her beliefs. She is also an educator at the school. Nzinga is a person who is prepared to go to great lengths to protect our children and help them to get in touch with their cultural selves.

She had the benefit of attending a school in St. Kitts, when she was four years old, where she was taught about Afrika by a woman who still spoke an Afrikan language, like her own grandmother. She is an example of a woman who is aware of the role of miseducation in undermining Afrikan children's educational and human potential. She has suffered in ways no one should suffer, but she is a warrior. Having gone through her own process of transformation, she sees that her children must know who they are in order to build a better world. She speaks of the undermining process that teachers practice to degrade Afrikan children and in turn degrade Afrikan people and the lengths that parents like her go to defend their children:

> You see . . . they tell them, "Oh stop speaking like that" because that's not the way to speak. And so I say, "Well, I speak like that in my house." So I stop work to look after my children. I wanted my children to believe in what I am and what they are gonna be.

Kumiwa's belief in Sankofa was fundamental to the building of the school. Her life has provided insights into the experiences of other Afrikan people trying to survive. It has shaped her activism and commitment to dedicate her life to providing advice and help to others who are or have been lost and traumatized.

Mothers like Nzinga and Kumiwa have always been, at whatever time in herstory that they existed, a critical element in the conscious development of Afrikan people in the process of creating social change.

Conclusion

The process of deculturalization begun by European domination was not able to eradicate all semblance of traditional institutions and certainly not the spirituality and the mind of Afrikan people as a collective consciousness. This understanding is important because the nurturing and reconstruction of Afrikan ideas and ways of being can only take place if there is a belief in their value. Such a belief is predicated upon the idea that understanding oneself as an Afrikan person enables one to reconnect with a world culture. In this way, one can free oneself from the limitations of parochialism, minority status, and a false European representation of Afrika and Afrikan people, whether these representations are condoned by people who look Afrikan or not. To look Afrikan or to have genetic features associated with Afrikaness is to suffer the ravages of racism, whether the recipient is aware of it or not. For example, of the four Afrikan mothers who do not send their children to culturally affirmative school, three, at the time of the study, were unable to see the significance of racism and its effect upon their children. It is my belief that their distrust of Afrikan people educating their children is based upon a fear that has its origin in Eurocentric culture and its validation of whiteness and devaluation of Blackness. While it is possible to find Afrikan people who have Europeanized minds, it is much more difficult to find European people who have been Afrikanized. This is a measure of the strength and validation of European cultural domination.

In the cultural context of Afrikan reality, past present and future, it is the Afrikan mother, the bearer of culture and humanity, who will be the determinant of the fruition of our future potential. Until the Afrikan woman is returned to her place of honor, there is no hope for the world. Her role as mother in the building of Afrikan-centered culturally affirming schools is the beginning of the journey of re-Afrikanization and self-transformation. As Diop said: "the degree of a civilization is measured by the relations between the man and the woman." (1991, 175). The legacy of Afrikan womanist[2] struggle borne by Afrikan women is one that has challenged patriarchal inhumanities from the earliest ravages of Afrika and her people, from ancient time to the present.

Thus, any liberationist theory and activism begin with the consciousness of the need to recover herstorically and culturally the complementary relationship between the woman and the man as a basis for our story and therefore the vision of the future world. The story of Afrikan struggle and survival in the cultural war is not the story of grandiose heroes and sheroes, it is the story of people like all the mothers in this study.

GREATNESS

It is well to understand our greatness.
Because what we have been
can shape what we may become.
Remember, however,
that Afrikan greatness grew
because of our value system.
Today, we live in and practice
the value system of the European.
Thus,
without reconstructing our own,
the greatest that we can ever aspire to become
is grounded in the vision of the European.

—Nah Dove (1995)

Epilogue

Since I began this study, Sankofa School in the United States has closed down. I do not believe that this situation diminishes the findings that center on the types of women who believe in the building and development of culturally affirming schools. The Marcus Garvey and Queen Nzinga schools in the United Kingdom still exist. The parents and children are still involved in the development and continuation of these schools. The independent schools that prevail are evidence of the necessary collective work that it takes to ensure their existence. It is evident in the movement toward public and chartered Afrocentric schools that Afrikan-centered ideas will remain an integral part of the Afrikan experience and expression despite all forms of oppression. We shall continue to learn and grow from our experiences both positive and negative.

Notes

Introduction

1. In the context of this work, "Afrikan" describes those women, men, and children who are continental Afrikan people or members of the Diaspora living in the West. This term recognizes the cultural and experiential specificity of a diverse people. Because of a need of the European "intelligentsia" to distinguish human types as "races," Afrikan people have been categorized as a Black race, based on skin coloring that may vary from brown to black. Psychological dimensions, cultural distinctions, and physical and mental attributes have been ascribed to the so-called races to differentiate them on a hierarchical scale. Afrikan will refer to Afrikan Caribbean, Afrikan American, Afrikan British, and continental Afrikan people.

2. This text utilizes the "k" rather than the "c" in Afrika because the Kemetic (Ancient Egyptian) word "Af rui ka", as Clinton Crawford (1996) notes, is the ultimate etymological root of the word *Africa,* which signifies "birthplace." *Recasting Ancient Egypt in the African Context* (Trenton, N.J: Africa World Press), p. 120.

3. "Deculturalization" is an integral part of the European colonization process. It includes any or all of these things, the removal of people from their lands, the forbiddance of people to speak their languages or practice their cultural forms, and the inculcation of alien values and practices either through forced or subtle means. It is, in this context, a dehumanizing, violent, and brutal process that includes denying people their humanity; taking control of or destroying traditional institutions; the violent

239

removal of real leadership; the use of torture and abuse on children, women, and men, physically, mentally, economically, and spiritually to achieve control; the withdrawal of access to cultural knowledge and the imposition of ideas that are hostile to the cultural continuity of a people. These aspects of deculturalization are supported by a belief in the morality and righteousness of this process.

4. The term "European" is used to describe the Caucasian people who now occupy and politically control Europe and most of the Americas, Australia, and New Zealand. As in the case of Afrikan people, there is a recognition of the diversity and differences in national interests among Europeans. However, as beneficiaries of global capitalism and as a result of their involvement with its development in the enslavement and colonization of Afrikans and others, and because of the similarities in their systems of governance and values and beliefs, I believe that it is possible to view Europeans as having as much in common in defending their positions as "White" people as Afrikans do to challenge the existing power relations.

5. In the book *The Destruction of Black Civilization*, Chancellor Williams constructs a scenario of the great tragedy that befell Afrika. He argues that the conquests of Afrika and her people by Asian, Arab, and European whites along with their religious impositions was exacerbated by the betrayal of "mixed races" created by the amalgamation of the conquerors with Afrikans who aligned themselves with white supremacy. The ensuing forced removals of peoples from traditional land-bases, the disruptions, famines, and diseases together played significant roles in this catastrophe.

6. "Maafa" is the Kiswhali word used by Dona Marimba Richards (later Marimba Ani) in *Let the Circle Be Unbroken* (Trenton, N.J.: Red Sea Press, 1980) to define the holocaust that Afrikan people have and continue to suffer under white domination.

7. Culturally affirming schools in the United Kingdom are supplementary schools that focus on the significance of understanding the story and culture of Afrikan people. Supplementary schools are mostly Saturday schools that run on a voluntary basis. They emerged during the 1960s to challenge the racism of state schooling. At the same time, in the United States culturally affirming schools, which include Afrikan-centered schools, emerged as private schools that run on a full-time basis.

8. The continent and lands known as the "Americas," North, South, and Central America, were named after an Italian sailor called Amerigo Vespucci around the end of the fifteenth century.

9. "First Nations" people refers to the indigenous and autochthonous peoples who inhabit what is known as the "Americas." The term "First Nations" is used in Canada by the indigenous nations as a way of claiming their rights as original people in lands that are still being contested and fought over by invaders. Like Afrikan people, their collective interests have been subordinated to the interests of Europeans in the construction of what is called "America," North, South, and Central.

Chapter 1

1. Afrocentrism is derived from the theory of Afrocentricity as it has been developed by M. K. Asante and K. Welsh Asante. This academic endeavor has striven to legitimize the struggle of Afrikan people within the scholastic arena in an ongoing effort to develop a global cultural paradigm that centers the story of Afrika and her people. In this way, Afrikan people may build on existing knowledge as a basis for developing knowledge that can effectively liberate the hearts and minds of people who are mentally incarcerated within European paradigmatic structures both inside and outside the academic world.

2. Herbert Ekwe-Ekwe, *Africa 2001* (Reading, U.K.: International Institute for African Research, 1993) provides a description of three "seasons" of invasion. The first, lasted for twelve centuries (525 B.C.E. to the beginning of the seventh century C.E.) during the civilization of Kemet (ancient Egypt). At that time, the Persians, Greeks, and later the Romans seized North Africa. The second season of Arab/Muslim conquest began in the seventh century and covered North and West Africa, while the third season saw the return of European conquest, from the fifteenth century until today, over part of the North and the whole of the South, East, and West (p. 1).

3. "Head Teacher" is a title used in Sankofa School to symbolize that role as one of a guiding nature rather than of an authoritative nature.

4. The definition of schooling is used in the context of Mwalimu Shujaa's research (1994) in *Too Much Schooling, Too Little Education*. He makes distinctions between the process of education and the process of schooling. Schooling is viewed as a method of institutional cultural imposition and subjugation used to transmit values and beliefs that support social inequalities in western-oriented societies. Education is a lifelong process of human learning and development. Within homogeneous societies, these

processes may overlap and work positively toward the fulfillment of the human potential of an individual and ultimately in the best interests of that society.

Chapter 2

1. For a concise explanation of neocolonialism, see Kwame Nkrumah, *Neo-Colonialism: The Last Stage of Imperialism.* (London: Panaf Books, 1974). His idea is based on his experience in Ghana, as prime minister and later president, after "independence" in 1957. Neocolonialism is a later stage in the development of colonization. It is a condition that exists when the system of colonial rule, while controlled economically by Europeans, is managed by colonized indigenous leadeship. The irony is that in the process of neocolonial development the colonized leadership believes that it has become independent of colonial rule.

2. The Labor Exchange is the government-run employment agency in the United Kingdom through which unemployment payments may be obtained.

Chapter 3

1. Infant school or primary school equals 4/5–7 years; junior school equals 7–11 years; and secondary school equals 11–16/17 years.

2. A-level GCE (General Certificate of Education) is a university entry level examination that is taken in many subjects. Ages range from 16–17. They can be school-leaving qualifications as well.

3. Ayinde Jean-Baptiste is a child protégé of Minister Farrakhan. He spoke at the Million Man March.

Chapter 4

1. The Combahee Women's Collective was a small group of Afrikan women who, as lesbians, considered themselves a "progressive, multi-issue, activist Black feminist organization" (p. 5). They wrote a statement in 1977 that encapsulated the ideas of their organization as well as many women who were not necessarily Black feminist or lesbian.

2. The term COINTELPRO came to mean the sustained, systematic, repressive campaigns directed by the FBI against perceived enemies

of the state. COINTELPROS originally refered to counterintelligence programs deemed domestic, covert, illegal operations.

Chapter 7

1. Anthony Browder's book *Nile Valley Contributions to Civilization* (Washington, D.C.: The Institute of Karmic Guidance, 1992) provides a readable, concise work of Afrikan-centered researchers of Kemetic beliefs and values.

2. "Caucasian" is a racial category created by Blumenbach in the 1770s, at the University of Göttingen in Germany, to refer to "White" women and men. He placed this "White" race at the top of a hierarchy of supposed races of human kind (Fryer 1987, 27–28).

3. Richard Hart. (1985). *Slaves Who Abolished Slavery*, 2 vols. (Jamaica: Institute of Social and Economic Research, University of the West Indies) for a detailed understanding of the strategies and thinking of Maroon activists in Jamaica.

Chapter 8

1. Re-Afriganization is a term used by Amilcar Cabral in a speech called "National Liberation & Culture" delivered in 1970 which is defined as a process of reclamation that Afrikan people colonized by Europeans (Portuguese, in this case) of necessity must undergo in order to appreciate their cultural heritage. This process provides a basis for challenging the imposition of European cultural values that serve to debase Afrika as an integral part of domination and conquest.

2. Womanist comes from womanism, a term coined by Alice Walker in her book *In Search of Our Mothers' Gardens* (1983). The concept of Afrikan womanism has since been shaped by the work of women like Clenora Hudon-Weems, Ifi Amadiume, Mary E. Modupe Kolawole and others. I further define Afrikan womanist struggle as the herstorical attempt by Afrikan women, particularly mothers, to regain, reconstruct, and re-create a cultural integrity that espouses the ancient Maatic principles of reciprocity, balance, harmony, justice, truth, righteousness and order. Such spiritual and social principles may only exist when feminine and masculine power relations are right(eous). This ancient struggle may be viewed as the foundation of Afrikan womanist theory. Moreover, it may be defined as voicing Maat.

References

Akbar, N. (1994). *Light from Ancient Africa*. Fla.: Tallahassee Mind Productions.

Akoto, K. A. (1992). *Nationbuilding*. Washington, D.C: Pan-African World Institute.

Amadiume, I. (1987). *Male Daughters, Female Husbands*. London: Zed Books.

Anderson, J. (1988). *The Education of Blacks in the South 1860–1935*. Chapel Hill: University of North Carolina Press.

Ani, M. (1994). *Yurugu*. Trenton, N.J: Africa World Press.

Asante, M. K. (1980). *Afrocentricity*. Buffalo, N.Y.: Amulefi.

———. (1991). *The Book of African Names*. Trenton, N.J.: Africa World Press.

Asante, M. K. and K. Welsh Asante. (1989). *African Culture: Rhythms of Unity*. Trenton, N.J: Africa World Press.

Battle, V. M. (1970). *Essays in the History of African Education*. New York: Institute of International Studies, Columbia University.

Baldwin, R. (1982). *Police Powers and Politics*. London: Quartet Books.

Best, W. (1990). "The Black Supplementary School Movement." In S. Olowe (ed.), *Against the Tide*. London: Inner London Education Authority (ILEA).

Bond, H. M. (1969). *Negro Education in Alabama*. New York: Octagon Books.

Browder, A. (1992). *Nile Valley Contributions to Civilization*. Washington, D.C.: The Institute of Karmic Guidance.

Bryan, B., S. Dadzie, and S. Scafe. (1986) *The Heart of the Race*. London: Virago Press.

245

Budge, E. W. (1895/1967). *The Egyptian Book of the Dead*. New York: Dover.

Bulhan, H. A. (1985). *Frantz Fanon and the Psychology of Oppression*. New York and London: Plenum Press.

Bullock, A. and O. Stallybrass. (1990). *The Fontana Dictionary of Modern Thought*. London: Fontana Press.

Burt, C. (1937). *The Backward Child*. London: University of London Press.

Campbell, H. (1987). *Rasta and Resistance*. Trenton, N.J.: Africa World Press.

Carby, H. (1982a). "Black Feminism and the Boundaries of Sisterhood." In Centre for Contemporary Cultural Studies (eds.), *The Empire Strikes Back*. London: Hutchinson.

Carby, H. (1982b). "Schooling in Babylon." In Centre for Contemporary Cultural Studies (eds.), *The Empire Strikes Back*. London: Hutchinson.

Carew, J. (1988). "Columbus and the Origins of Racism." *Race and Class* 29.4.

———. (1994). *Rape of Paradise*. Brooklyn, N.Y.: A & B Publishers.

Carruthers, J. (1994). "Black Intellectuals and the Crisis in Black Education." In M. J. Shujaa, (ed.), *Too Much Schooling, Too Little Education*. Trenton, N.J.: Africa World Press.

Chinweizu. (1975). *The West and the Rest of Us*. New York: Vintage Books.

Churchill, W. and J. Vander Wall, eds. (1990). *Agents of Repression*. Boston: South End Press.

Coard, B. (1971). *How the West Indian Child Is Made Educationally Subnormal in the British School System*. London: New Beacon Books.

Cohen, S. (1985). "Anti-Semitism, Immigration Controls and the Welfare State." *Critical Social Policy*. 13.

Collins, Hill P. (1990). *Black Feminist Thought*. London: HarperCollins Academic.

Commission for Racial Equality. (198?). *Race and Society* 84, no. 1323.

The Combahee River Collective. (1986). *The Combahee River Collective Statement: Black Feminist Organizing in the Seventies and Eighties*. New York: Kitchen Table Women of Color Press.

Dadzie, S. (1990). "Searching for the Invisible Woman: Slavery and Resistance in Jamaica." *Race and Class* 32.2.

Davis, A. (1982). *Women, Race and Class*. London: The Women's Press.

Dhondy, F. (1982). *The Black Explosion in British Schools*. London: Race Today Publications.

Diegues, C. (1984). *Quilombo*. New York: N.E.W. Yorker Video.

Diop, C. A. (1974). *African Origins of Civilization: Myth or Reality*. New York: L. Hill.

————. (1990). *The Cultural Unity of Black Africa*. Chicago: Third World Press. (Published originally in 1959 as *L'Unité culturelle de l'Afrique noir*)

Dove, D. (1988). "The Underdevelopment of the Black Child." Unpublished dissertation. North London Polytechnic, London.

————. (1990). *Racism and Its Effect on the Quality of Education and the Educational Performance of the Black Child*. London: Institute of Education, University of London.

Driver, J. (1980). "How West Indians Do Better at School, Especially the Girls." *New Society*, January 17.

Du Bois, W. E. B. (1969). *Black Reconstruction in America, 1960–1880*. New York: Atheneum.

————. (1982) *The Souls of Black Folks*. New York: New American Library.

Ekwe-Ekwe, H. (1993). *Africa 2001: The State, Human Rights and the People*. Reading, U.K.: International Institute of African Research.

Fanon, F. (1983). *Wretched of the Earth*. Harmondsworth, Middlesex, U.K.: Pelican Books.

————. (1986). *Black Skin, White Mask*. London: Pluto Press.

Fatumbi, A. F. (1993). *Oshun: Ifa and the Spirit of the River*. Bronx, N.Y.: Original Publications.

Finch, C. (1990). *The African Background to Medical Science*. London: Karnak.

Finch, J. (1984). *Education as Social Policy*. London: Longman.

Fryer, P. (1984). *Staying Power*. London: Pluto Press.

————. (1988). *Black People in the British Empire*. London: Pluto Press.

Gerima, H. (1994). *Sankofa*. Washington, D.C: Mypheduh Films.

Giddings, P. (1988). *When and Where I Enter*. New York: Bantam Books.

Ginsburg, R. (1988). *100 Years of Lynchings*. Baltimore, MD: Black Classic Press.

Gould, S. J. (1984). *The Mismeasure of Man*. Harmondsworth Middlesex, U.K.: Pelican Books.

Hanke, L. (1959). *Aristotle and the American Indian*. Bloomington: Indiana University Press.

Hart, R. (1985). *Slaves Who Abolished Slavery*. Vol. 2, *Blacks in Rebellion*. Jamaica: Institute of Social and Economic Research University of the West Indies.

Hilliard, A. G. (1984). *Kemetic Concepts of Education*. London: Hackney Black Peoples Association.

————. (1987). *Free Your Mind: Return to the Source*. Videograph. East Point, Ga.: Waset Educational Productions.

Her Majesty's Stationary Office. (HMSO). (1973). *Educational Reconstruction*. London: Department of Education and Science (DES).

Inner London Education Authority. (1988). *Characteristics of Pupils in Special Schools* (Report No. RS1198/88). London: Research and Statistics Branch, Inner London Education Authority (ILEA).

James, G. M. (1989). *Stolen Legacy*. New York: United Brothers Communications Systems.

Jones, V. A. (1986). *We Are Our Own Educators*. London: Karia Press.

Joseph, G. (1981). "The Incompatible Ménage à Trois: Marxism, Feminism and Racism." In L. Sargent (ed.), *Women and Revolution*. Boston: South End Press.

Karenga, M. (1989). *Selections from the Husia: Sacred Wisdom of Ancient Egypt*. Los Angeles: University of Sankore Press.

King, K. J. (1971). *Pan-Africanism and Education*. Oxford: Clarendon Press.

King, R. (1990). *African Origin of Biological Psychiatry*. Hampton, Va.: U.B. & U.S. Communications Systems.

Krippendorf, K. (1980). *Content Analysis: An Introduction to Its Methodology*, vol. 5. Beverly Hills, Calif.: Sage.

Ladner, J. (1971). *Tomorrow's Tomorrow*. Garden City, N.Y: Doubleday.

Lesko, B. (1977). *The Remarkable Women of Ancient Egypt*. Berkeley, CA: University of California Press.

Lusane, C. (1991). *Pipe Dream Blues: Racism and the War on Drugs*. Boston, MA: South End Press.

Lyons, C. (1970). "The Educable African." In V. M. Battle (ed.), *Essays in the History of African Education*. New York: Institute of International Studies, Columbia University.

Mackay, L. (1988). "The Nineteenth-Century English Preparatory School: Cradle and Crèche of Empire?" In J. A. Mangan (ed.), *Benefits Bestowed*. Manchester, U.K.: Manchester University Press.

Mac an Ghaill, M. (1988). *Young, Gifted and Black*. Milton Keynes, U.K.: Open University Press.

Mangan, J. A., ed. (1988). *Benefits Bestowed*. Manchester, U.K.: Manchester University Press.

———. (1990). *Making Imperial Mentalities*. Manchester, U.K.: Manchester University Press.

Marable, M. (1983). *How Capitalism Underdeveloped Black America*. London: Pluto Press.

Marx, K. (1976). *Capital*. London.: Pelican Books and New Left Review.

Mies, M. (1987). Patriarchy and Accumulation on a World Scale. London: Zed Books.

Mohawk, J., O. Lyons, V. Deloria Jr., et al. (1992). *Exiled in the Land of the Free*. Santa Fe, N.M.: Clear Light Publishers.

Nkrumah, K. (1974). *Neo-Colonialism: The Last Stage of Imperialism*. London: Panaf Books.

Nobles, W. (1985). *Africanity and the Black Family*. Oakland, Calif.: Black Family Institute.

Ogbu, J. U. (1978). *Minority Education and Caste*. New York: Academic Press.

Opoku, K. A. (1978). *West African Traditional Religion*. Accra, Ghana: F. E. P. International.

Rashidi, R. (1992). *Introduction to the Study of Classical African Civilizations*. London: Karnak.

Ratteray, J. and M. J. Shujaa. (1987). *Dare to Choose: Parental Choice in Independent Neighborhood Schools*. Washington, D.C.: Institute for Independent Education.

———. (1988). "Defining a Tradition: Parental Choice in Independent Neighborhood Schools." In D. T. Slaughter and D. J. Johnson (eds.), *Visible Now*. Westport, Conn.: Greenwood Press.

Ra Un Nefer Amen. (1990). *Metu Neter*. Brooklyn, N.Y.: Khamit.

Rich, P. J. (1988). "Public School Freemasonry in the Empire: Mafia of the Mediocre." In J. A. Mangan, (ed.), *Benefits Bestowed*. Manchester, U.K.: Manchester University Press.

Richards, D. M. (1980). *Let the Circle Be Unbroken*. Trenton, N.J: The Red Sea Press.

Robinson, C. (1983). *Black Marxism*. London: Zed Press.

Rodney, W. (1982). *How Europe Underdeveloped Africa*. Washington, D.C.: Howard University Press.

Scott, Y. K. (1991). *The Habit of Surviving*. New York: Ballantine Books.

Shujaa, M. J. (1994). *Too Much Schooling, Too Little Education: A Paradox of Black Life in White Societies*. Trenton, N.J: Africa World Press.

Steady, F. C. (1987). "African Feminism: A Worldwide Perspective." In R. Terborg-Penn, (ed.), *Women in Africa and the African Diaspora*. Washington, D.C.: Howard University Press.

Sudarkasa, N. (1996). *The Strength of Our Mothers*. Trenton, N.J: Africa World Press, Inc.

Sweetman, D. (1984). *Women Leaders in African History*. London: Heinemann.

Stone, M. (1976). *When God Was a Woman*. San Diego, Calif.: Harcourt, Brace, Jovanovich.

Tedla, E. (1995). *Sankofa: African Thought and Education*. Washington DC/Baltimore: Peter Lang.

Terborg-Penn, R. (1987). *Women in Africa and the African Diaspora*. Washington, D.C.: Howard University Press.

U.S. Government. *Negro Education: A Study of Private and Higher Schools for Colored People in the United States*. (1917/1969) vol. 1. NY: Negro University Press.

Van Sertima, I. (1992). *Golden Age of the Moor*. New Brunswick, N.J.: Transaction Publishers.

Waddel, J. O. and O. M. Watson. (1971). *The American Indian in Urban Society.* Boston: Little, Brown.

Welsing, Cress F. (1991). *The Isis Papers.* Chicago: Third World Press.

Williams, C. (1987). *The Destruction of Black Civilization.* Chicago: Third World Press.

Williams, E. (1966). *Capitalism and Slavery.* New York: Capricorn Books.

Wolfe, E. R. (1982). *Europe and the People without History.* Berkeley: University of California Press.

Woodson, C. G. (1968). *The Mis-Education of the Negro Prior to 1861.* New York: Arno Press and The New York Times.

Woodson, C. G. (1933). *The Education of the Negro.* Philadelphia, Pa.: Hakims Publications.

Wright, C. (1985a). "Who Succeeds at School and Who Decides?" *Multicultural Teaching* 4.1. 17–22.

Wright, C. (1985b). "Learning Environment or Battleground?" *Multicultural Teaching* 4.1. 11–17.

Index

251